Exposure

Exposure

Inside the Olympus Scandal:
How I Went from CEO to Whistleblower

MICHAEL WOODFORD

PORTFOLIO
PENGUIN

PORTFOLIO PENGUIN

Published by the Penguin Group
Penguin Books Ltd, 80 Strand, London WC2R ORL, England
Penguin Group (USA) Inc., 375 Hudson Street, New York, New York 10014, USA
Penguin Group (Canada), 90 Eglinton Avenue East, Suite 700, Toronto, Ontario, Canada M4P 2Y3
(a division of Pearson Penguin Canada Inc.)
Penguin Ireland, 25 St Stephen's Green, Dublin 2, Ireland (a division of Penguin Books Ltd)
Penguin Group (Australia), 707 Collins Street, Melbourne, Victoria 3008, Australia
(a division of Pearson Australia Group Pty Ltd)
Penguin Books India Pvt Ltd, 11 Community Centre, Panchsheel Park, New Delhi – 110 017, India
Penguin Group (NZ), 67 Apollo Drive, Rosedale, Auckland 0632, New Zealand
(a division of Pearson New Zealand Ltd)
Penguin Books (South Africa) (Pty) Ltd, Block D, Rosebank Office Park,
181 Jan Smuts Avenue, Parktown North, Gauteng 2193, South Africa

Penguin Books Ltd, Registered Offices: 80 Strand, London WC2R ORL, England

www.penguin.com

First published 2012
005

Copyright © Michael Woodford, 2012
All rights reserved

The moral right of the author has been asserted

Set in 12/14.75 pt Dante MT Std
Typeset by Palimpsest Book Production Ltd, Falkirk, Stirlingshire
Printed in Great Britain by Clays Ltd, St Ives plc

Except in the United States of America, this book is sold subject
to the condition that it shall not, by way of trade or otherwise, be lent,
re-sold, hired out, or otherwise circulated without the publisher's
prior consent in any form of binding or cover other than that in
which it is published and without a similar condition including this
condition being imposed on the subsequent purchaser

HARDBACK ISBN: 978–0–670–92222–2
TRADE PAPERBACK ISBN: 978–0–670–92223–9

www.greenpenguin.co.uk

Penguin Books is committed to a sustainable
future for our business, our readers and our planet.
This book is made from Forest Stewardship
Council™ certified paper.

ALWAYS LEARNING   PEARSON

Dedicated to Koji Miyata and Waku Miller,
the best friends a person could ever have.

Contents

Dramatis Personae

(Positions where relevant as at 14 October 2011)

Tsuyoshi Kikukawa Born 1941, joined Olympus in 1964. In 1999 he became a main board director responsible for the finance department, and in 2001 was appointed president and representative director. Ten years later, on 1 April 2011, Kikukawa handed the title of president to Woodford, but remained chairman and assumed the new title of CEO. Kikukawa continued in his role as chairman when Woodford was promoted to CEO on 1 October 2011. Two weeks later, Kikukawa reassumed the titles of president and CEO when Woodford was dismissed. Kikukawa resigned as chairman, president and CEO on 26 October 2011. On 24 November 2011, he resigned from the board.

Hisashi Mori Born 1957, joined Olympus in 1981 and became a main board director in 2006, rising to become an executive vice-president, until his dismissal from this role on 8 November 2011. On 24 November 2011, he resigned from the board.

Hideo Yamada Born 1945, joined Olympus in 1963, becoming a main board director in 2003, and rising to the level of executive vice-president. In June 2011 he was appointed a standing corporate auditor up until his resignation, some five months later, on 24 November 2011.

Shuichi Takayama Born 1950, joined Olympus in 1970, becoming a main board director in 2006. In April 2011 he was made president of the company's consumer business, Olympus Imaging Corporation. Also a director and senior executive managing officer of Olympus Corporation. On the resignation of Kikukawa on 26 October, Takayama was appointed Olympus president and representative director. He resigned from all his positions and left the company at an extraordinary general meeting on 20 April 2012.

Dramatis Personae

Haruhito Morishima President of the company's medical business, Olympus Medical Systems Corporation, and a director and executive vice-president of Olympus Corporation.

Masataka Suzuki Chairman and executive managing director of Olympus Corporation of Asia Pacific Limited, responsible for Olympus's twenty-two companies in China, South-east Asia, Oceania and India. Also a director and senior executive managing officer of Olympus Corporation. (Up until April 2008, Suzuki had been the executive managing director and Chairman of the Board of Olympus Europa Holding GmbH, and for the preceding five years had worked closely with Woodford. When Suzuki returned from Europe, Kikukawa appointed Woodford as the new head of the European business.)

Kazuhisa Yanagisawa A director of Olympus Corporation, responsible for the company's Corporate R&D activities. Promoted to senior executive managing officer in June 2011.

Hironobu Kawamata A director and executive officer of Olympus Corporation who in effect fulfilled the role of the company's chief financial officer.

Hiroshi Kuruma A former senior executive at Nikkei Inc., which publishes Japan's largest business daily newspaper, and one of the three outside (non-executive) directors of Olympus Corporation.

Yasuo Hayashida A medical doctor and one of the three outside (non-executive) directors of Olympus Corporation.*

Akihiro Nambu General manager of Olympus Corporation's Public Relations and Investor Relations department. He negotiated the Gyrus Group PLC acquisition in 2008 and became a director of the subsidiary alongside Kikukawa and Mori.

Toshiro Shimoyama Olympus president from 1984 to 1993, succeeded by Kishimoto.

---

* The third outside director was Junichi Hayashi, who also served as an auditor of the ITX Corporation, an information technology group acquired by Olympus in 2003. He resigned with Takayama and all the other board members at the extraordinary general meeting on 20 April 2012.

Masatoshi Kishimoto Olympus president from 1993 to 2001, succeeded by Kikukawa.

Hajime 'Jim' Sagawa A banker who had previously worked for Nomura, Drexel Burnham Lambert and PaineWebber before setting up Axes America, of which he was president. He was also a part-owner of the affiliated firm Axes (Japan) Securities. A report of 11 October 2011 by accountants PricewaterhouseCoopers (PwC) established that Sagawa had signed official documents with Olympus as a 'Director' of Axam, the Cayman Islands-based fund which had received $670 million of the $687 million paid in so-called 'fees', in relation to the acquisition of Gyrus Group PLC. The remaining $17 million had been paid to Axes.

Akio Nakagawa Head of equities at PaineWebber in Japan in the early 1990s where he worked with Hajime Sagawa. He and Sagawa were also colleagues at Drexel Burnham Lambert. After Nakagawa left Wall Street in 1998, the pair again joined forces at Axes America.

Nobumasa Yokoo Former investment banker with Nomura who by 1998 had become head of its prestigious Shinjuku Nomura Building branch. Here he dealt with some of the firm's leading clients including Olympus. He founded Global Company in the late 1990s, the conduit for Olympus's investment in three small, unprofitable companies.

Akinobu Yokoo Older brother of Nobumasa Yokoo. In 2003 he was chief financial officer of the ITX Corporation, which was acquired by Olympus that year. He was an Olympus executive officer between 2005 and 2009.

Takeshi Kunibe Born 1954. President of Sumitomo Mitsui Banking Corporation (SMBC) – Olympus's main bank and one of its largest Japanese shareholders

Koji Miyata Born 1941. Former president of Olympus's medical business who, already a friend, became one of Woodford's most trusted confidants and advisors in the months following his dismissal. Founder of the Grassroots website which provided an unofficial forum for Olympus employees.

Waku (aka Brian Miller) Born 1954. An American by birth, Waku has lived in Tokyo for thirty years and became the voice of Michael Woodford in Japan. His son, Doug, provided the technical support to Koji Miyata in establishing and maintaining the Grassroots website.

Josh Shores Senior analyst and principal for Southeastern Asset Management, Olympus's largest foreign shareholder.

Mark Hewland A senior partner at the law firm of Simmons & Simmons in London, and the lead lawyer globally coordinating the many legal issues affecting Woodford.

Tatsuo Kainaka Born 1940. Retired supreme court justice who chaired the Third-Party Committee investigation into the Olympus scandal. His committee's report deemed Olympus's senior management to be *rotten to the core.*

A Happier Time: 10 February 2011.

The press conference in Tokyo at which Olympus CEO Tsuyoshi Kikukawa announced that the company's next president would be a *gaijin* (foreigner): Michael Woodford.

Kikukawa talked about me to the assembled audience: 'I firmly believe that his experience and knowledge, as well as his strong leadership, will be vital for our corporation.'

When I spoke, my words held a glimpse of the future: 'One thing I think Japan is known for is that it is very good at managing and protecting the status quo. Change in Japan can be difficult to implement.' I went on to tell the reporters: 'It can be done, it will be done, but I need a Japanese "umbrella".' I was referring to Kikukawa, whom I trusted would support and protect me. Eight months later that umbrella would close.

Prologue

Sometimes I feel like I've spent my life at 38,000 feet. Strapped in above the clouds, whiling away the hours as I cross continents with my briefcase and laptop. I know the drill. The check-in, the unsmiling passport official, the shoe removal, the phone in a tray, the over-lit duty-free stores. The long hike to the gate, down the air-bridge, over the threshold, and turning left to the sanctuary of the first-class cabin. Remove the jacket, take a glass of champagne and wait as the final stragglers board. At last the 'armed and cross-checked' announcement. Then hour after hour above the clouds, until the pre-landing procedures and touchdown. Finally, the bleary-eyed exit to another place.

But this flight was different. All Nippon Airways 202 from London Heathrow to Narita, Japan, departing 23 March 2011 at 7 p.m. Less than two weeks before there had been an undersea megathrust earthquake measuring 9 on the Richter scale, its epicentre forty-three miles east of the Oshika Peninsula of Tohoku. The largest earthquake ever to hit Japan and the fifth biggest on earth since they started recording such things back in 1900. Within thirty minutes a tsunami, peaking at a height of 133 feet, struck the country's north-eastern coastline.

The world watched on television as the surging wall of grey water, with cars, boats and trucks bobbing on its surface, worked its way up to five miles inland in Sendai province, smashing most structures in its path. It destroyed 129,225 buildings. Nearly 16,000 people were killed, 27,000 injured and 3,155 were still missing. I was flying into a disaster zone.

Below me, as we descended, another threat remained. The Fukushima Daiichi nuclear power plant located on the coast was thumped by the full force of the wave. It remained upright but its back-up power systems failed and the plant's workers, soldiers and firemen were fighting to keep the radiation-spewing reactor cool.

If things took a turn for the worse, the Japanese authorities were secretly contemplating the possibility of evacuating the whole of greater Tokyo, a megalopolis with a population of 35 million. And Tokyo was precisely where I was headed.

I appeared to be the sole Westerner on the plane. Many foreigners based in Tokyo were rapidly heading in the opposite direction, out of the country to safety. As the plane flew through the night I slept fitfully, my mind returning to the days before I had left my home for Heathrow. With the twenty-four-hour news channels showing the desperate efforts to bring the Fukushima reactor under control, my wife had told me not to be a hero. To think about her and our two children.

She said that everyone would understand if I delayed my return. It would be foolhardy and irresponsible to go back now. I knew that other *gaijin* (foreign) company presidents were not in Japan, and perhaps my colleagues would understand, but for me there was never a decision to make. I had to return – how could I possibly be the president and not be there with the rest of the company just because it was dangerous?

As we prepared to land, the softly spoken young stewardess who had looked after me so conscientiously for the last twelve hours came over to my seat and smiled sympathetically. She passed me a plastic duty-free bag containing six bottles of Tŷ Nant, Welsh spring water. Without any alarm in her voice she explained that tap water was best avoided due to possible radioactive contamination, and that bottled water in the city was fast running out. It all felt decidedly ominous.

Then came the anticipated bump and screech of the wheels as we touched down and I looked through the small window to the familiar surrounds of Narita Airport. I needed to focus my mind on the job I was there to do. A brand-new role for me – the top job in the organization for which I had worked long and hard. I was a foreigner, yet I had been chosen to lead this huge Japanese corporation and its 40,000 employees.

I had joined Olympus thirty years earlier as a salesman and never imagined that I would become its president. But I would be heading a company that was in trouble. Even before the earthquake its balance sheet was worryingly over-leveraged, and costs were out of control. It was one of the most indebted businesses in Japan and urgently needed to start paying back its colossal borrowings. It was my job to lead Olympus back to the land of milk and honey. I was sure I knew how.

Coming back to Tokyo was a test of my character, demonstrating that, whatever the personal risks, I was committed to my Japanese colleagues. Like most governments around the world, the advice of the British Foreign and Commonwealth Office was not to travel to Japan; many airlines were flying to Seoul in South Korea and then running a shuttle service to Tokyo so that the aircrews didn't have to stay overnight in the city.

As I stood on the moving walkway I could feel the dosimeter, a device the size of a mobile phone used to measure radiation, in my jacket pocket. I stepped out from arrivals to meet my driver, Nick, an immaculately turned-out Japanese Marlon Brando lookalike. He had become a friend. He had dropped me off at Narita just two weeks before, and was clearly delighted to see I had returned despite the aftershocks and what might travel down on the wind from Fukushima. He greeted me with a smile, a bow, and took my bag.

With him at my side, what could go wrong?

Rumours and Revelations

It was high summer when the email arrived. A quiet ping into my inbox. It lay there quiet and unattended. That July of 2011 Europe sweltered in the grip of an unusual heat wave. I was travelling, as so often, chairing meetings in Hamburg, the north-German city where Olympus has its European headquarters. The board sat expectantly round a large circular table, a change I had made so people actually looked at and listened to each other.

I had been presiding over meetings there for years, but was doing so now as president of the entire global company, and the deference I was newly accorded was palpable; a novelty which nevertheless also prompted a slight sense of unease. We went through the agenda with me fulfilling my usual role of questioning and challenging, always endeavouring to solicit the views of everyone around the table. We were finished by late afternoon.

I got back to my hotel room and flipped open my laptop to greet the stream of incoming emails. I was known for always responding promptly to messages, meaning I put myself under a relentless pressure. As I looked at the screen, there it was – a tiny time bomb of a missive that was to change my life for ever.

The email's subject read: URGENT NEWS. A friend in Tokyo, Gorō, had read an article in an obscure Japanese magazine called *Facta* in which all sorts of wild allegations had been made about Olympus. I had never heard of *Facta*, but I later discovered that it was a small business title run by a maverick, a rare phenomenon among Japanese media: a campaigning journalist who was unafraid to expose things that demanded to be exposed. Had I been a pessimist, I might have worried. But I was no pessimist.

'Have you received the translation on the Olympus piece?' Gorō asked. 'No,' I emailed back. 'Why? Something I should know?' After four months as president, I was used to being written about particularly in Japan. Newspapers and magazines were always running stories on me, about the *gaijin* boss, the novelty, the curiosity. Guessing that Gorō might be referring to yet another profile, I hoped it was at least flattering.

His return email was swift. The article was not about me. It was about Olympus, and made serious allegations. The message was clear: 'You should come back immediately.' As to what had supposedly taken place, all I could infer from his words was that the accusations against the company involved large sums of money, but the detail was vague. I didn't believe we could have done anything wrong and assumed the article must be either malicious or sensationalist.

Funny how everything around you can unravel so quickly, unstitching the fabric of all you know, or rather of everything you thought you knew. I flew back to Japan, unaware of precisely what awaited me.

The day after I returned to Japan we had our monthly board meeting. It was Friday, 29 July. By then, with the assistance of friends and trusted colleagues who, unlike me, spoke Japanese, I had the gist of the *Facta* article. It alleged that the company had been spending hundreds of millions of dollars on inexplicable transactions relating to the acquisition of strange and unlikely takeover targets. This *was* serious.

Today's meeting agenda would surely now be ditched in favour of getting to the bottom of what had apparently taken place. Who was involved? Tsuyoshi Kikukawa, who had preceded me as president, possibly, but who else? How many people?

On entering the boardroom, I expected the atmosphere to crackle with tension. As was the case when I returned from overseas, everyone was friendly in welcoming me back. There were no signs of anything untoward. The meeting progressed as normal, humdrum in its ordinariness, with no one mentioning any kind of irregularity. I didn't raise the issue as I felt I should keep my counsel until I knew exactly what I was talking about. As the meeting ended I made my way back to my office, wondering if *Facta* had got the wrong end of the stick, although a large part of me remained suspicious. Something felt wrong.

In most companies, the president has a principal influence over events, but at Olympus my authority as the new incumbent had already proved diluted, much to my frustration. Before my appointment Kikukawa had fulfilled the role of both president and chairman (not the ideal model for good corporate governance), but when I became president, he introduced for the first time in the company's history, the title of CEO, which is a Western concept. In general in Japan the president is the CEO and the chairman's position is an honorary one. But I could see things at Olympus were now going to be different in that it quickly became clear that the new CEO title trumped the presidency. This gave Kikukawa ultimate power, at board level, to hire and fire, and also gave him control over the key issue of determining the remuneration of his fellow directors. This situation had troubled me enough to raise the matter with him in a non-confrontational way on more than one occasion. I had asked him politely, 'Why promote me, but effectively limit my ability to manage?' But Kikukawa brushed these concerns away, telling me, 'These titles don't matter; you are the boss.' This did nothing to assuage my unease at the division of roles between CEO and president. I knew full well that I was the person with whom the buck stopped. As the president, I had legal responsibility for signing the company's accounts, along with the letter of representation with the auditors.

Perhaps I was always seen as a *gaijin*, an outsider without Japanese attributes, and the kind of president from whom secrets were kept. But my relationship with Kikukawa dated back decades. He had promoted me in the US, where he had given me responsibility for the company's then loss-making surgical business. He had also promoted me to run all Olympus's businesses in Europe, which had gone on to become the most profitable part of the corporation. He had been my patron. But my loyalty was not blind.

Much as I enjoyed Tokyo, I also craved escape at weekends. That Sunday afternoon I caught a train out of the steaming city with Gorō. He is a generation older than me and very much part of Tokyo's business elite. Our friendship is an unlikely one and many people would be surprised if they knew we were close. As I'm now a controversial figure in Japan, to be publicly associated with me could be harmful to him, and to protect his identity I've changed his name. We were bound for a hot springs retreat a couple of hours out of the metropolis. During the journey, Gorō painstakingly translated the *Facta* article in full for me. The allegations seemed so preposterous that I could not quite believe what I was hearing.

Olympus Runs Amok, shouted the headline. *Runs up massive losses on inexplicable mergers and acquisitions. Dumps ¥70 billion into three minuscule businesses only to write off nearly the whole amount as impairment losses. We expose the shenanigans by Kikukawa and Co. that threaten to decimate Olympus's net worth.*

The whole thing was made even odder by the quirky and melodramatic style of the writing. *Stranger than fiction*, it began:

> Olympus spent ¥70 billion in the 2008 financial year on three companies unrelated to its core operations. It then quietly wrote off most of the investment as impairment losses the next year.
>
> The acquisitions, all unlisted: Altis, which disposes of industrial waste from hospitals; News Chef, which develops and markets microwavable dishes; and Humalabo, which sells mail-order cosmetics and health foods. These subsidiaries are all but invisible in Olympus's securities reports, and information about their business performance is unavailable. Clearly, the company is eager to hide something.

This was bad enough but it was not all. As we sped through the Japanese countryside it kept on coming. *Facta* was asking questions in relation to the acquisition of a British company we had made for ¥270 billion ($2.2 billion):

THE BIZARRE ACQUISITION OF A BRITISH COMPANY FOR 270 BILLION YEN

Olympus raised eyebrows in the equity market when it announced plans to acquire the London-listed manufacturer Gyrus [Gyrus Group PLC] for the princely sum of ¥211.7 billion: a 40 per cent premium over Gyrus's market capitalization. Incredulity turned to stupefaction in the 2010 financial year, when Olympus purchased preferred shares of Gyrus for ¥59.9 billion. The identity of the seller was a mystery, and equity analysts were aghast at the lack of proper financial disclosure.

What is more, goodwill [the excess of payments for corporate acquisitions over the book value of the companies acquired] accounted for more than half of Gyrus's total assets. Observers strained to recall whether they had ever seen a manufacturer with such a balance sheet. Olympus was essentially buying a massive clump of goodwill wrapped in more goodwill. It subsequently declined to provide any information about Gyrus's fiscal performance other than some rudimentary sales figures.

The accusations were wild, and yet each was meticulously detailed. The article alleged that Olympus had purchased three essentially 'Mickey Mouse' companies. Unbelievably, a mail-order face-cream company, a microwave dishes company and a recycling company had all been quietly placed in the Mergers & Acquisitions shopping basket. Each had posted only small turnovers, and yet we had paid approaching $1 billion for them at current exchange rates. A few months earlier, Kikukawa had given me a bottle of 'Lift Essence Lotion' from the newly acquired face-cream company for my wife, Nuncy, to try. (She didn't trust it and this remains unopened in the bathroom cabinet!) I supposed Olympus had spent a small amount of money on some silly distraction; I couldn't imagine why we might have paid huge sums for it. The existence of the other two companies was news to me.

The Gyrus Group PLC deal, however, I remembered all too well. The British medical equipment group had been bought for over $2 billion in 2008, a price which always seemed excessive. But now a further $700 million of payments seemed to have been linked to that acquisition. Why?

Facta had actually thrown down the gauntlet to Olympus before publication. On getting wind of the financial high jinks, its publisher, Shigeo Abe, had sent a letter to Olympus's public relations/ investor relations division in late June. The letter contained questions about the acquisitions and payments and a request for an interview with the chairman Kikukawa. Olympus had stonewalled, refusing to make him available for an interview and declining to answer any of the questions.

So you think you can just blow off Facta *like that, do you?* railed Abe in a blog entry of 15 July. *Well, we'll see soon enough . . . Our upcoming issue is your worst nightmare. Until then, sweet dreams.*

Facta had certainly made good on Abe's threat. As the train travelled on, I sat silent and motionless as Gorō continued to translate. When he finished, we both remained quiet, with the Japanese countryside racing past us and Mount Fuji seemingly holding still in the distance.

It didn't need to be said. We were thinking the same thing: *This had huge implications.* Now it was public knowledge and impossible to ignore. Even if a small part of the article was true, heads would roll, and the company's reputation would be irreparably damaged. And where, as president, did this leave me?

As the train drew up at the station, Gorō and I were greeted by Daisuke, a senior Olympus executive. He is one of the company's most able managers and he had met Gorō in the past with me. Again I've used a false name to protect his anonymity.

The coastal *onsen*, hot springs, were in beautiful surroundings. The temperature was cooler here, the air almost sweet to the taste. According to lore, the minerals to be found within the springs provided all manner of health benefits, and the *onsen* were supposed to have a relaxing effect on both body and mind. I decided to go for a run along the coast because I needed to clear my head. It was out of season in the resort town and there were few people around. Being a 6" 2' Westerner in fluorescent running kit, I must have looked a bit of an oddity. But I had grown comfortable in being different. As I jogged along the seafront, a slow trickle of sweat ran down my face, I entered a rhythmic trance-like state, and my mind went back over the events of the last nine months.

It was in November 2010 that I had been called over from England to Japan by the then president, Mr Kikukawa, or Tom as I knew him, for a meeting without an agenda. When I entered his office he smiled warmly and said straight away, 'Michael, I would like you to be our next president. I haven't been able to change this company, but I believe you can.'

Olympus was a sizeable enterprise, with approaching 40,000 employees and over 70 per cent of the world's medical endoscope market. The healthcare business was performing strongly, with annual sales of around $4 billion delivering an impressive $800 million in profits. The company's products were extraordinarily well engineered and designed. They included cameras, digital voice recorders, microscopes and, most successfully of all, endoscopes coveted by doctors around the world. I was humbled by my engineering colleagues, who to me were the true heroes of the corporation: because of their quiet and understated efforts, Olympus was globally recognized for its formidable strength in design and engineering.

Aside from the golden child of its medical company, other parts of the organization were performing poorly, in particular the camera business. Olympus could undoubtedly make world-class cameras but in the high-end segments, which offer most profits, we were lagging way behind our main competitors Canon and Nikon. Within a decade, our dominance in the point-and-shoot digital camera business had been eroded.

In fact we now lost money on cameras. Net sales in Olympus Imaging Systems had fallen from $3.3 billion in 2008 to $1.7 billion in 2011. By 2011 the division's losses had reached $175 million. Overall our total operating income as a corporation had slumped from $1 billion in 2008 to only around $400 million in 2011. Considering the strength of the medical business, these results were dismal.

But I was not deterred. I understood what had to be done and which difficult decisions needed to be taken. If managed in the right way I knew the medical business, in particular, could deliver even more impressive results. With the help and support of the small talented team I had personally chosen, I was sure things could be quickly turned round.

In facing the challenges ahead, I clearly had the confidence of Kikukawa, who had long been my mentor, an unfailing and vocal supporter who was prepared to grant me a privilege almost unheard-of in Japan: to be the Western president of a ninety-two-year-old Japanese icon.

Were I to take the job, I would become a celebrity of sorts in my host nation, an object of fascination but also of respect, for Japan was known to reward loyalty, and, with thirty years at the company behind me, I had certainly demonstrated that.

This was my moment. I gazed out beyond the seated Kikukawa from his executive suite on the fifteenth floor of the Monolith building and focused on the twin-spired Tokyo City Hall which dominated the Shinjuku district skyline. In some ways I considered Kikukawa a fatherly figure. After just a few seconds, I answered him with a simple 'Yes, I'll do it.'

Back in my room at the Park Hyatt Hotel, I phoned Nuncy and told her the news. I was in a state of high excitement but was quickly brought back down to earth. She went quiet and started to cry – and not out of happiness.

'But you love working in Europe, and living here,' she sobbed, referring to our family home in Southend on the Thames estuary. 'We've got a good life already. Why on earth do you want to change it?'

She was, as is her fashion, quietly persistent. 'Okay, so Everest is there. But you don't have to climb it, do you?' 'My love,' I answered, 'let me change this company for the better. It'll only take a few years and I owe so many people that.' She knew what I was like and that my mind was already made up.

What worried her above all was that the distance and physical separation could destroy our marriage. We both recognized the turmoil that the change would bring to our lives. Little did I know just how right she would turn out to be, and that our sense of security would soon be lost, and our everyday existence would turn into a living nightmare.

My promotion had come on 1 April 2011, April Fools' Day.

On the first official day in my new role I had greeted and addressed the annual intake of new graduate employees, at a time when Japan was still traumatized by the devastating earthquake and tsunami just a few weeks earlier. Foreigners were staying away, and the nation was in a kind of helpless lockdown, further perpetuated by the uncertainties of the unstable Fukushima nuclear reactor which had led to fears of widespread contamination. The dignified, stoic way that the Japanese people were dealing with these disasters reminded me of just why I loved the country so much.

Now I was back in the executive suite on the fifteenth floor, in my own grand office with windows overlooking the teeming, yet entirely organized, chaos of Shinjuku. I was one of only four foreign company presidents in all Japan, but the only *gaijin* ever to have climbed the corporate ladder within the same company, and the only *gaijin* 'salary-man' to have made it to the top.

My appointment was made public in February 2011 and generated headlines in the financial media around the world. The Olympus stock price rose sharply in anticipation that the *gaijin* president would wake up this sleeping corporate giant, and deliver the financial expectations of a company with probably the best medical equipment franchise in the world.

I had given a lengthy interview to the *Financial Times* as part of a feature which considered me alongside the three other *gaijin* presidents: Howard Stringer of Sony, Carlos Ghosn of Nissan and Craig Naylor of Nippon Sheet Glass. 'If I had been Japanese, then I wouldn't be the president,' I had told the paper's correspondent Jonathan Soble. Describing myself as a 'rationalist and stubborn, "dog with a bone" problem-solver', I speculated that with my direct, straight-talking style I would have been sidelined in Japan, where cultural pressure to achieve consensus and to respect hierarchy is all that matters. 'The Japanese have a saying,' I had reminded Soble: 'If you're the nail that sticks out, you get hammered down.'

And Soble, who seemed to find me intriguing subject matter, then continued: 'But while Mr Woodford built his reputation by cutting fat – for a time he was called "Darth Vader" to Mr Ghosn's "le cost killer" – his CV reflects the growing general diversity among Japan's *gaijin* bosses. For a start, he is not an outsider to Olympus, having worked for the company for thirty years, starting as a junior salesman at a European medical equipment company that was part-owned by the Japanese group.'

I made it clear to Soble that I had hard decisions to make: 'Harmony and consensus have their place and time but scrutiny and challenging – devil's advocate, whatever you want to call it – leads to better decision-making. You have to be able to confront, and to say "Oi!" too, because much of your management is going to be outside of Japan.'

Helped by positive media coverage of this sort, my acceptance as president appeared to be going well. The message of change was getting across to both our employees and our shareholders. At the company AGM in June 2011, the most important event in any corporate calendar, I had received more votes of endorsement from shareholders than any other director. The final anointing had occurred at my formal inauguration on 12 July 2011, at the Imperial Hotel in Tokyo, where I was instructed to appear in morning dress to be presented to the world. The great and the good were summoned. Now it was all up to me.

It was never going to be an easy job, but in the months before my formal appointment as president, I had assembled a management team across the world whom I knew could deliver and whom I could trust. It was critically important to get our costs down quickly and this inevitably involved dealing with the most sensitive human issues, principally redundancies, something the Japanese never find easy.

I found that, at least at a middle-management level in Japan, if you explained what needed to be done in a rational and logical way, there was an understanding that by making the difficult choices you ultimately improved the future of the whole company – you made it stronger. Many of the middle managers in Tokyo embraced this new approach, although the men in grey suits at board level were perhaps more comfortable with maintaining the status quo. Nevertheless, I was making rapid progress and was determined to realize the potential of the business.

In the first weeks of my presidency, I had introduced a company-wide programme named 'Cost Cutting 20' an initiative to reduce Olympus's ratio of Selling, General and Administrative (SG&A) expenses (excluding R&D costs) as a percentage of sales by 20 per cent within four years. I discussed this publicly and in detail at a number of presentations to financial analysts who easily understood my logic that by reforming the company's internal structures and processes, there was enormous potential to address its bloated cost base. We needed to have an organization that reflected the international nature of the business, respecting but not being constrained by national boundaries. Logistics is a perfect example where it could be more attractive to ship a product directly from the factory to the customer, as opposed to it going through the internal regional and country structures. Cutting costs in Japan has negative implications and my message to employees was a simple one. By vigorously reducing the cost of the bureaucracy, we could safeguard and build upon what was important: designing and manufacturing products people wanted to buy. I put together a small team of managers to oversee the global programme and we quickly started to see results. When you stopped talking in generalizations and focused on the specifics, people understood. After a few months there was a general acceptance that the temptation to maintain the status quo was the real barrier to the future prosperity of the company.

I was now spending more time in Tokyo, a city which had always delighted me – its people, its sprawl, its conformity, and of course its food. Thirty-five million people live and work in the Japanese capital. It's so colossal that nobody knows for certain where it starts. Or where it stops. The flat plain on which it was founded has long since filled up with people. Now they are creeping up the mountains to the west and land is being hungrily recovered from Tokyo Bay in the east. The guides, as soon as they are written and printed, are out of date.

Next to skyscrapers nestle single-storey family homes with carefully tended roof gardens. Rooms in houses are small and even bedrooms often don't have the space for a permanent bed: you roll out your futon to lay your weary head at night and then roll it up again in the morning. Things are constantly on the move both above your head and beneath your feet. And there is no space. Unless you are wealthy and can use your funds to spread out – get a little elbow room – you are forever cheek by jowl on the subway, the pavement, the park jogging tracks, in the bars. Almost everywhere.

In such confined space, people have to get on and be civil to one another. I loved the intense level of politeness and decorum. Some of my female friends will be appalled at this, but I admit to enjoying the way when you are led to your first-class seat on ANA, the stewardess kneels in front of you and places the slippers on your feet. People care about how they treat others.

My secretaries in Europe had never bowed to me upon leaving my office; in Tokyo, my assistant Michiko did. She had been a first-class purser on Cathay Pacific. After a few weeks, I told her not to walk backwards out of my office and just to call me Michael, which eventually she did.

I loved the countryside, the mountains and the hot springs. I loved the bullet trains that always left and arrived on time. I loved the culture beneath the Japanese stereotype of the automaton salary-man with his sake and karaoke-fuelled nights; I had developed deep friendships with people to whom I would remain close for the rest of my life. Someone once said, 'If you're expecting Japan to be very Westernized, you're astonished at how oriental it remains. If you're expecting it to be very oriental, you're dismayed by how Westernized it has become.' I know now just what they meant.

I could settle here happily. Previously I had always stayed at the Park Hyatt, a hotel made famous by Sofia Coppola's film *Lost in Translation*. It had become like a second home to me with its contemporary design and colour scheme of brown and beige, its supremely attentive staff, its dramatic forty-seventh-floor pool with ceiling-height glass windows where Bill Murray and Scarlett Johansson take a dip because, tortured by jet lag, they are always awake at twenty past four in the morning. At its New York Bar and Grill, high up on the fifty-second, looking out at the winking lights of night time Tokyo, big shot businessmen consume costly Kobe beef steaks in the company of attractive younger women about whom their wives at home know nothing.

To show my commitment to my Japanese colleagues, I had rented an apartment in the Shibuya district in a smart new development called Grosvenor Place. It cost an absolute fortune but was comfortable, had a roof terrace and was near the city's biggest railway station and densest shopping areas. All the best tourist photos feature Shibuya in the background. Typically, Tokyo apartments are small, cramped affairs, as real estate is at such a premium. But mine was unusually large and beautifully appointed. Importantly, it was big enough to accommodate friends and family, allowing them to spend time with me and experience the metropolis for themselves.

I had moved to Japan alone, with Nuncy unwilling to follow just yet, retaining our home in England as our main base. Our children, Edward, eighteen, and Isabel, sixteen, were still at school, with our son university-bound and our daughter soon to be a boarder at a Hogwarts-like establishment. I had a plan: that I would work at full throttle in Tokyo, without distraction, for fourteen to sixteen hours every day, weekends included. Then every two weeks or so I would fly back via London to chair the European or US board meetings, allowing a home visit. The Woodfords could be together in Tokyo during the school holidays, and Nuncy would visit when she could.

I was fifty years old. Having left school in Liverpool at sixteen with only modest academic qualifications, since joining Olympus as a salesman I had steadily climbed up the corporate ladder. I was now ready for the ultimate challenge, leading the organization in which I had worked for almost my entire career. A new life would reboot the system, and refresh my senses. I had never lost sight of my good fortune, all too conscious of how differently things might have turned out. I was also acutely aware that my good luck had risen exponentially.

But my luck had been interrupted by *Facta*'s revelations. The evening we arrived on the coast, the three of us stayed up late in our hot-spring *ryokan*, lingering over dinner and late-night drinks until birdsong interrupted our conversations and sent us, tired but unsettled, to bed. For a while I lay awake wondering what the mainstream Japanese press would make of the *Facta* story. Surely it could only be a matter of time before the headlines appeared. All we could do was wait.

2.

'Who do you work for?'

Monday, 1 August. I woke with my head unexpectedly clear, despite the quantities of alcohol consumed the night before. Filled with resolve, I walked down to the reception area for the English-language morning papers. Not only had the story not made the front covers, it hadn't made it anywhere inside, either. Nobody appeared to be interested, and I couldn't understand why.

But then I remembered the Japanese sense of propriety. Investigative journalism, *Facta* aside, seemed to be anathema here, almost as if illegal business practices were best left uncommented upon.

We took a private car back to the city, to ensure I was in the office before the working day began. Before we reached Shinjuku, I dropped off my hot-spring friends, telling them that we would stay in close touch, hourly if necessary, with updates. When I arrived on the fifteenth floor, Michiko greeted me with my normal café latte and egg croissant. The routine of the day continued with no sign that anything was out of the norm – it was business as usual. By lunchtime I could take it no longer. I needed to talk to someone and summoned to my office two Japanese colleagues I knew I could trust.

'Have you seen this?' I enquired, holding up the magazine. Their expressions cowed, they both admitted they had. They had been instructed not to tell me.

'By whom?' I asked.

'By Kikukawa-san.'

I could not sleep that night. The reply from my confidants had been deeply unsettling. As I tossed and turned, I decided that the next day I would have to confront Kikukawa. After all, I had my own sense of propriety, of right and wrong, and I felt a responsibility to act. We could not just sit there and ignore *Facta*. Someone had to do something.

At 8 a.m. on the Tuesday I had a meeting with the president of a major national camera retailing business, which only Kikukawa and I were due to attend. I arrived that morning at the customer's office in my black Lexus limousine, Kikukawa in his, enacting the public pageantry of our collective power. The meeting was perfunctory, progressing with well-oiled smoothness. Our revered host knew nothing of any awkwardness between his guests, and at the end of the meeting he presented us both with gifts. The giving of tokens of appreciation is normal practice in Japan, part of business culture. He gave us tickets to a forthcoming major baseball game, two to me, two to Kikukawa. The *thank you* had barely left my lips when Kikukawa lurched forward with a speed that belied his seventy years and snatched the tickets from my hand.

'He will not be needing those, as Michael doesn't like baseball,' he told the president. 'He is British; he likes soccer.' My pair of tickets joined his, and all four disappeared into the breast pocket of his suit jacket. This rudeness annoyed me. The retailer's president rewarded Kikukawa's tight smile with one of his own before departing. As we left the building, I half-expected Kikukawa to suggest that we go for a coffee to talk about the revelations made in the *Facta* article.

He didn't. Unsure of the etiquette when you suddenly suspect all those around you of conspiracy, I phoned Michiko in my car on the way to the office to arrange an urgent meeting with both Kikukawa and his 'right-hand man', the senior vice-president Hisashi Mori. Within ten minutes, she phoned back and told me, 'Michael, Mr Kikukawa's secretary has told me he's very busy today and the only time he can meet with you is over lunch.'

I arrived at the meeting room. Both men were already sitting in the gloomy surroundings of beige walls and dark wood. Like something out of the 1970s and with blinded windows that seemed to keep out unnatural amounts of light, the effect was heavy and oppressive. I had never liked that room.

On the long table in front of them was a magnificent platter of sushi; in front of where I was clearly expected to sit was a rather sad-looking tuna sandwich of the sort that you would expect to find at a suburban train station kiosk. I adored sushi, as the two men knew full well. Some none-too-subtle point was being made here. No matter, I did not have much of an appetite. A game was clearly being played, and nobody was informing me of the rules. I was going to have to pick them up as I went along.

A minute earlier I had been superficially warmly welcomed, but after my own friendly greetings the atmosphere immediately changed when I placed the *Facta* magazine on the table, showing its headline 'Massive Hidden Losses on Reckless M&A'. Lifting the magazine, I began to speak: 'I am really worried about this story, which several different people have drawn to my attention.' I said. 'Aside from friends, you know I have many contacts here at a senior level in the business community and also at the embassy.' This remark was intended to blur things and hopefully avoid being asked just who had drawn my attention to the magazine's revelations. I certainly didn't want to start being evasive myself. Kikukawa made no response, sensing I had just started. I lingered on the back page headline and then without commentary, but with several heavy sighs, slowly flicked through the pages of the Olympus exposé. The extensive feature included a particularly sinister-looking image of Kikukawa which I thought made him look like Doctor Evil. I pointed to the schematic diagram explaining the strange and tortuous routings of the acquisitions. There was also a photograph of a sign taken in front of the building that housed the headquarters of the three 'Mickey Mouse' companies, on which their logos and the Olympus one appeared together. In a deliberately calm and quiet voice I asked, 'Why has nobody told me anything about this?' After a pause, I continued: 'The allegations in here are really serious.'

Kikukawa responded, trying far too hard to be friendly: 'Michael, I instructed the staff on the Executive Floor not to tell you.' 'But why, Tom?' I asked. 'Because you're the president working so hard and are much too busy to be bothered by domestic issues like this,' he replied.

This was not what I wanted to hear. Sighing again deeply, I said, 'Tom, I need to communicate with all those who have an interest in our company. I have just returned from our Investor Relations Road Show and, in the process, have been to New York, Boston, Paris and London, meeting with our overseas investors and potential new ones. I have done the same here in Japan.' Kikukawa started to tilt his head to one side, looking puzzled and anguished. I continued, 'As the president of the company, surely at the very least I should have been briefed about something like this? They are, after all, extremely serious allegations.' There was an uncomfortable silence and then, with my voice falling away, I asked, 'Are they true?'

Kikukawa nodded. 'Some of them, yes.'

'Which parts are true, Tom?'

'Well,' he replied, a study in evasion, 'we did make some provisions. There were some write-downs for the acquisitions.'

It was all highly unspecific.

I watched his face, framed by a large pair of glasses that sat heavily on his nose, fight a losing battle to maintain a smile. The watchfulness in his eyes matched the tension in the room. I pressed for more details. None were forthcoming.

I switched my stare to Mori, his face unresponsive beneath his thick black eyebrows and head of soft white hair. Mori was looking into the middle distance as if transfixed.

We were getting nowhere. I insisted that I needed to know more and agreed to meet Mori alone after a ten-minute washroom break. Away from Kikukawa, Mori would hopefully open up more. Mori was a bureaucrat but an intelligent one who very much played the monkey to Kikukawa's organ grinder. With Mori, I felt I would be able to get into the detail of what had actually taken place. So much of what was in the magazine article still didn't make sense. I needed to be enlightened. I wanted the truth.

On reconvening the meeting with Mori now alone, I tried hard to keep our discussion civilized. I started with Gyrus. Why, I asked, if we had bought Gyrus in 2008 for over $2 billion, were we now paying out a further $700 million two years on? He mumbled his response, referring to something about A-preference shares, but then dried up. That made no sense whatsoever as I knew that we had acquired the company outright, with no minority interests remaining.

We were interrupted by Kikukawa, who marched in with another magazine and asked me if I recognized the person in the photograph he showed me. I answered that it was the president of one of Olympus's main banks. He translated the unflattering article, commenting with disgust that the tabloid press was always creating sensational and groundless stories. Companies needed, he continued, to be treated with more respect. He left as abruptly as he had entered.

For Kikukawa to come back into a meeting that he had already left showed me just how unsettled he was. Alone again, I pressed Mori further, but he fell into total silence. He just sat there, my questions bouncing off him. Requesting answers from someone who looks at you with such unswerving blankness is a disorientating experience. The crows' feet around his eyes may have deepened, but otherwise he was entirely immobile. I tried to lighten the mood and with an ironic smile said, 'Mori-san, come on, you can't be serious about this. Olympus is a high-tech enterprise that adds engineering know-how to our products. And now we want to enter the cosmetics business? Is this part of our new global strategy, getting into competition with the likes of L'Oréal, Shiseido and Estée Lauder?' His face remained passive and inscrutable. 'And what about these *microwave plates*?' I laughed, hoping to break through his wall of silence. At least this time Mori responded, albeit in a whisper, that 'the plates are good for those with diabetes'. I could not help but laugh again at the desperate explanation. I went on: 'Aside from the obvious lack of "strategic fit", how did we value these companies so obscenely high? Surely we have overpaid, and by a grossly high multiple too?' Mori continued to be impassive but I wasn't going to allow him to escape my probing. I continued: 'How could these acquisitions possibly benefit the company, much less our shareholders?'

Mori had fallen silent again. I now grew annoyed, then angry. I raised my voice and told him that I was the president, and he the vice-president of whom I was asking reasonable questions. These related to transactions with a value in excess of $1.5 billion. Still not getting any answers, I leaned towards him and looked him in the eye. Moving close to him physically, raising my voice and being so direct in my approach would in Japan be considered unusually assertive.

'Mori-san,' I asked. 'Who do you work for?'

I imagined his response would be that he worked for Olympus, or that he reported to me. Momentarily, Mori's mask fell away. 'I work for Mr Kikukawa. I am loyal to Mr Kikukawa.' That was quite possibly the first truthful answer I had received since we had sat down.

The temperature in the room seemed to drop, and I suddenly felt cold and numb. I was desperately trying to process his response. I felt an ominous mix of disillusionment and foreboding. I could also hear Nuncy's voice inside my head: *Why go to Tokyo? We have a good life here. Why change it?*

Mori left. I returned alone to my office wondering just what it was that I had stumbled upon. Something sinister had taken place in the past and I was now caught in its web. I wanted to walk away, to run, but knew that I could not. That the mainstream Japanese media had self-imposed a silence on the story to date was ominous, and only heightened my anxiety.

I knew that I was going to have to deal with this myself, and quickly.

For the rest of that week I went through the motions of my role in a daze. Meetings came and went. Formal dinners, one after another. My annual leave was approaching, and having worked ludicrously hard since my appointment, I desperately wanted to spend time with Nuncy and the children. We had booked eleven days in Majorca, which meant a breathing space away from *all of this*. I could not wait. On the Friday night I finally flew to the Balearic island via Paris.

In Majorca, we were in an idyllic spot far from the crowds in the Cap Rocat Hotel, a converted fortress on the Bay of Palma. It was hot, quiet and beautiful. Our family's week and a half of relaxation was disrupted only by the endless chiming of my iPhone. And the competing noise inside my head. To Nuncy's overtures of disapproval, and my children's weary indifference, I continued to work each day, speaking frequently with the English office, and went to bed, tired but constantly wired.

This was far from the most restful family holiday we had ever taken. Nuncy and the children were only catching up on my new story, whereas I was immersed in the intensity of it. So I tried to get them engaged and told them about the meetings and Kikukawa's behaviour but, understandably, they couldn't grasp the full magnitude. I am a worrier with a tortured soul; it takes a lot to make me switch off, and this was not going to be a holiday to find inner peace.

I found myself self-medicating by drinking. Each evening as the sun descended in the west, in a futile attempt to escape my cares, I would have a large gin and tonic, followed by half a bottle of powerful Ribera del Duero red wine and then a good Spanish brandy. I drank quickly for its seductive sedative effect.

I woke each night dehydrated in the sweltering early hours with those figures dancing before my eyes: $800 million here, $700 million there. I just couldn't come up with a plausible explanation. Kikukawa, a man I had previously thought rather benign, now began to take on an entirely different persona.

We are a dysfunctional family but a loving one and despite my worry I wanted to catch up with Edward and Isabel, both of whom were awaiting vital exam results. But I could not connect fully with them. So I often just sat on the beach, getting brown and brooding.

My mood was not helped as back home it seemed as if the whole of the UK was on fire, with rioting and looting spreading from London to six other cities. These were the first 'social media-orchestrated' riots as groups roamed and plundered, linked by Facebook, Twitter and BlackBerry instant-messaging. We watched the disturbing images as all police leave was cancelled and Prime Minister David Cameron was forced to cut short his holiday. Not for the first time while abroad did I feel ashamed of being British.

There were some happy moments caught by the photographs taken during those days on the island. To create diversions and prevent myself from lying still on the beach thinking about *Facta*, we hired boats. On the third day we chartered a small yacht and had eight beautiful hours in the Mediterranean sun with the warm sea breeze cooling us. Another time we took a motorized RIB to explore the turquoise seas along the Majorcan coastline. For a few hours, I actually forgot my troubles.

But these periods of relief were short lived. With Isabel in particular I tried hard to disguise my anguish about events left behind in Tokyo. Nuncy could see I was worried, but sometimes in a family you can be very alone carrying your cares. I was desperate for support from my family but I didn't want to ruin their holiday and instil them with my own sense of foreboding.

I had the English translation of the *Facta* article with me, which I must have read a hundred times. I was obsessed with it. Its level of detail was comprehensive, which meant the information could only have come from an Olympus insider, from a whistleblower. Yet how, with over 40,000 employees, would I track that person down? I found myself hoping that he or she would reach out to me. After all, I already had a certain reputation within the company. I was known to be very black-and-white, to operate with a strict moral code.

I had, you could say, form. In Hamburg, back in 2005, I reported serious internal wrongdoing which led to a director leaving the company without compensation. Then, three years later, a tax audit carried out by the German authorities highlighted that company managers, Italian and German nationals, were linked to four payments totalling €640,000 ($883,000) made between July and October 2003, where no services appeared to have been rendered. I went immediately to Tokyo to report the matter, and again I was supported. I was, however, forbidden to sue in a civilian court for the recovery of the monies, for Kikukawa insisted that to do so would have caused Olympus reputational damage. The German prosecutor eventually pressed charges against the three individuals involved, but not until March 2011.

I lay in the blistering heat of the Majorcan sun wondering about what sort of person Kikukawa really was. I was very much his man, his project, his anointed one. Everyone thought I was close to him. Most relationships in business are splendidly superficial but ours was complex but warm. It is remarkable how you can be intimate in that way with someone, spend so much time with them travelling and in meetings, and then discover you don't really know them at all.

To the outside world we were an intriguing team. Me tall and Western, him short and Japanese. A dynamic duo. The perceived ideal answer to the problems of a Japanese industrial conglomerate – the Westerner who could implement the tough cost-cutting that the *ringi-sho* or consensus-built decision-making made so difficult for a native.

At the press conference in Tokyo some six months earlier, when I had been presented to the media as president elect, I had described Kikukawa as my greatest supporter and a protective 'umbrella'. I explained he would be able to help me extend the sort of changes I had made in Europe to Olympus as a whole. 'When you're changing an organization, there are lots of sensitivities, lots of human issues, and we've always been able to talk about these things very easily,' I had remarked at the time. How hollow all that looked now.

In response to questions, Kikukawa had commented he would leave operations and strategy to me and focus mainly on relationships with the banks, Japanese shareholders and the company's suppliers. Everyone in the audience of journalists laughed heartily when Kikukawa said he disapproved only of Mr Woodford's hobbies: running and sailing. 'I have ordered him to learn how to play golf,' he had pronounced with a thin smile. 'Golf is essential to a Japanese executive.' On the phone that evening I told a colleague in Hamburg that 'I loathe and detest golf. If ever I take it up, you have my permission to shoot me.'

Except at formal meetings with outsiders, I always addressed Kikukawa simply as Tom, his chosen Westernized name. This informality was a privilege extended only to me. Our closeness was made possible by his excellent English, learned during the many years he had worked in America.

He called me Michael or Mr President when I became the president, or the Japanese term for the position: *Shacho*. He was always very respectful – it was Mr Woodford in public. He often showed me genuine kindness. In 2002 I was made a Member of the British Empire. After I received the award from Prince Charles, Kikukawa took me to a famous Italian restaurant in Tokyo to celebrate. He told me how proud he was of my achievements and presented me with a black Montblanc fountain pen. I still have it in my sock drawer at home as otherwise I would have lost it within a few weeks – my habit with watches, pens and keys.

There were limits to this closeness. Although I met his sons in London, both of whom were charming and likeable, I never met his wife. Kikukawa was always much more keen to talk about his pair of miniature poodles. He adored those dogs, dressing them up at weekends in their little suits. Their image in a couple of kitsch out-fits was even the screensaver on his computer.

We used to joke when I would tell him about the trials of being married to a strong-minded Spaniard. In return he would smile and note that when his wife went away she would leave him all his meals in individual dishes in containers in the fridge, so that he only had to heat them up. 'You're joking,' I replied. 'When my wife goes away, I have to go to the supermarket, buy a frozen ready meal and put it in the microwave.' He would laugh at my exaggerated self-pity, and with daily exchanges like that, I felt there was an understanding and connection.

We were very different but complemented each other. I thought we would work effectively as a partnership. If we could laugh easily together and always discuss things in an honest way, it was surely the right basis for the strongest of working relationships to develop.

Kikukawa had, however, some serious weaknesses. When he got involved in issues concerning the medical business – which made the majority of the company's profit – he revealed a surprising, and to my mind worrying, lack of knowledge of the detail. While it was often patently obvious he didn't understand what he was talking about, my colleagues never dared expose this. I quickly learned that no one ever asked why the Emperor wasn't wearing clothes.

Whatever Kikukawa's pronouncements, however wide of the mark, they were taken as words of wisdom, thanks to the prevailing assumption in Japan that those in the most senior roles are infallible and all-knowing. Indeed, often when I spoke at meetings or events in Japan, people would diligently and meticulously write my com-ments down, even if, in my opinion, they weren't noteworthy. The most egregious forms of management-speak would be especially treasured, as if they were religious proclamations. One of my former colleagues would refer dryly to the obsessive use of mindless management-speak as 'bullshit bingo'!

My management style is fundamentally different. I am much more questioning of human nature. I rarely automatically accept what I am told and constantly question to get beneath the platitudes of PowerPoint presentations and the like. Whenever a manager made claims I would ask for supporting evidence. I have seen, too many times, things accepted as fact or the God-given truth just because it was on a PowerPoint slide and the presenter spoke with a loud and confident voice. I have been accused of being cynical in my management style, but any senior manager is foolhardy to work on any other premise – there is nothing wrong in seeing the best in people but you also have to see their weaknesses.

Nevertheless, I have met a handful of Japanese managers who've worked for Western companies, for example Johnson & Johnson and Apple, where through their experience they also had learned not to simply accept things at face value. These were exactly the type of questioning and challenging Japanese managers I wanted in Olympus's senior team.

From my experience, there remains a lot of meaningless noise and clutter in Japanese corporate life. I always tried to concentrate on results; in simple terms, what was being delivered and by whom and where. This gave me the data to question why one part of the organization performed so much more strongly than another. This type of questioning often created uncomfortable tensions but was how you objectively focused on strengths and weaknesses, which in my opinion is what management is about. Kikukawa was unable to read weaknesses and strengths in this way.

I would often contrast him in my mind with my greatest Olympus hero, Ichizo Kawahara. He had been president of the medical business, an engineer and effectively the father of the modern endoscope. Although his English was limited, he understood the strengths and weaknesses of Westerners and could see immediately who was 'bullshitting'.

Aside from his understanding of the products and medical proce-dures for which they were used, he had a great insight into human nature, which made him one of the most remarkable and effective managers I have ever worked with. Kawahara was notorious within Olympus, not least because of his legendary red pen. In the pre-email days, he would go through memos or letters and annotate with *This is rubbish* or *You should have thought about what you are writing*. But he remained exemplary to me of all that is good about Japan. He had worked his way up, becoming the president of the medical business, but never lost that obsession about the company's products and cus-tomers. He should have been made the group president but was passed over in favour of Toshiro Shimoyama, a much lesser entity who was subsequently identified as starting the 'Tobashi' some two decades earlier. (*Tobashi* is the Japanese for 'fly away'. It describes the once common practice in Japan where external investment firms typ-ically take loss-bearing investments off the books of their client company at the original valuation. This conceals the investment losses from the clients' financial statements. In that sense, the losses are made to disappear, or 'fly away'. I will explain more later in the book.)

Such was Mr Kawahara's contempt for Shimoyama, he used to deal with his in-tray in board meetings, preferring to put the time to good use, rather than listen to the utterances of the president.

Mr Kawahara retired from Olympus in June 1994. I last met with him, after becoming president, on a Saturday afternoon in the sum-mer of 2011, when we had lunch together at the Chinese restaurant in the Keio Plaza Hotel. He is a man in his seventies but his mind and wit are as sharp as ever. We laughed and talked for many hours, reminiscing about the old days. I often dream of what would have happened if Mr Kawahara had been made group president instead of Shimoyama.

Kikukawa, by contrast, was vain and self-obsessed. Always nattily dressed and impeccably manicured, he had installed a treadmill in his office behind an opaque glass partition. In July 2011 when we were at the Imperial Hotel rehearsing for my inauguration ceremony, we passed a small boutique in the hotel's shopping mall and he proudly announced that the week before he had bought three ties there at $500 apiece. I found such boasting vulgar and ostentatious. I once bought a pair of Prada shoes at the duty free in Heathrow and the P fell off. A warning perhaps to me on the perils of vanity.

There had been one bizarre occasion doing the photography for the company's 2011 *Annual Report and Accounts*, a document which was beautifully and expensively presented. Kikukawa and I had to pose for a joint photograph for the inside cover – I was instructed to arrive in a grey suit and he would wear a blue suit. Of course he had to choose the ties: 'I'll have that one, and Michael will have that.' (Naturally he chose the nicer one.) In one shot he stood on a box, and had me carefully positioned to minimize the apparent height difference. That process went on for hours with make-up artists and fifteen people from the PR company. And there was Kikukawa, in the middle, preening himself like a peacock.

I had watched the deference, the kow-towing towards him. Everyone knew there was a hard side to Kikukawa, which I had seen on a few occasions in his treatment of previous directors and managers who he felt had challenged him. One talented director chose to leave the company, realizing that Kikukawa held all the cards and his obedient board would always support him. This told me of a darker side, a side that would not tolerate dissent of any kind. I had certainly found it odd that he personally decided the salaries of both Mori and Hideo Yamada, our so-called independent standing corporate auditor who most days had lunch with Kikukawa. They, in turn, approved his.

From a governance point of view, this is unacceptably cosy. But

Olympus, not unusually for a Japanese corporation, had no formal remuneration committee. In the West, where executive pay levels are controversial and increasingly disputed by shareholders, such an approach would be unthinkable. In the culture of the Kikukawa era, there were no effective controls, no checks and balances, and that increased the likelihood that board members would act in mutually back-scratching ways.

As I lay there on that Majorcan beach, I recalled one aspect of Kikukawa's behaviour which had irked me from my very first meeting as president. At every Executive Committee meeting he would sit next to me, and smoke. Olympus has a strict no-smoking policy but he would happily puff away because he was the boss. I'm slightly asthmatic and would start coughing. When I got home I stank of his cigarettes. I found it a terrible example for the chairman to have no regard for the rules, and to smoke openly in the office. It was just like in *Animal Farm*, where there is one rule for the masses and another for the few. I reflected on the man, whom I had seen a different side of since I had come to Tokyo. He enjoyed luxuriating in being the big shot in town. And how he liked attention. He loved it. He was controlling, and I am not very good at being controlled. As he would discover.

Sad to leave Majorca and my family, at the end of August I found myself in a black mood as the aeroplane touched down back at Narita. This was despite the fact that my son Edward, happy after getting his desired A level grades, was accompanying me with his friend Toby. Before we left I had thought that Tokyo was the very last place I wanted to be. But it proved fun having this pair of late teenagers at my apartment, talking and observing. It turned out one of the most rewarding and enjoyable weeks I had in Japan. I had put 'the problem' to one side. The two of them had a wild time, including a visit to one of the infamous maid cafés, where you can choose a coffee but have to beg for your milk and sugar by making meowing noises. I even introduced them to Kikukawa when I took them into the office – they asked after his beloved poodles. I trust Edward's judgement and he knew about the *Facta* allegations. One night during his visit he provided a prescient warning: 'Dad, he comes across as a very likeable, charming man. If you are going to go against him, you need to make sure you have all the facts to prove that he's not the man he appears to be.'

The period ahead gave me precisely that opportunity. Fortunately, my immediate schedule involved visiting our European and US manufacturing companies. Over the next few weeks I was to visit our plants in Hamburg, Přerov in the Czech Republic and then New Hampshire in the US, ending with an Olympus of the Americas board meeting in New York. Hisashi Mori was due to accompany me on the European leg of the trip, together with manufacturing colleagues from Germany and Japan.

In Hamburg, the plant had an enviable reputation and I found the factory people welcoming and extremely positive. Mori was distant and withdrawn but he still went through the motions of asking questions of those we met. I tried to be professional and show interest but my mind was preoccupied. I wanted to ask Mori a question; what about the $1.7 billion. Where has that gone?

They were long days with full schedules. After each one, a group of us would head out for dinner to unwind. I had always valued these opportunities on business trips to get to know my colleagues better. After all, you can't effectively run a global company by sitting in your office on the fifteenth floor of a Tokyo skyscraper. I was also grateful that there were so many of us eating together each night. This avoided the need to dine alone with Mori, who, since our frosty meeting the previous month, had become even more distant and detached.

A dutiful cog in the boardroom, Mori was different in social situations. He would focus his implacable gaze on the plate in front of him, the only effort he expended being the methodical movements of his jaw, turning his meat to mulch and slowly swallowing. On the two nights that we ate together on that trip, hardly a word of conversation passed between us.

One night while we were in Hamburg I went back to the Park Hyatt for a nightcap with a trusted Japanese colleague. We talked until very late and I outlined the potentially catastrophic consequences of my continuing along this road of enquiry. If I went much further, there would be no question of turning back.

He was a very conservative, loyal company man. And he still is. So his view was very important to me. 'Michael,' he said, 'I know if you don't do this, the wrongdoing will just go on with power being passed on from one generation of bad men to the next.' He mentioned one of Kikukawa's cohorts by name and forcefully said, 'I hate him.' And then mournfully, 'I have a very bad feeling about the company's fate. But you must continue because there's no one else who can do it. Only you as the president can find out what has happened. Only you can do that. The sickness will stay for ever if you don't remove it.' It was that conversation more than any other which convinced me to keep going.

3.

Antisocial Forces

On 19 September I flew to New York for the American section of my itinerary. On my first evening there, I had arranged to meet with Joel Young, a former board member of Olympus Surgical & Industrial America (OSIA), a US subsidiary in New York which I had established. Joel is a tall handsome man with the physique of an athlete and I had teased him in the past for looking like Christopher Reeve of Superman fame. In a management reorganization in 2008, I lost responsibility for OSIA and the company was closed in 2009. After twenty years of loyal service Joel was made redundant. He suffered greatly in his feelings of rejection. In that difficult first year when he was searching to find another job, we kept in regular touch and grew close. I am hugely fond of him.

That night we ate dinner at the Andaz Hotel on Fifth Avenue. Within a few minutes he presented me with a package and told me excitedly to 'open it now'. He had bought me an American first edition of one of my favourite books, George Orwell's *Animal Farm*. It was a perfect gift, as Joel had remembered that I had referred to the novel frequently in talking about the dangers of power and that in any large company it's the most senior managers who are most prone to becoming deluded and separated from reality. We both said, almost in unison, 'All animals are equal but some animals are more equal than others,' quoting the character Napoleon the pig, and we both knew which of our colleagues had become pig-like themselves.

I told Joel everything because I trusted him. He was shocked but listened carefully. I stopped talking and there was a short silence between us. 'You get these moments in life,' he said, 'when you are presented with a choice which offers two paths.' He recalled how in 1994 in Bridgeport, Connecticut he had seen a young woman being kidnapped at knifepoint in a car park. Without thinking about his own safety, he jumped into his car and pursued the kidnapper and terrified victim. With his inherent modesty, Joel would be embarrassed if I retold the full story but what I will share is that the police later made it clear that his actions probably saved the woman's life. Few would have acted in the way Joel had.

When you are on edge, it's hard to overstate how uplifting it is to have people telling you you're doing the right thing. I was starting to realize that the road to becoming a whistleblower was a lonely one and sets you apart. You become an island. There are times when some people are on the island with you, but generally speaking you remain like Robinson Crusoe, or Tom Hanks talking to a basketball. It's very isolating. After sharing the confidences in that Manhattan restaurant, Joel stuck with me even closer. As the drama unfolded in the weeks that followed, he wrote or phoned me almost every day with wise advice.

The next day I flew up to Lebanon, New Hampshire to visit a company Olympus Corporation had recently bought – Olympus Biotech. It makes blood protein to enhance bone growth, a radical departure from the normal kind of business activity with which Olympus had traditionally been involved. It was an unusual acquisition and I wanted to understand more and determine whether it was going to be yet another disappointment.

It turned out to be an interesting company with obvious potential, and meeting the people involved was uplifting for me. It was exactly the thing I should have been doing as the president: celebrating and encouraging new ideas that would ensure everyone's future.

Generally my view for Olympus was that we should invest in our existing businesses, especially medical. We had impressive engineering know-how and there were so many areas where we could build upon our existing strengths. This is a much cheaper and more productive way of running a corporation than making expensive acquisitions such as Gyrus, the biggest by far. But the real reasons behind that acquisition were becoming clearer and clearer as each day passed.

I flew from the Granite State back to New York that same evening with my Olympus Biotech colleagues in a small private jet, landing at Teterboro Airport in New Jersey. It is located only twelve miles from Manhattan but the traffic was heavy and I arrived back at the Andaz with only a few minutes to shower and change before dinner. The venue was the Capital Grille, a large, noisy and atmospheric steakhouse on East 42nd Street, where I was joined by the other board members of Olympus of the Americas (the north American subsidiary, covering the US, Canada and Latin America).

Looking around the table made me think of the management consultants I'd so often heard waxing lyrical about the need for 'globalization'. Among us were Welsh, Spanish, German, English and Japanese. The group represented a multinational management team that would have made the United Nations proud.

After dinner they came back for a drink at my hotel. It was already gone 11 p.m. and the basement bar at the Andaz was throbbing. We found a corner booth. The *Facta* revelations were now common knowledge as they had, after all, been published in Japan, and were much talked about among the senior management. My colleagues were anxious to know just what lay behind the allegations. I promised them I would do everything I could to get to the truth. Everyone was supportive, urging me to investigate and find out exactly what had gone on. They were all behind me, but ultimately it was still my decision as to whether I should write to Kikukawa and the Tokyo board and get things out into the open. I do not judge my colleagues harshly in not becoming directly involved, because what could they do? They had their own careers and families to look after and a lot was at stake for them if things went wrong. But a lot was at stake for me too. Everything.

The following morning I woke up at 3.20 a.m., due to the adrenaline in my system and a disrupted body clock acquired from working and living around the globe. With only a few hours' rest, last night's alcohol, and a sleeping pill in my bloodstream, I moved around the room in a zombie-like state. As was my habit, the first thing I did was open up my laptop. There in my inbox was what I had half-expected and hoped for.

The previous day *Facta* had published a second story on Olympus and here attached to the email was the English translation. I clicked to open it with a mix of fascination and dread. What grim revelations could be in store in the latest episode from that weird, quixotic little magazine? What did they know about my company that I didn't?

The reporter was cross that Olympus was stonewalling him and refusing to answer any questions. *I get it. You think you can just blow off Facta like that. However, I'm afraid I now have you by the tail. You can look forward to a spotlight being pointed to the Olympus cover of darkness in our upcoming issue. And, by all means tremble as you wait.*

In the darkness of my room, the only light coming from the laptop screen, I read on slowly and with increasing dismay. This new article revealed the share structure of one of the 'Mickey Mouse' companies, Altis. Apart from Olympus, the other shareholders included two outfits with curious names, Neo Strategic Ventures and Dynamic Dragons II – two Special Purpose Companies (SPCs) registered in the Cayman Islands. *Now we are starting to see money flows that had been shrouded in thick darkness are coming to light*, wrote the *Facta* journalist in his thriller-like style.

It got worse. *Facta* then established a link between these two SPCs and another outfit called J Bridge. It was explained that J Bridge was a company suspected of having a relationship with 'antisocial forces' and was shunned by the capital markets.

I can't believe what I'm seeing, wrote the wide-eyed *Facta* scribe. *Here is Olympus, a company with a proud history, posting mountainous*

losses on account of management carelessness of momentous proportions
and funnelling cash behind the scenes to antisocial forces. The mind fairly
boggles. This is simply too over the top, too pathetic to be real.

My heart sank. I got up from my chair in my bathrobe and walked
around. 'Antisocial forces' is the standard euphemism for organized
crime. Even a clueless *gaijin* like me was well aware of that.

This new article opened a fresh chamber of horrors. I wasn't just
worried about alleged white-collar fraud, but now something much
worse. The Yakuza, a Mafia-like organization, had been around for
decades in Japanese society but had been brought centre stage for us
non-Japanese speaking foreigners by the publication in 2009 of
Tokyo Vice by the acclaimed American investigative reporter Jake
Adelstein.

Jake is a highly unusual character; a complete one-off. At the age
of twenty-four this Jewish man from America's Mid-West somehow
got a job in Tokyo as a crime reporter for the *Yomiuri Shimbun*, the
world's most-read newspaper with a daily circulation of 13.5 million. Jake was the first American to work for the Japanese press as a
Japanese-language reporter. His position gave him a unique Westerner's view of Japan from the underbelly up as he toiled away
doing eighty-hour weeks at crime scenes for twelve years.

His near undoing came when he got the scoop of his life after
discovering a leading yakuza had travelled to the United States for a
liver transplant. The Mob tracked Jake down and requested a meeting to warn him off the story. A henchman from the Goto-gumi
gang, a particularly nasty sub-set of the Yamaguchi-gumi, sat him
down and calmly told him, 'Either erase the story, or we'll erase
you. And maybe your family. But we'll do them first, so you learn
your lesson before you die.' Adelstein is like something out of a
Raymond Chandler novel, and a Tokyo legend whose revelations
led him and his family to be placed under police protection.

It was Jake who had urged readers to rethink their views of the
Yakuza and revise their image from one of a bunch of tattooed

nine-fingered thugs in white suits wielding samurai swords and running extortion plus prostitution rackets, to something far more white collar. They had observed the world of high finance with its attractive margins and liked what they saw. Jake called them 'Goldman Sachs with guns'.

Japan likes to have everything organized – even its crime, according to Adelstein – and I wasn't keen to form an appendix to an updated edition of *Tokyo Vice*. The latest claims in the October issue of *Facta* changed the magnitude of what I was facing.

Things had gone far enough. I knew then that I had to formalize my concerns in writing. I decided that I wasn't going back to Japan if I didn't get some answers. I needed to deal with this straight away; I couldn't put it off any longer. In reading the *Facta* article what frightened me most was that I simply couldn't work out just what and who was a risk, but there was clearly good reason to be worried.

Everything felt surreal and my imagination was on fire with possibilities. It was a 'normal' autumn day in New York, but I felt I was living in parallel worlds. The Monolith building in Shinjuku was a long way away but my mind was filled with its murky goings-on.

That day's American board meeting was being held at the Four Seasons on East 57th Street. My hotel was on 41st Street, but I needed some air and time to think, so rather than take a cab I dragged my suitcase the sixteen blocks. And as I went along, crossing roads, the wheels clacking against paving stone cracks, I kept thinking to myself, *Here I am in New York, I'm going to a routine business meeting and there are yellow cabs. Drivers are honking their car horns, steam is streaming out of vents in the street, and pedestrians are crowding sidewalks on their way to work. All appears normal. But I've just discovered the company for which I have worked since my early twenties has been involved in something very bad. What is going on? What is happening to me? It can't be real.*

Somehow, though, being lost in the crowds and noise of NYC was reassuring. Nobody could get to me here. During the coffee breaks I met individually with each of the directors with whom I had shared drinks and my anxieties the night before. I updated them on the latest and profoundly worrying revelations from the most recent *Facta* article. They appeared confident that I would bring in forensic accountants and that Kikukawa and his cronies would have to leave. There were words of disbelief, and entreaties to 'be careful'.

That evening I took a 'red eye' flight back to the UK. As it landed at London City Airport, located in the old docklands area of the city, with its runway perilously positioned between two sections of open water, the sun was rising. I travelled back to the company's British headquarters in Southend. I wanted the best possible secretarial support and the input from my colleagues, whose intellect and accounting skills I valued greatly. They all understood why I was doing this. I started to write the first letter.

Although I was tired, I knew we had reached the point where I had no option but to get my concerns down in writing and to create a paper trail of evidence. I spent the rest of that day and all of the following one agonizingly drafting and redrafting my letter. Finally, late on the Friday evening, it was finished. I addressed it to Mori-san, its subject title shouting out boldly from the page in capitals.

SERIOUS GOVERNANCE CONCERNS RELATING TO
THE COMPANY'S M&A ACTIVITIES

I am writing to you in your capacity as the Olympus Group Compliance Officer. I have carefully gone through the translation of the latest feature published in the October issue of Facta (released 20 September) and, whilst already extremely concerned about the content of the July edition, this further article has only added to my anxiety.

It not only raises many issues relating to the reputation of Olympus, but also to the governance and internal controls applied in the context of the company's M&A activities over recent years. I don't want to appear

righteous or detach myself from being a member of the senior manage-
ment group, but clearly, as the president of the company, I have a
responsibility to understand all of the issues involved, and indeed have a
personal exposure if there are any areas where the company has not acted
in the interests of our shareholders.

It was a long letter, over 2,500 words. It was polite but pointed, and raised my concerns in such a way that they could no longer go ignored by the board. I requested the details of the purchase price paid for each of the three companies, and to whom the payments were made. I requested the nature of the relationship between Olympus and the parties from whom the companies were acquired, and also the rationale: why had we invested in them? I called for due diligence reports, and for records of any commission payments made. I asked how the purchase price was determined for each of the companies, how the sanctioning of the purchases transpired, and also how they were funded. I asked to know about any further payments due, and details of any connected-party relationships that might create conflict of interest. I asked for an explanation of how these acquisitions had been accounted for since their purchase, their current financial performances and future expectations.

That weekend we were staying with friends who lived in Bournemouth, on the south coast. Delayed by several hours finishing the letter to Mori, I arrived by train just before midnight. I had phoned Nuncy earlier in the day to explain that I would be late and she had driven down that afternoon with Edward and Isabel. Our friends were warm hosts and, after accepting several nightcaps, I slept well. It was my first decent night's sleep in a long while.

Waking refreshed on the Saturday morning, I switched on my laptop. An emailed reply from Japan was pleasingly prompt. But it revealed nothing, with Hisashi Mori proving as infuriatingly enigmatic on screen as he was in person.

I had so been looking forward to this long-planned weekend with our friends, who are both lawyers, and their two young boys. But, being the party-pooper whose work so often intruded into other people's lives, my late arrival the preceding evening meant that our precious time together had already been eaten into.

To everyone's annoyance, I set up office in our hosts' kitchen. When they had all gone out to leave me in peace I started to draft the second letter. *Your reply is unsatisfactory*, I began, and went on to make clear that if I didn't receive substantive answers then I would insist that independent accountants from an eminent firm were brought in to investigate. I explained that until I received the answers I wanted, in writing, I would not return to Tokyo. I was due to return on the coming Monday's overnight flight for that month's board meeting, but was fully prepared to postpone my travels if necessary.

A response arrived by return email. More details this time – Mori had clearly made an effort, but again ultimately insufficient. Another email followed, this time from Kikukawa, saying that he didn't think my communications were productive, and that I should cease them forthwith. It was like a game of chess conducted by letter.

Our friends were generous and forgiving when it became increasingly obvious our weekend was not going to be the relaxing one we had all envisaged. Even their two young children had picked up on the drama, sensing that Michael was having a battle with some 'bad men'.

The weather on the Dorset coast was ugly and grey. Nuncy was getting thoroughly fed up with the fact that I had become obsessional and focused on the task in hand, ignoring her and everyone else. I tried to explain to her why it was so important but she was used to me saying every situation was important and discounted my words accordingly. Our friends remained good-natured and sympathetic, but of course life carried on. That just made me feel even sorrier for myself because I could see the others were continuing to have fun without me.

That evening we returned in near-silence to our home in Southend.

But the day was not yet over and I went to the office to meet some colleagues from my inner circle and worked late finishing my third letter of the weekend, as detailed and fraught as the first. The next day, a fourth ensued, this time addressed to Kikukawa. As with all the preceding communications it was formally copied to the whole board. I had purposely started writing to Kikukawa directly as he ultimately was the source of power and I didn't want him to hide behind Mori.

Another day, another letter – the fifth in as many days and one in which I said I had no option but to resign if I didn't receive satisfactory answers to my basic and straightforward questions. Things were gathering momentum now, and my threatened resignation, if it happened, would ensure the revelations would become a major story in Japan and around the world. A *gaijin* president quitting and publicly stating his concerns about the way the corporation was conducting itself: that would guarantee headline news.

In writing these missives I felt like I was turning into a lawyer, pinning down my own board of directors with precise language that gave them no wriggle room. This helped structure my thoughts and took away any ambiguity. If they were being deliberately evasive, hiding something dreadful, then every detail needed to be closed down so that I could substantiate my case.

I had also copied the last two letters to the senior global partners of the company's auditors, Ernst & Young, not just in Japan but in Asia, Europe and the United States, as well as James Turley, the partnership's global chairman and CEO. I was after total transparency here. I was no whistleblower, not yet. Indeed, I had wanted to keep this all within the company as much as I possibly could. But for that I required a degree of cooperation from my board colleagues, which was blatantly unforthcoming.

By formally alerting our accountancy firm in such explicit terms, I knew that whatever now happened to me, the genie was well and truly out and that the concerns I had raised could never be put back in the bottle. Whatever happened, Kikukawa and Mori would now be held to account.

For I was already certain from the answers provided to me in response to my five letters that something was very wrong, and that the knowledge now in my possession had to be spread more widely. Whatever I might be accused of later – and there were several accusations – would be nullified because I had copied the world's senior partners at Ernst & Young, making it impossible for anyone to suggest that I could be silenced thereafter by offering me inducements. It was a tactical process; it was almost like war.

I must have turned into Kikukawa's worst nightmare. But he knew what he was taking on with me. He only had himself to blame. I'm organized, I'm structured, and I could defend myself. The answers to my fifth letter had finally arrived. It was from Mori. He had endeavoured to answer my questions but his explanations as to why we had bought the three 'Mickey Mouse' companies and paid the huge amount in advisory fees were simply not credible. Nevertheless, they were sufficient to get me back to Tokyo. I flew to Japan a day later than planned on the overnight Air France flight from Paris, landing early in the evening of Wednesday, 28 September.

The next day I got to the Monolith in good time for the 9 a.m. private meeting with Kikukawa and Mori, which I had requested before I left London. I entered the room and there they were, sitting behind a long table with an unnaturally large gap of two empty seats between them. I sat down facing them with Kikukawa on my left and Mori on my right.

They had been somewhat taken aback when at the start of the meeting I insisted on an English colleague joining as a witness. Although they reluctantly accepted this prerequisite to my sitting down with them, having to insist upon it illustrated just how far trust had broken down. It was the oddest of meetings, made even more so as we had to continually adjourn to attend a series of retirement ceremonies in an adjoining room.

Kikukawa and I presided over these ceremonies jointly, giving our best smiles, bowing and cheering. We were the epitome of senior-managerial togetherness. It felt utterly bizarre – as if we were acting in a *kabuki* drama. We were certainly giving a performance, and what people were seeing masked a completely different reality. It was surreal to be smiling and finding the right words to thank a person for their lifetime of service to the company, and then returning to the meeting room to face two people whose actions were putting the entire organization at risk.

But at least I could finally look into their eyes and make clear that these were big issues that would not go away and had to be dealt with. We needed to see things through to a conclusion. I also asked to be given the CEO's responsibility to oversee this process. I *was* president, after all. Moreover, I wanted to bring in a team of forensic accountants as that was the only way we would get to the facts.

Hearing my requests, Kikukawa smiled with a pained expression at the suggestion he relinquish the CEO's position, explaining that our Japanese shareholders would never accept such a move. Starting to pack my papers away, I answered, 'Fine. Then I'll resign.'

This was not what Kikukawa wanted to hear. The meeting degenerated into a slanging match. 'Do you hate me?' Kikukawa blurted out. 'No I don't hate you,' I assured him. 'But you've got to understand that I simply want the authority to manage the company in the right way.' Was that not why I had been hired in the first place? He started to shout, his face filling with blood and turning purple with anger. That was a first for me. 'Don't shout at me,' I yelled back. 'I'm not one of your poodles,' Mori chipped in, trying to calm things down, but the gloves were off. It was ugly and very un-Japanese, with the veneer of calm politeness stripped away.

In his ten-year reign Kikukawa had rarely, if ever, been held to account. Nobody challenged him; everyone just fawned at his utterances. Even at this stage he clearly still saw himself as the all-controlling, all-powerful Emperor who could not be questioned, and who believed I could be similarly controlled.

After the shouting came the charm offensive. Kikukawa asked me whether I would like to go back to my old job in Europe. He was exploring every possible way to save his own skin. I was very careful in how I responded to this solicitation and explained in a calm and considered way that I wasn't going anywhere until the matters I had raised had been satisfactorily dealt with. I remember saying, 'Tom I am the president and it is my responsibility.' I wasn't going to take the easy option and walk away. Kikukawa nodded his head with a look of resignation, knowing he would have to go away and think again. The meeting was adjourned, presumably to be reconvened once Kikukawa had talked to the other board members about my intransigence.

It was a difficult day but I felt I was master of the facts, and I knew it wouldn't be easy for Olympus just to bundle me away. Think of the publicity. In Japan I was a celebrity in my own right, being the first *gaijin* who had worked his way up to the top, a salary-man, loyal and faithful to the company. While knowing it was only a small chance, if I was made CEO I believed it would be more likely that I would be allowed to do what was necessary, in particular inviting forensic accountants to go through the books. I knew that I needed to speak to the board and tell them what I proposed to do. I couldn't begin the huge clean-up operation, the purging of all this wrong-doing, unilaterally.

That night I had to leave the office by 6 p.m. for a private dinner at the British embassy with David Warren, the ambassador to Japan, and a fellow *gaijin* president, Sir Howard Stringer of Sony.

At ten minutes to six Kikukawa returned with Mori for what appeared to be a dramatic climbdown. Suddenly warm and conciliatory, Kikukawa spoke first: 'Michael, at the board meeting in the morning I will propose to make you CEO in addition to your presidency.' He went on, 'I will no longer attend the Executive Committee [EXCOM] management meetings, and you alone will be responsible for nominating future directors to the board.' His eyes looked at mine, soliciting my approval, and I smiled modestly, trying to appear conciliatory. He ended by saying, 'So, Michael, my future role will be limited to that of chairman and representative director,' adding after a few seconds, 'Is that okay for you?'

There was hardly any time left before I had to leave but I said, 'Tom, thank you. I'm relieved. I'm sure we can now move ahead in the right way and I'll do everything I can to get us through this.' I didn't want to appear triumphal; I knew how difficult it must have been for Kikukawa to back down in this way. We smiled and shook hands like it had been just another day in the office. As I left the room I caught the eye of my English colleague. From his knowing expression, I could see that, like me, he had never believed that Kikukawa would agree to all of this. Was this now the beginning of the end?

As I entered the empty lift to go down to the basement where Nick would be patiently waiting for me, I breathed in deeply several times – I now understood what a sigh of relief meant. I arrived at the embassy, where I said nothing about the day's events. Stringer looked exhausted, weighed down by his own set of Japanese problems, as Sony was showing no sign of the turnaround he had been put in place to effect. I went to bed feeling optimistic. Perhaps now I could get to the bottom of what had taken place. But I hadn't reckoned on the extent of Kikukawa's capacity to surprise.

The next day there was a long board meeting with some delicate and challenging issues to address which were unrelated to the concerns I was raising. I'm not sure why, but during the course of the endless discussions and PowerPoint presentations I became temporarily obsessed with the shirts of several of my fellow board members, with their fancy stitching and buttons. I was the child round the table trying to work out why they went in for this sort of peacockery.

At the end of the pre-agreed agenda, Kikukawa made a short statement in which he said he would like to make me CEO as well as president, confirmed that he would withdraw from the EXCOM meetings, and agreed that I could nominate future board members. He then put his three proposals to the vote and there was unanimous agreement. I was then given the opportunity to talk to the board and I explained my concerns in a constructive way, trying to avoid any unnecessary confrontation. For a few moments I thought we were making real progress. Then Kikukawa asked, 'Are there any questions?'

Immediately, three hands shot up. The movements were so fluid it was obvious something had been rehearsed.

The first director to speak was Masataka Suzuki, whom I had worked with for many years in Europe, where he had chaired the European board. Looking uncomfortable, and directly at me, he started his attack: 'You've known about the Gyrus acquisition all along and have been openly critical about it. Why bring it up again now? You have been president for six months already, yes?' I responded calmly that I had of course known about the acquisition, and had indeed expressed concerns at the time over the high multiples paid – indeed, I had pointed out that we already made greatly superior products in Japan and Germany. My concerns now, I explained, had nothing to do with the $2 billion acquisition in 2008, but why some two years later we had paid an additional $700 million over the original purchase price. 'Did you know about that, Suzuki-san?' I asked. He went silent.

The second to speak was Kazuhisa Yanagisawa, the director responsible for Corporate R&D, who was sporting the most fancy shirtwork with elaborate stitching and coloured buttons. He berated me for threatening not to come to that day's board meeting and remain in the United Kingdom. He was wary of me because about a third of the company's total R&D expenditure went under the generalized heading of 'Corporate R&D' and was under his control. During the last few months I had been questioning exactly on what and where the money was being spent. Untypically assertive, he asked: 'Should a president of a major company behave in such a fashion?' I reiterated what I had said in my series of letters, namely that I was not prepared to turn up to a meeting blind to the facts, where I might be asked to make decisions without knowing the essential detail. I concluded, 'Having now received some answers [to my letters] from Mori-san, which has only prompted more questions, I have nevertheless returned and am here today.'

I was then criticized by the non-executive director Hiroshi Kuruma, a former senior executive at the prestigious Nikkei Inc. business media organization, for copying my letters to Ernst & Young. By doing so, he said, 'you have brought "outsiders" in. Why act in this way?' His message was clear to me: Olympus was a family, and families require loyalty.

It reminded me of the speech Michael Corleone delivered to his hapless brother Fredo when he disagreed with him in front of the Las Vegas crowd in *The Godfather*. 'Fredo, you're my brother, and I love you. But don't ever take sides with anyone against the Family again. Ever.' A similar sentiment I sensed applied in my case, except that the Olympus board members didn't love me. They just wanted to silence me or get rid of me.

'Why on earth should we have anything to fear from our auditors?' I demanded. 'Given the huge sums and the specific accounting issues involved, I would do the same again.' That put Kuruma-san back in his box.

This was the first time I had been subjected to such openly hostile questioning since becoming president. The board members were clearly getting a lot off their chests, and I now knew that the real decisions had been taking place in forums to which I hadn't been invited. ·

A terrible blackness came over me. I felt utterly alone, profoundly depressed by what my colleagues' behaviour implied. My new CEO title was pure window-dressing and I was leaving the room with even less authority than when I had entered. All the other directors would stick tightly together, acting as one entity and I was now more of an outsider than ever. Kikukawa's eyes met mine and he sat there passively, looking victorious.

With the overwhelming litany of condemnatory facts presented to them in the five letters sent to date, and in the subsequent replies received from Mori and Kikukawa, my fellow board members must have surely had some reservations. Where was their collective conscience and their sense of what constituted proper corporate governance? But they all chose to stay silent, to remain subservient and obedient to their master. I alone had crossed some invisible line and I would now pay the price for doing so.

I left the board meeting dazed but confident in what I had to do next. I had to go public. It didn't help that the original whistleblower, whoever he or she might be, had gone quiet again, resuming their role undetected somewhere within the company.

Later that afternoon the EXCOM meeting was held. I chaired it and, as had been agreed, at the end Kikukawa said, 'I've been coming to this meeting for twenty years and this is my last one. So goodbye.' He bowed and everyone clapped. I clapped, too, just one more strange event in an increasingly surreal world. A dark fog was enveloping me. It was as if I had taken a potion which had transported me to an *Alice in Wonderland* world. Curiouser and curiouser.

I left the office and walked the five minutes to the Park Hyatt, where I was a member of the health club. The genial welcome of the receptionists, who over the years I had grown to know, softened my mood. I stepped onto the running machine in the fitness centre and ran mile after mile, gazing out through the window of the forty-seventh floor, staring at the city below and trying to burn off the anger and frustration. It didn't work.

A few hours later I boarded the Air France overnight flight back to Europe. I was exhausted but couldn't sleep. A stewardess, sensing my unease, asked if I was all right. I blamed the jet lag, but having hardly slept for a week, the truth was that I was tortured by indecision.

As we crossed Siberia I realized that, before I could go public, I needed further evidence. I decided that the first thing I would do when back in the UK, in my capacity as the president of Olympus, would be to commission PricewaterhouseCoopers (PwC) in London to review just one aspect of the accounting – the inexplicable payments for the so-called fees of $687 million, $620 million of which had been paid through London to the Cayman Islands to a shadowy company called Axam, and the recipients of the funds were impossible to identify.

First thing that Monday the wheels were put in motion and eight days later PwC's report was completed. It was shocking in its conclusions:

> The eventual cost of the Transaction to Olympus is extremely significant and is as a result of a number of actions taken by management which are questionable and which give cause for concern . . . We were unable to confirm that there has been improper conduct, however, given the sums of money involved and some of the unusual decisions that have been made it cannot be ruled out at this stage . . .
> In addition, there are a number of other potential offences to consider including false accounting, financial assistance and breaches of directors' duties by the board.
>
> It is important that Olympus takes appropriate steps to fully investigate and understand the acquisition of Gyrus and the arrangements made between Olympus, AXES and AXAM and whether there are wider regulatory issues such as money laundering and, if so, consider what action and remedial steps it should take.

PwC went on to warn that the company might face questions from the government regarding its risk controls and procedures: *In addition, there are a number of other potential offences to consider including false accounting, financial assistance and breaches of directors' duties by the Board.*

Early evening on Tuesday, 11 October I completed my sixth and, as it would transpire, final letter. It was the most difficult that I have ever had to write, but also the most necessary. I wrote to Kikukawa:

In putting the company first, the honourable way forward would be for you and Mori-san to face the consequences of what has taken place, which is a shameful saga by any stretch of the imagination. It is clear that the current situation is now untenable, and to move forward positively the necessary course of action is for you both to tender your resignations from the board. This approach will allow the situation to be managed in a discreet manner, and minimize the reputational damage to both Olympus and yourselves. If your resignations are not forthcoming, then there is a principal obligation upon me in respecting my fiduciary duties to raise, with the appropriate parties, my fundamental concerns in relation to the governance of the company. Tomorrow I am visiting Tohoku [the northeast region of the country where the devastating 2011 earthquake and tsunami hit] and therefore suggest that I meet with you and Mori-san on Friday to discuss exactly where we go from here.

I had to leave the office in a rush at around 7 p.m. for Southend Airport, from where I took a small Cessna jet to Charles de Gaulle Airport in Paris, en route for Tokyo.

As I was a VIP traveller, a limousine was waiting to transport me from the aircraft directly to the Air France first-class lounge, which in Paris is uniquely different from the aseptic transitory environment of such places around the world. An oasis of tranquillity has been created for those privileged travellers and *Animal Farm* came to mind. There is a restaurant with incomparable cuisine, conceived by Alain Ducasse, the famous restaurateur, but I was so hyped up I couldn't eat anything. I had made this journey many times but this was horribly different. I fiddled with the beautiful food while at the same time working on my laptop drafting the covering email which would accompany letter number six, but was too tired to structure my thoughts coherently.

Just before midnight, as we taxied in the Boeing 777 towards the runway, I could see the tail fins of the British Airways and Iberia planes which always bring me back to the places I feel most secure – England and Spain. This trip was going to be conclusive.

After a seemingly interminable flight, I landed at Narita on Wednesday, 12 October at around 6 p.m. I still needed to finish the covering email to accompany the letter and to then get it translated into Japanese. It was 10 p.m. before I was satisfied with my wording. My old friend from Olympus, Koji Miyata – who would play a pivotal role in the months of turmoil to follow – worked on the translation.

The finished communication read:

Subject: LETTER 6: SERIOUS GOVERNANCE CONCERNS RELATING TO THE COMPANY'S M&A ACTIVITIES

Dear Colleagues,

You will find attached a letter dated 11 October 2011 to Mr Kikukawa in relation to the above issue – I hope when you read through the detail and the accompanying PricewaterhouseCoopers' report, you will not consider the fact that I'm a foreigner or allow long-established personal loyalties to override logic, and will focus on the specific issues involved.

The events detailed are extraordinary and have profoundly weakened the financial position of the company and to move on from here, there has to be accountability by those responsible. I hope there will not be an attempt to 'ride out the storm' or believe this matter can be 'brushed under the carpet' which is impossible with the existence of the PwC report which is truly condemning in relation to what has taken place with regard to the Gyrus payments to AXES/AXAM, aside from the huge amounts of wasted monies involved with the bizarre acquisition of companies (Altis, Humalabo and News Chef) which have never had any real value in the context of what was paid for them.

I have a four-year contract with fixed terms and there is no personal gain for me whatever my change of status – my only motivation and concern is for the best interests of the company and I will move ahead to do what's right with conviction and resolution.

Michael

I was in effect begging my colleagues to look objectively at the facts, and not to dismiss them solely because I was a *gaijin*, or to put long-established personal relationships ahead of what was best for the company.

It was after 2 a.m. Sitting on my bed, I re-read the letter and covering email one last time. With my finger hovering over the 'send' button, I hesitated and then firmly pressed the key down. There was no going back. It felt reckless and daring, but something had to be done to rid the company of the malady from within. I checked the 'sent mail' box and re-read my letter. As I did so, I drew comfort from the knowledge that I had several colleagues backing me, some of them trusted friends with whom I had worked closely for many years.

4.

Showdown

It was 13 October and I sensed the endgame was upon me. At 7 a.m. to the second, after I'd had only four hours' sleep, the doorbell rang. It was Nick, my driver. Taking my briefcase, he smiled warmly and asked, 'How are you this morning, sir?' 'Tired,' I replied, not wanting to burden him with my worries.

Nick and I drove to Tokyo Station, from where I was scheduled to take the Shinkansen – the bullet train – to Tohoku with Sakuo, my special assistant. I had worked with him for several years in Europe and we knew each other well. He understood my management style, and I had made it a prerequisite of becoming president that he would be appointed to assist me. Sakuo translated both the meaning and intention of my directions. We had an easy-going relationship. I liked listening to him talk so lovingly about his daughter's dance lessons and his son's soccer games.

Tohoku is the hilly region to the north of Sendai and its coastal plain had been badly damaged by the earthquake and tsunami. As president, I was there to observe and encourage the extraordinary efforts of Olympus volunteers from factories and offices across the country. My colleagues were trying to bring back some normality to one small area struck by the tsunami. The assembled group were quite lovely: sweet, positive and laughing and joking with me. Such a contrast to the boardroom machinations back at the Monolith and another reminder of the decency of most Olympus employees.

It had been only seven months since almost 16,000 people had died, a fact that threw all my anxieties into sharp relief. I watched as my colleagues cleared a former paddy field so that rice could grow again. The soil was riddled with so much debris – small pieces of metal, wood and cloth, and we all knew that these were bits of people's previous lives.

I left the devastated area with even greater resolve, having been reminded of just how special a place Japan was, full of kind and warm-hearted people like our volunteers. I did not want to let a few deluded and egotistical individuals ruin it, not just for me, but for the way the rest of the world perceived the country.

Sakuo and I got back on the bullet train. As we sped along at 250 kilometres per hour, there was another ping on my phone. I read the text message announcing that an extraordinary board meeting had been called for the next day at 9 a.m. I knew immediately that there was a 95 per cent chance I was going to be dismissed, because if the board were going to take the easier option, which would mean Kikukawa and Mori resigning, they would have asked to meet with me privately. That is the way things are done in Japan. Anything awkward or difficult is discussed behind closed doors, with the preordained conclusions announced and rubber-stamped at meetings. I had not been invited to any behind-closed-door sessions this time. But I'm sure others had.

The meeting agenda had one item: 'Governance concerns relating to the company's M&A activities.' I realized that the real item up for discussion was me. 'I'm going to be fired,' I said to Sakuo. He went quiet. I tried to tell him not to worry and that I had done the right thing. That made him even quieter.

On our arrival back at Tokyo we were met by the usual teeming sea of thousands, heading into or leaving the station via its south and north exits. Nick greeted me, and I felt relieved to be in the quiet air-conditioned cocoon of the Lexus. I told him about what I had seen in Tohoku and he just nodded, knowing that any words in response would be clumsy and redundant. Within just ten minutes I was back in my apartment.

That evening I met with three Olympus colleagues at the Keio Plaza Hotel where they were staying. We set up camp in one of their bedrooms, with me teasing them that they were luxuriating by staying on the recently refurbished 'Executive Floor'. Defensively, they explained that the corporate rate meant that the room charge was under £150, which was very modest, by business standards, for a hotel in central Tokyo. I laughed when they emphasized that this included a buffet breakfast. Working around one laptop, we drank mineral water and Diet Coke. There was a wonderful sense of comradeship and mutual support. These three had helped me most in investigating what had gone on. Whenever there was opportunity we joked to relieve the tension, and agonized over almost every word preparing a statement for me to hand out at the board meeting – now less than eight hours away.

It was just past 1 a.m. but they all came down in the lift to say goodbye and wish me good luck. In the deserted lobby we found out that we needed several ¥100 coins to use the photocopier, which somehow I found amusing in the context of the billions of yen which had been squandered by the company

The statement to the board, which, as it turned out, I was never allowed to hand out, summarized in one document all the salient points from my six letters and the responses received from Mori and Kikukawa. It read as follows:

STATEMENT TO
THE OLYMPUS CORPORATION
BOARD OF DIRECTORS' MEETING:
FRIDAY 14 OCTOBER 2011

1)   *As detailed in my letter to Mr Kikukawa, dated 11 October 2011, and the report prepared by PricewaterhouseCoopers of the same date, I have serious concerns in relation to the company's governance, in particular the monies paid to AXES and AXAM, financial advisors in connection with the purchase of Gyrus.*

2) *There is no evidence of any due diligence having been carried out on AXES or AXAM, a company registered in the Cayman Islands and struck off in June 2010 for non-payment of licence fees. Furthermore, according to a note filed at the local corporate registry, as such, the company is not legally authorized to continue being active.*

3) *No professional advice was obtained as to the reasonableness of the fee structure within Agreement 2, dated 21 June 2007, to establish whether this was competitive in relation to the market rate for such financial advisor services.*

4) *There was no formal Board approval prior to the signing of Agreement 2 on 21 June 2007, which was approved on a 'ringi basis' by Mr Kikukawa, Mr Mori and Mr Yamada and only retrospectively approved by the Board of Directors' meeting on 19 November 2007, some five months later. [A ringi is a collective decision-making process involving the circulation of a document called the ringi-sho. This is annotated and amended as it circulates, and continues around the decision-making loop until everyone signs up to it using their own name stamp.]*

5) *The Olympus officers involved chose not to accept the professional advice provided by KPMG and Weil, Gotshal & Manges to settle the liability for the share options by making a cash payment and decided instead to proceed with the issue of preference shares as requested by AXES/AXAM.*

6) *The Olympus officers involved took no professional advice in relation to the calculation of the value of preference shares and the annual rate of return applied to these shares. The calculation basis employed resulted in the liability in respect of the share options granted under the terms of Agreement 2, increasing from USD177 million to a liability of between USD530 million and USD590 million.*

7) *The company eventually settled on a value of USD620 million to repurchase the preference shares.*

8) *The total fees paid to AXAM/AXES in respect of the acquisition of Gyrus Group PLC totalled USD687 million, equivalent to approaching 35% of the purchase price of Gyrus Group PLC. This compares with a market rate for services of this type of around 1% (USD20 million), up to a maximum of 2% (USD40 million).*

9) *In relation to the acquisition of Altis, Humalabo and News Chef, the total purchase price paid for the three companies was JPY73.4 billion, approaching USD800 million.*

   As part of the year-end closing for the year ending 31 March 2009, the investment in these three companies was written down by approaching USD600 million in the same fiscal period as the final tranches of shares were purchased, which represented 76% of the value of these companies. [See detail in the table below.]

Company	Purchase Price	Purchase Dates	31 March 2009 impairment	% of value amortized
Altis	JPY28,812m	May 2006–April 2008	JPY19,614m	68%
Humalabo	JPY23,199m	Sept 2007–April 2008	JPY18,370m	79%
News Chef	JPY21,408m	May 2006–April 2008	JPY17,699m	83%
TOTAL	JPY73,419m		JPY55,683m	76%
	USD773m		USD586m	

10) *There is no evidence of the Olympus officers involved carrying out appropriate due diligence on the third party shareholders (Dynamic Dragons II SPC, Neo Strategic Venture, Tensho Limited, Global Targets SPC, New Investments Limited, Class Funds IT Ventures), from which the shares of Altis, Humalabo and News Chef were purchased.*

11) *Olympus made investments in these three companies totalling approaching USD800 million, yet the value of this investment was written down by almost USD600 million, to only 25% of*

the value, within the same financial year that the last share purchases were completed.

In summary, aside from the disturbing circumstances surrounding the purchase of Altis, Humalabo and News Chef, the findings in relation to the extraordinarily large and disproportionate payments made to AXES and AXAM, whose ownership remains unknown to the Board and the company's auditors, to this day, totally justifies my concerns in relation to the governance of this company.

It is truly incredible that a leading Nikkei publicly-listed company, has made payments of approaching USD700 million for 'financial advice', to an entity in the Cayman Islands, which has not allowed the auditors to determine whether there are any related parties, with all the associated implications.

Finally, I formally request that this statement, my six letters dated 23rd, 24th, 25th, 26th, 27th of September and 11th of October, together with the PricewaterhouseCoopers report, dated 11th of October, in both Japanese and English, are attached to the minutes of this meeting of the Olympus Corporation Board of Directors, as a matter of record.

Michael C Woodford

14 October 2011

I walked out of the hotel's lobby through the automatic glass doors and took a taxi back to Grosvenor Place. As the driver suddenly braked in preparation to turn off the busy road into my building's glamorous entrance, which is sited on a bend, I started worrying about a completely different issue. After years of being involved in road-safety campaigns, I had become concerned about the road outside the building: the exit was dangerous because a line of hedging which ran alongside the carriageway blocked the view of approaching vehicles.

I had called meetings with the landlord's representative and engineers from the Shibuya local government, who had promised to remove the hedging and replace it with low-level planting. I also remembered that I was yet to receive a conclusive answer from the landlord addressing my concerns that there weren't enough fire alarms in the apartment, should a fire break out in the kitchen. Such is the power of anxiety.

I showered and took a can of ice-cold Asahi Dry out of the fridge. I walked up the stairs to my apartment's rooftop garden and looked out across to the flashing lights of Shinjuku. The cool night air helped calm me. My mind was now crystal clear – maybe this is how it feels knowing you're about to face your executioner. As with an emotional shock such as bereavement, things come into the tightest of focus.

I eventually made my way to bed, feeling strangely peaceful but anticipating the inevitable in the morning. Just as I wanted to sleep, I was struck by a glimmer of hope. 'Perhaps, just perhaps they will do the right thing. Something can be resolved.'

Having got used to surviving on four or five hours' sleep, I got up early to be greeted with a text – 'Go get the fuckers' – sent by one of my colleagues who had worked with me the night before drafting the statement. I was surprised by the expletive as he was not the type of man to use such language, but I felt all the more the force of what he meant.

I arranged to meet up with a close friend (who subsequently asked to remain anonymous) and gave him my two Sony Vaio laptops. These needed to go back to the UK and be wiped of any information that would incriminate the many colleagues who had assisted me. I was now prepared; I had never been sacked in my career but for the previous fifteen hours had known precisely what awaited me.

As I entered the Monolith building I glanced at my phone: it was 8.41, Friday, 14 October. I entered the lift in silence, a deference to the etiquette in Japan, where everyone seems to keep fixed, unreadable expressions in such situations. I wondered if my Japanese colleagues around me knew what was about to happen. I got out on the fifteenth floor, walked the twenty or so yards to the electronically controlled double doors into the executive suite. Normally I would enter the secretaries' office by the reception desk and say: '*Ohayou gozaimasu*' (good morning), and then, having exhausted my Japanese repertoire, would in English ask the four secretaries who shared the office how they were and spend a few minutes talking and joking. That day I went straight to my own office.

There was a knock at the door and Michiko entered. She had clearly been crying. I could see in her eyes that those wretched men had told her what was going to happen and no doubt had forbidden her from saying anything to me. In that moment I felt such warmth for her, remembering all the funny times we had together. We had laughed a lot when we had gone out shopping to buy my tailor-made shirts (which were necessary to accommodate my long limbs), my fancy Porsche-designed electronic pepper and salt grinders and my beloved Nespresso coffee machine. Every morning before I arrived she would go down to the building's subterranean shopping arcade and in Café Croissant buy me my favourite egg croissant for breakfast. She knew how to look after me – a useless *gaijin* who didn't speak Japanese – and had made my time in Tokyo go smoothly. She loyally watched my back, and now she couldn't stop her own colleagues from stabbing me right between the shoulder blades. But she was completely professional. She didn't say a word.

I wanted to say goodbye to her properly but subsequently found out she had been instructed to go across the road to wait in the Keio Plaza Hotel, until I had left the building. They didn't want her to bump into me when I came out of my last board meeting as president.

The meeting was scheduled for nine o'clock, and in a culture where nobody is late for anything, ever, the boardroom was full at the appointed hour. The roll call that day was thirteen board members, two translators, four attending auditors and one secretariat member. But somebody was conspicuously absent. Having called this extraordinary meeting, Kikukawa was late. *Late?* How could he be late?

At 9.02 I looked to my right and caught Hisashi Mori's eye. His gaze, as ever, offered nothing. I made an exaggerated play of checking my watch and raising my eyebrows. He leaned slightly towards me and, in a feeble attempt to humour me, asked about my visit to Tohoku the preceding day.

'Michael, how was it? You must have been affected?' With my mind fresh from the scenes of devastation I had witnessed the day before, I felt an overwhelming revulsion that he would use this of all subjects to try and distract me. A low-level fury rose from my stomach. In a raised voice, and deliberately omitting the honorific 'san', I replied: 'Mori, stop playing games. Just get on with it.' Realizing that I knew my fate, Mori shrugged nervously and scuttled off to find his master.

Kikukawa eventually arrived, with Mori dutifully in his wake. It was 9.07. Kikukawa waddled in like a duck, wearing a shiny blue suit. He nodded at those present, and anxiously, perhaps even a touch excitedly, fiddled with his tie. I immediately recognized the tie. It was one of the three he had recently bought from the Imperial Hotel boutique, at a price of $500 each, about which he had later boasted. A little puffed-up duck in a five-hundred-buck tie. He didn't go to his normal chair, immediately to my right, but stood at the podium as if he were to give a routine PowerPoint presentation on the last quarter's financial results.

He cleared his throat. 'Today's board meeting to discuss concerns relating to M&A activity has been cancelled.' (I was listening in my earpiece to the translation.) 'There is instead to be a new agenda: firstly the dismissal of Mr Woodford as president, CEO and representative director.'

I waited for a ripple of murmured astonishment, perhaps even dissent. Everyone stayed silent.

Kikukawa put the motion, as company law directed, to a vote, and almost before he had finished speaking, all fifteen members simultaneously raised their hands in approval. I was reminded of young children in a classroom who know the answer to a simple question, all stretching their arms up, desperate for the teacher to call on them. There was to be no discussion, no debate, just acquiescence.

Kikukawa was now talking again. 'Mr Woodford,' he said, looking into the middle distance, 'is not permitted to make any comments here, because he has a vested interest in the outcome.' Oddly, I had an overwhelming desire to laugh. I was in a room full of people – of colleagues, some of whom I had known for over thirty years – who were now operating beyond all the recognizable codes of conduct, not just in Japan but anywhere in the business world.

I stared at Kikukawa: at the cut of his expensive suit, at the precision of the knot in that silk tie, at the curt, pinched smile that played beneath his nose, and the reflection of the overhead lighting on the lenses of his glasses. He struck me as a ludicrous figure, and so delusional. He resembled little more than the captain of a sinking ship who believed that by throwing out the deadweight, his vessel would suddenly right itself and resume its calm drift into the horizon.

He read out a second motion: 'Mr Woodford is stripped of all his directorships of Olympus's subsidiary companies, including Olympus Corporation of the Americas and Olympus Europa Holding GmbH' (the American and European organizations at both of which I was CEO and chairman of the board). Tellingly, he went on to announce, 'Hisashi Mori will replace Mr Woodford in these roles.' *Mori*, I thought. The Emperor's trusted sidekick, a bureaucrat, a creature of the corridors – he knows nothing about the real business of customers and products.

It was no comfort to know that I was making history, for the forced removal of a company president is almost unheard of in Japan. No one is let go unless they are guilty of major malfeasance such as when, in 1997, the chairman of Japan's then largest bank, Dai-Ichi Kangyo, was convicted of lending billions of yen to members of organized crime groups.

So why were Kikukawa and his board cronies acting this irrationally? They knew waves of publicity would be generated by my dismissal, but they were obviously scared of something far worse.

But now they were going to hold a press conference to announce their bizarre decision to the world.

I checked my watch; it was 9.15 a.m. Just eight minutes had elapsed. An eight-minute corporate execution. I was now officially the ex-president. I remained a director, albeit one without portfolio, thanks to a quirk in Japanese corporate law whereby, if you don't resign, only the shareholders can remove your directorship.

I rose quietly, left the room and, deliberately holding my head high, walked back to my office. I immediately opened the safe in the corner of the room, retrieved my bank book, about £1,000 worth of yen and, most importantly, my Japanese name stamp. If massive fraud had been taking place, the very last thing I wanted was these people getting hold of my name stamp. The red Japanese characters it leaves on a page are legally as good as my signature and are crucial for endorsing all official documents in Japan. Made out of wood and beautifully painted, the stamp was the size and width of my index finger. I kept it in a small leather box with a red ink pad. Using it always reminded me of my childhood Post Office set, but it was no plaything.

The only thing on my mind was to escape as quickly as possible. I just couldn't understand why the board members were acting in this way. They had seemed scared, but of what? I was confused and disorientated. My thoughts turned again to the second *Facta* article, and its suggestion of connections to organized crime, to the Yakuza. I was both frightened and angry.

Somebody entered my office, and I turned to see Hironobu Kawamata, who in effect fulfilled the role of Olympus's chief financial officer. He was accompanied by the recently appointed head of the secretarial division, a quiet and unassuming man who had clearly been 'volunteered' to make this encounter two against one. He remained silent during the exchange that followed. Kawamata was smiling broadly enough to reveal his teeth. Japanese people often smile or laugh when nervous, but this was not the case. There was too much relish in his expression.

'Michael, there are a few points I need to go through with you,' he said, as if what had just taken place in the boardroom was routine. 'Firstly, I want your two phones.' His manner was so rough that I became angry again. I looked him in the eye and, passing him the Samsung Galaxy, which I had used most frequently in Japan, said, 'You can have this one.' I could not help but add, 'I've already wiped it.' My other phone – an iPhone – had been issued to me by the British subsidiary.

I held it up. 'I'll keep this one because my wife will be worried if she can't make contact with me.' I walked towards him and with my face just a few inches from his I said, 'Or are you going to take it off me? Are you a policeman?' He buckled slightly, which pumped me up all the more. I wanted to shout, *Who the fuck do you think you are?* My fingers curled, I clenched my hands at my sides.

Kawamata took a step back, relocated his resolve and demanded my two Sony Vaio laptops. It was my turn to smile. I told him, 'I know your games and they have already been sent back securely to London. I'll drop them off at KeyMed [Olympus's UK headquarters] once they've been wiped of all data.' Numerous colleagues from around the world had assisted or written to me, expressing in the most explicit language their contempt for the Olympus board's behaviour, so my overwhelming priority was to protect them. Next, Kawamata demanded that I relinquish my company-issued credit card. I passed it to him with no comment.

'Your apartment,' he said, moving through his to-do list, 'you have to vacate it by the end of the weekend.' This I found extraordinary: I paid more than half of the rent personally. I stayed calm, telling him that I would pack a bag and return the keys in due course. Lastly, he said, 'And by the way, when you go to the airport, you are not allowed to use Nick. You can take the airport bus.'

His smile had returned. Over my many years visiting Japan, I had never seen or heard of anything like this. This aggressive rudeness was all so very atypical, simply not the way business was carried out here. My efforts to highlight wrongdoings had brought out a bully-ing mob mentality in my colleagues.

My hands turned cold. I wanted to get out.

Kawamata did not accompany me the fifteen floors down to the ground floor, and for that I was grateful. I breathed heavily through my nose as the lift descended, my hands like ice, a cold sweat break-ing out across my forehead and the back of my neck. Once at the foyer I strode briskly from the lift across the gleaming marble floor and out into an unseasonably warm and sunny Tokyo morning. Rush hour was over, so I had no trouble hailing a taxi. It was a relief to be inside, amid the curious frilly white doilies that cover the seats, and being driven away. I gave the driver a laminated card with my address in Shibuya, his hands white-gloved and resting at a calm ten to two on the steering wheel, and resisted the urge to ask him to drive quickly.

We arrived at Grosvenor Place and there were two men in suits loitering downstairs in the foyer. They looked hefty and officious. One of them gave me a sidelong glance. Did they have all their fin-gers? I went upstairs.

My apartment, technically no longer mine, was silent. I went straight to the bedroom and packed my bags, pulling clothes from drawers and cupboards, taking photos of my wife and children and stuffing them into a case, my ears alert to any sounds outside the window or the front door. I crossed the floor to the kitchen, sud-denly feeling thirsty; I drank deep from the tap. Zipping up my bags, I hesitated by the front door. I took a very careful look through the fisheye lens spy hole which revealed an empty corridor. I opened the door, stepped out, and allowed it to close quietly behind me.

Back downstairs, the two suspicious men still loitered. I passed the reception desk where the three uniformed ladies bowed, not knowing it would be the last time they would see me. Out on the street and hurrying along the pavement, I was soon sweating as I lugged my large silver suitcase in one hand and my black leather briefcase in the other.

5.

Escape

There are not many open spaces in Tokyo, but Yoyogi Park, a five-minute stroll from the apartment, was one of the largest. I used to enjoy going there at the weekends when it was filled with people. As industrious as Tokyo is, like London and New York it needs its breathing spaces – and it knows how to let off steam in its deeply idiosyncratic fashion. In Yoyogi Park people would practise martial arts alongside young rockabilly dancers, styled to resemble latter day James Deans going through their own fifties moves. Gilding the periphery were young women dressed as living dolls, part Barbie, part geisha, decorated in ornately embroidered pink, and twirling parasols. Their attention to detail was fascinating, and the length they went to stand out in a country of such uniformity was some-how admirable. More 'nails' trying to stick out.

I approached an empty bench outside a small ice cream kiosk I knew. It was in the centre of a wide-open space and facilitated 360° vision around me. I watched the children playing, in particular a small boy on a tricycle who was simultaneously endeavouring to pedal while licking his ice cream. Recognizing the demands of multitasking, he stopped and the ice cream won his full attention. It was reassuring to watch and hear the sounds of children playing.

Everything seemed so normal. Nobody appeared to be watching me. I took out my one remaining mobile phone and called Jonathan Soble, the *Financial Times* correspondent for Japan based in Tokyo. He had interviewed me back in the spring shortly after I had become president. It had only been on the train heading back from Tohoku that I had decided that, if my assumption was correct and I was to be fired, Jonathan would be my first port of call. If he hadn't answered, then the *New York Times* and the *Wall Street Journal* were next on the list.

Mercifully, Jonathan picked up. 'Hey, Michael. I've just read on the wires you've been fired. They're saying you've been dismissed after acting in an "arbitrary manner". You haven't been following the Japanese way, apparently.'

'Well there's a lot more to it than that. Can we meet? Now?' I asked him.

Sensing an exclusive, he dropped everything and hurried over, suggesting Violette, a quiet café nearby, as a rendezvous. (He later told me he'd never had a story fall in his lap like this, perfectly choreographed and sourced.)

As I approached the café, I noticed a chalkboard with a message written in English: 'For *gaijin* people. Happy Hour 11.30–19.00' – one could be happy all day. It was empty except for a young couple who kept giggling. Opposite, I could see through the window some school children playing football in a mesh-fenced playground. Still sweating, I ordered an iced coffee to cool down and put lots of sugar in it, remembering that was supposedly good for people suffering from shock.

The short wait for Jonathan seemed like an eternity. When he arrived I handed him a large black lever-arch file, complete with copies of all six of the letters that I had sent, the responses from Kikukawa and Mori and the PwC report. I even included English translations of the *Facta* articles. Jonathan ordered himself some tea and started going through the documents. He said little but now and again nodded in recognition of something he was reading. He asked me the occasional question for clarification. At one point, seeing I was agitated, he broke off from his review and asked, 'Are you okay?' I wasn't going to play games and was completely honest in my response. 'I'm scared, Jonathan. Something is very wrong here. *Facta*, which seems to be right on so many things, has mentioned links to organized crime.'

We talked for about forty-five minutes. I ended our meeting by saying, 'Jonathan I need you to expose all of this. And please do it quickly.'

'What are you going to do now?' he asked.

As I answered, I could hear the panic in my voice as surely as could he. 'I'm getting out.'

'When?'

'Now.'

He followed me to the street corner where we said goodbye. I hailed another taxi.

Haneda Airport, thirty minutes away down on Tokyo Bay, was busy, and I took instant comfort from that, still convinced that I might have been followed. Even so I kept seeing people who looked like they were watching me. As I walked into the terminal building, a man in a blue military-like uniform began to walk towards me and my hands and feet were again ice cold. He kept on walking.

By now it was early afternoon. I realized I was trembling. I scanned the departures board, displaying the details of planes leaving for all over Asia, Australia and beyond. Anything that would get me out fast. The next London flight was nearly twelve hours away. Too long. I found one leaving shortly for Hong Kong and bought two tickets – one for me, and the other for an English colleague who had joined me. He had been 'the witness' in my meeting with Kikukawa and Mori just two weeks earlier and I knew it was not advisable for him to remain in Japan. We got in the Cathay Pacific queue.

Waiting in line, I remembered the Livedoor scandal in 2006, when its CEO Takafumi Horie, the then thirty-three-year-old, Ferrari-driving chancer who for nearly a decade had given two fingers to the Japanese establishment, wound up getting sentenced to several years in jail.

Livedoor was one of Japan's hottest internet companies when it was revealed to be mired in financial scandal, accused of artificially increasing the value of the stock price for enormous gain. Everything associated with the company started to implode. Just one day after the scandal broke, Hideaki Noguchi, an executive at a firm raided by prosecutors in connection with the controversy, was found dead in an Okinawa hotel room, an apparent suicide.

Leading members of Japan's business establishment had been barely able to contain their glee. The pleasure among the staid suits of Tokyo came from what Horie had come to represent. He had become the 'Leader of the Pack' of internet entrepreneurs who hung out in the contrived but chic Roppongi Hills enclave.

Horie was a 'love me, love my money' full-in-your-face type of man. The chubby, self-described geek eschewed business suits for loud T-shirts and designer jeans. He drove flashy red sports cars and dated sexy models and actresses. He had numerous enemies and relished identifying them in public. He has often said that 'all evils come from aged business managers', a view that I have come to share.

After losing 90 per cent of its stock price and amid strong evidence of securities fraud, Livedoor was delisted from the Tokyo Stock Exchange in April 2006, eventually being acquired by a Korean company. During his lengthy appeal process against his prison sentence, Horie published an autobiography, *Complete Resistance*. He claimed that he was targeted by the government due to his infamy, not for the actual nature or severity of any crimes. His case had always disturbed me because executives charged with such white-collar crimes generally avoid prison terms. In June 2006, to prevent a recurrence of the scandal, Japan passed a law similar to the US Sarbanes–Oxley Act, nicknamed J-SOX. But it didn't stop Olympus taking the wrong road. (The Sarbanes–Oxley bill was enacted in 2002 as a reaction to a number of major US corporate and accounting scandals, including Enron and WorldCom, bringing about far-reaching reforms to the regulation of financial practice and corporate governance.) I couldn't help but compare myself to Horie; I, too, had challenged the established order. I wondered what could happen to me.

At last my colleague and I made it to the front of the Cathay Pacific queue and discovered – to our relief – that there were just two seats left. We shuffled nervously through security and the immigration desk, where the official looked at my picture and then at me for what seemed too long. He finally nodded indifferently and handed back my boarding pass – my ticket to freedom.

In the lounge I called my sister Lou Lou at her home in Sydney, explaining what had happened and asking her to phone Nuncy and let her know that I was safe and would call her from Hong Kong. I started thinking about the movie *Lost in Translation* and how the time difference with Japan made everything out of kilter. Bright sunlight came through the glass panels in the airport lounge, but it was still the middle of the night in the UK. I thought Nuncy would still be sleeping, unaware of everything. (I found out later she had been awake all night worrying about me.)

After a short time in the lounge, we walked to the departure gate. If I got as far as Hong Kong, I knew there was no way they would extradite me to Japan. With the unhealed wounds of history, there continues to be a mutual wariness between the Chinese and the Japanese governments.

The flight was called and I boarded. Never before had I derived such comfort from the buckling of my seatbelt, the roar of the engines, and the tilt of the aeroplane as we left the tarmac, and Japan, behind. As we climbed I could see the sacred Mount Fuji. *I won't be flying over you again for a while*, I thought. I treated myself to a double gin and tonic and sat back.

Three and a half hours later we touched down in Hong Kong. The first thing I did was phone Nuncy. 'So they have done it – those devils,' she said. I reassured her that there was nothing to worry about, which was a big white lie, but a necessary one. We could worry together later.

I called Jonathan Soble, who was making good progress in speaking to all involved and getting the paper's lawyers to approve his copy. While the story had yet to go to the editor, Jonathan could hopefully meet the print deadline for the *FT*'s Saturday edition and the story would be out. He wished me well.

The London flight, an old Cathay 747, was so full that the only seat available was next to the noises and smells of the toilet. I can still smell that toilet now, with an endless line of overweight businessmen eating and drinking too much and traipsing towards it, all night long. The sucking whoosh as they flushed. I was developing an irrational hatred towards that lavatory.

With the aid of several glasses of red wine, the shock and fear started to subside, and sadness overwhelmed me. I began to worry about my colleagues around the world and what would happen to them. Exhausted, I nonetheless stayed wide awake, eating whatever was put in front of me.

Unable to concentrate on any of the films on the entertainment system, but too filled with adrenaline to sleep, zombie-like I simply followed our flight path on the screen, the successive yellow flashing dashes leading a safe route back home. How on earth had I come to this?

Intermission

Liverpool 1967: Walking Alone

My life changed the day my mum left my dad.

It was November 1967 and I was seven years old. When I got up that morning expecting to go to school, my dad had already left the house for work. My mum took me aside and gave me a crisp pink ten-shilling note. The deal was that it would remain mine on the condition that I didn't cry on the train we were about to take. At seven you don't take much in, and my mum didn't explain what was going on, but ten shillings was more than enough to buy my silence. So my two sisters – Yvonne, who was eleven, and Louise (aka Lou Lou), who was three – and I packed our little suitcases and the four of us went to Stafford Station and caught the InterCity to Liverpool, where our mum's parents lived. I didn't cry on the train and kept my ten shillings. Seventy-five miles away my father had arrived home to find the house empty. I wasn't to see him for many months.

My father, Noel, was a university lecturer and an electrical engineer who had run power stations. We were a middle-class family – I had grown up listening to classical music, and even though I was seven, Dad would talk to me about literature and art. He was also a talented photographer. His photographs from the 1960s are innocent but in another way very erotic. He would take black and white pictures of long-legged girls in Mary Quant-style dresses, never showing their faces. My favourite is a beautiful image of a woman with the bombed-out Coventry cathedral as a backdrop; it hangs in our living room to this day.

My dad was great fun to be around, but he could be selfish and infuriating in his intransigence. We lived in a comfortable modern house on an estate with trimmed, neat lawns, where every husband cleaned the car on Sundays. The road in which we lived was near the three-spired cathedral in Lichfield, which is an attractive historic small city in the Midlands. Our town was the birthplace of Doctor Samuel Johnson, one of the greatest English writers, who famously stated, 'When a man is tired of London, he is tired of life.'

Well, my mother was clearly tired of life with my father. My mum's upbringing had been far more modest. She was bright and clever, but by her own admission had been relatively unsophisticated when they had met.

I sense Mum at times found being a mother difficult, and she was not the most physically demonstrative of people. But she was strikingly beautiful, like a cross between Audrey Hepburn and Marilyn Monroe. With long legs and blonde hair, she was quite a catch. Later in life my father told me how he had fallen in love with her legs. I think he took her on as an apparently innocent girl, a project to mould. But he got far more than he bargained for. The final straw had been a huge row about a room extension my father wanted to build. Leaving was mum's way of saying no.

In Liverpool, we stayed on Orford Street, a row of Victorian terraced houses in a working-class part of the city. George Harrison had been brought up just around the corner at 12 Arnold Grove, but by 1967 he was long gone, and my time in Liverpool consisted of few warmth-inducing 'Penny Lane' and 'Strawberry Fields Forever' moments.

The house had a single outside toilet in a backyard shed. There was no bath or shower, so we had to go once a week to the local public bathhouse, an old Victorian building with huge cast-iron baths that were rusty at the bottom. I was suspicious of this brown coating – I took one look and convinced myself it was almost certainly something unpleasant. I refused to get in and created a scene for which my mum soundly scolded me.

The house was crowded, containing my grandma, grandad and my great uncle George, who was doubly incontinent. There were only three bedrooms – one for Uncle George, one for my grandparents and one for my mum and the three children. There were two beds in our room. I would sleep with Yvonne and Lou Lou with my mum.

Things did not begin too well in Orford Street. Within a few days of our arrival, all our bodies were covered by huge red blisters and we soon discovered we were allergic to the cat . . . He was jet black and went by the name of Whisky. My mum carted us off to hospital where we were prescribed large jars of grey unguent to smother all over our bodies. But the allergic reaction wouldn't stop, so poor Whisky had to be put down. I'm not sure my grandmother, who understandably could not have wanted us there in the first place, ever forgave us for bringing about Whisky's demise.

Money was short, so my mother and grandmother would often cook oxtail stew, then the cheapest cut of meat. I will never forget the horrible clear soup with big chunks of fatty cow end in which you could make out the bony structure of the tail. Yvonne and I would put it in our mouths, go silent and then ask to be excused to go out to the backyard toilet where we would spit it out. I still cannot bring myself to eat oxtail stew, despite its resurgence of late in high-end restaurants.

On my first full day in Liverpool I went out on my bike, a Raleigh RSW14 that my mum and grandmother had bought me. I must have looked and sounded like a little toff because David Murphy, the boy who lived opposite, came over and pushed me off. His behaviour didn't impress his mother, who rushed out, told David off and invited me in. David later became my best friend and partner in a series of entrepreneurial activities for which I became renowned in the neighbourhood.

Many theories have been advanced about what turns children into entrepreneurial, mercantile adults. For me, it seems to have been a mixture of factors: insecurity about the absence of my father; a strong sense that we were poor; an urge to find something I was good at and, maybe most importantly, a desire to be different from the pack. I was, even in those days, a bit of a lone wolf.

Liverpool was where I developed my insecurities. When I went to school I couldn't have a new blazer, unlike the other children, because they cost too much. On a brand-new blazer the school badge is bright and stands out; mine was always dull and worn. I was different because divorce was at that time still relatively unusual and because of my somewhat exotic look, with slightly Asian features inherited from my father's side of the family. Children are always cruellest to those who are different.

The Woodford siblings received free milk and free lunches at school because of our low household income, and our peers knew it. So even in the working-class district of Wavertree where we lived, we were poor. Children can easily feel ashamed. When the teacher was collecting the dinner money I did not go up with my coins. My classmates never deliberately tried to humiliate me, but everyone knew.

That is where my drive came from. I never wanted to go back to the public baths, or to being the one with the frayed blazer. This is something that I have never entirely shaken off, even when I was earning a seven-figure salary as president of Olympus, albeit for a mere six and a half months. But it also taught me that life is random and conditioned by luck. Things can be taken away from you through no fault of your own.

Trying to earn money was important. I used to pick blackberries then put the fruit in cleaned-out yoghurt pots (hygienically sealed with cling film!), and sell them to my neighbours door-to-door. Chocolates were also a source of revenue. At that time, if you collected a large number of wrappers, Cadbury would send you a £3 voucher. I used to go out in the streets and pick up Cadbury papers, even if they were dirty. I remember foraging through all the back alleys and I must have appeared like a juvenile litter obsessive. I then sent the bundles away to receive my £3. Only one voucher per household was permissible, but I got round that by using the addresses of all our friends and relatives. I spotted another lucrative source of income in newspaper money-off vouchers, which I would collect by scavenging for old newspapers. I had a deal with the owner of our local corner shop who totalled up all the vouchers and gave me the face value in goods.

I thought, why not go into business myself? With my voucher-obtained goods I set up a shop in the house with a little red toy till. When we had any visitors, they had to buy something from my shop. They used to complain that it was more expensive than the local supermarket, but I would pester them relentlessly until they gave in.

By the age of ten I also had a car-wash round where I would knock on people's doors and ask if they wanted to have their cars cleaned and built an extensive and loyal clientele. Special opportunities came round every now and then. There was a biscuit factory in Liverpool and one year, just before Christmas, David Murphy and I bought a special consignment which was being offloaded at less than half price. We sold the tins on to small shops and made hundreds of pounds. Growing in confidence, we went to a cash-and-carry wholesaler and bought a variety of toys, just in time for Christmas. But we didn't have any unique offering. We had acquired all these plastic nasty bits and pieces made in China. And, for the life of us, we couldn't sell them. This was my first deal where my heart got the better of my head. My mum had to take us back to the cash-and-carry and attempt to bail us out. The Indian owner looked at my mum with her humbled son in tow, thought about it and said, 'Okay, I'll take them back. But when your boy is sixteen, let me give him a job.' That pleased me a lot, although I learned more from this failure than the successes before it.

Getting into the King David High, a Jewish secondary school, was a stroke of luck – the other alternatives were large, rough, Liverpool comprehensives. I had little street awareness or ability to protect myself, so if I had gone to one of the comprehensives, my life may have been very different. But the King David High was a high-achieving school, and I found most of the other pupils were also potential willing customers. I got a little business going at break time selling, among other things, smoky bacon crisps. When word got out and I was challenged by the deputy headmaster that such snacks weren't kosher, I replied that there was no actual pork in the product, merely artificial flavourings. He was not amused and I stopped selling them.

To get home with my earnings, I had to go past either of the two comprehensive schools, and I would be stopped. 'Are you a Yid, la?' the students used to shout. And I used to tell them, 'I'm not Jewish, I'm a gentile.' But they didn't understand the word 'gentile' so that got me pushed around even more. With gangs of lads, you don't fight back. If I wasn't being accused of being a 'Yid', my tormentors assumed that, with my Asian features, I had to be Chinese. So they would ask me, 'Are you a Chink, la?' or taunt me with 'Two number 29s,' referring to the menu at Chinese takeaways. Or they could always fall back on a Liverpudlian expression, 'Have you got the touch of tar brush in you, la?' To which I would reply, 'No I haven't, I'm English.' And I would get clipped around the head for my impertinence.

Daily experience of anti-Semitism and racism forges your character. I grew to loathe discrimination of any type, which is why when Kikukawa suggested that I didn't like Japan because of some spurious racial prejudice, I found it so utterly offensive.

I'm not angling for pity here. Those early years didn't crush me and many children have endured far worse. You just have to brush it off and get on with it. I had good friends and we had good times. But I never really felt happy at home. I remember seeing the film *Oliver*. There's a scene where the orphaned Oliver is thinking of his mother, and sings the song 'Where Is Love?' Alone, just like in the film, I used to sing it out aloud and make myself cry. That's how I felt, like Oliver. To this day I sing the song for my own children, and tears will always come to my eyes.

Love, I probably convinced myself, was back in Lichfield with my father. I saw him twice a year. But it distorts everything when you see someone for only a few hours after not having seen them for months. When Dad came to Liverpool we always went to the Golden Phoenix restaurant a few minutes' walk from Lime Street Station. I always ordered Chicken Maryland (fried chicken, fried banana and fried pineapple) because it was exotic. And it wasn't oxtail. But it was strange to see someone for only four hours. Dad was not allowed to come by our home and I could sense he was in pain. He never spoke badly of my mother. My mum would tell me that he wasn't generous with his financial support. But I always found him generous in spirit. After a while, my father's significance waned as he became a distant figure. It wasn't until I left home at eighteen that I re-established contact with him. It was only then that I finally got to know him. He died twenty two years later, at the age of seventy-three, and I'm grateful for every moment we had. I loved him a lot.

I learned from my mum some of the harder lessons of life. Once, at thirteen or fourteen, I criticized her ironing by pointing out a few creases. She took all my shirts – we were living next to an allotment – and put the whole lot in the mud. After that I had to iron them myself. I was careful never to complain again.

After a few months in Liverpool, we moved out of our grand-mother's home to our own place in Rathbone Road, with the luxury of an indoor toilet.

Despite being a single parent, my mum put herself through teacher-training college and was determined to better her family's prospects. These first years were easier than the ones which would follow. At the age of seven I had become the man of the house.

Then, when I was eleven, everything changed. My mum married Terry, a very different type of person from my dad, and he moved in. When he met my mum, Terry was a non-commissioned officer in the RAF. As is often the case with step-relationships, children clash with the new incoming adult, especially of the same gender. Stated simply, we never got on.

Terry wore thick black bifocal glasses and had slightly pink skin. We had no common ground: he loved snooker and it bored me. He was good to my mother, but even at that age, being somewhat snobbish, I felt superior to him because he read the *Daily Express*. My father would read the *Guardian* or *The Times*. After leaving the air force, Terry became a salesman, which makes it somewhat ironic that I went into sales.

Every night my sisters and I followed a strictly enforced washing-up rota. When it was my turn, Terry always came out into the kitchen to inspect my endeavours. There would be a tiny speck of something in the drain – perhaps a solitary pea – and he would say, 'Look, you haven't done it properly. Do it again.' He would then re-inspect to make sure everything was to his satisfaction.

Terry would watch quiz shows on the TV and guess the answers out loud, looking around to everyone for acknowledgement of his genius. I sat quietly, seething, and developed a pathological hatred of panel shows where the host and guest celebrities are so infuriatingly smug. But at the core of my problems with Terry was the ineluctable fact that my mum's allegiance was towards him more than me.

The atmosphere in the house was uncomfortable. I spent a lot of time in my room and always ended the day by listening to the BBC Radio 4 10 p.m. news, followed by *The Financial World Tonight*. Life was happier for all parties if I stayed out of Terry's way.

This might sound all a bit bleak, but on the positive side, my mother did have the virtue of being the origin of my moral standards. There are two incidents from my childhood which I recall with the utmost clarity. Aged nine, I stole a packet of Wrigley's double-mint chewing gum from Woolworth's. It was a green packet, and when I had gone to pay for it, the assistant had been called away to another counter. And I thought, 'Ah, I'll just turn around and take it. No harm done. Who will know?' But even before I got outside the shop, I knew it was wrong. I took the packet home with me, but I didn't eat it, and began to be tortured by the realization I was a common thief. The following morning I took it back, and that was much scarier than taking it in the first place. I dropped it near the 'pick-'n'-mix'. It made me realize how you have to live with your own conscience. I had heard in school or at church that you can never cheat yourself, and came to realize that this was true.

Another formative incident occurred when I was ten or eleven. One day I took a fifty-pence piece from my mum's purse to buy my favourite Caramac chocolate bar. I knew that if my mum ever found out I would be skinned alive, and on returning to the house, to my horror, she had indeed noticed that the coin had disappeared. But she didn't get angry. She just said, 'If I can't trust my own son, then who can I trust?' That's all. I felt so wretched. It was just for a chocolate bar, but I never forgot the lesson.

By this time we were living in Thingwall Road in a semi-detached archetypal suburban house. I suppose we would have been deemed lower middle class, just a rung below where we had been in Lichfield. So in a material sense we were relatively comfortable, but on an emotional level not much had changed, and as I grew older and more independent, things at home became ever more strained. In the years before Terry arrived on the scene, I have happy memories of my mum cooking a midnight feast of chips, and sitting in the bed eating them with salt and vinegar. Or when she took me on the ferry across the Mersey to New Brighton, to celebrate my eighth birthday. I was given a huge paper cup of coins to play with in the slot machine arcades. The chiming noises and bright lights had always captivated me. I appreciate that my mother had gone through a lot, and she demonstrated a resilience which should be respected. But there just wasn't much warmth. I'm sure my mum loved me as a child, but it didn't feel like she did. This left me highly insecure. If you're an insecure child, that mind-set will never leave you. It will stay with you. You learn more by pain than by happiness. It made me very driven and that's why I will still get up at 5.30 a.m. to work, after going to bed at midnight. I will push myself to the limit.

If Terry did one thing for me, it was to make me determined. I remember one occasion which involved my uncle Pat, who was my father's brother and owned a stationery shop. I used to go to visit his shop in Hoylake, and it was like an Aladdin's den for me with pens, paper, hole punches and tapes. I can smell it now and recall it was a rare place where I felt truly happy. Pat would allow me to take whatever I wanted. Pat had maintained an amicable relationship with my mother after my parents divorced. He came to our house one day, when Terry and my mum were there, and of course he had to buy something from my 'shop'. He said to Terry, 'This boy is going to be successful in life. You just watch him.' Terry said, 'I'm not so sure.' *I'm going to show you*, I thought.

Leaving Home

It was September 1971 when I first went to King David High. There were three classes in each year and on joining the school, I was assessed and placed in the bottom stream. That wasn't surprising as I had been affected by the divorce, which manifested itself in making me a very distracted and unsettled young person. I nevertheless worked hard and received a prize at sixteen for the best overall CSE results. I was interested in Economics and English but I never really caught fire with learning in a formal environment. Maybe if I had been brought up by my father, I would have gone to university. But that was not to be and I simply wanted to leave school and get away from Thingwall Road as fast as I possibly could.

One tragic event also had a profound effect on me. At the age of fourteen, I witnessed a fatal crash involving a car and a motorcyclist. I had no connection with the accident and was just walking along the pavement, but the way a split second can suddenly change lives profoundly altered how I viewed the world. It was a common accident where the car driver exiting from a side road, simply hadn't looked properly and seen the approaching motorcyclist, and had moved out in his path.

I can still vividly remember the motorcyclist lying on the ground with his white helmet removed and blood coming out of his ears. It started a lifelong passion for road safety and in my teenage years I began a campaign to make the use of daytime running lights on motorcycles compulsory, eventually meeting with the Transport Minister of the time, Peter Bottomley. In such accidents the motorcyclist is almost inevitably the innocent party, but having a bright light on during daytime makes them much easier to see. Whenever I travel on the roads and see potential accident sites, wherever they may be in the world, I take photographs and then write to the authorities. I've helped make over a thousand locations safer.

In the heatwave summer of 1976, when 10cc's 'I'm Not In Love' seemed to be on the radio almost continuously, I said goodbye to the King David High. I went on to attend Millbank Business College in the evenings for business studies. But I never completed the course as I had found a real job as a pub chef. Then I spotted an opportunity at Lucas Aerospace, which made fuel injection units for Rolls-Royce RB2-11 engines. It was a huge industrialized plant, and I applied for the grand-sounding role of 'commercial management trainee'. For some reason, they gave it to me and for the first time in my life I felt I was somebody. During training I was moved around all the different departments – personnel, finance, IT, and administration. This suited me perfectly and I liked simply being there in the factory: watching, listening and learning.

The factory was unionized and industrial relations were strained in the classic fashion of 1970s Britain. I would chat with the craftsmen working the vast lathes on the factory floor who were paid by the number of units they produced. For a period I was the post boy and walked around the factory delivering the mail. Liverpool is banter-filled – they are famously great talkers and as I passed would shout out: 'You all right, la? Love the suit.' They would tease me but it was warm; unlike at school I felt I belonged.

I learned at a very young age how to speak to people across the social spectrum. My mum was so well spoken that she was known locally as 'The Queen'. But around us were some of the most deprived kids in the country. So later in life, I was able to talk comfortably with anyone, a janitor or a senior banker, without it feeling forced or unnatural. Of course the nicest people in any organization are often those at the junior level, and some of the shittiest, the most senior.

The personnel manager at the aerospace factory had an inflated sense of his own importance, and our relationship was difficult because, naïvely, I always said what came into my head. There was a suggestion box, which most people ignored, so one day I put in a recommendation that the relationship between employees and management would improve if the personnel manager spent more time walking round the factory floor rather than remaining in his office. I was sixteen. I signed it and was convinced I would get £20 for making such a suggestion.

Before long, I was called into the personnel manager's office and he went absolutely berserk. I received such a savage dressing-down that I became convinced I was going to get fired. I went to seek advice from my trade union representative, who told me that I had done nothing wrong.

Britain's industrial relations in the seventies were a terrible mess with widespread industrial strife. The coalminers went on strike and the government introduced a three-day working week. The power cuts meant food went bad in our freezer and, most depressing of all, we couldn't watch television. Rubbish piled up in the streets and there was a sense of anarchy in Liverpool. Soon Margaret Thatcher was on the horizon. A woman for her times, she was courageous enough to confront and challenge practices that simply could not continue if we were going to stand any chance of getting out of the mire.

I felt insecure at Lucas because the factory was under threat of closure – an event that came to pass not long after I left. Having made my start in working life, to have wound up so quickly on the dole would have been a disaster. I bought the local paper and went through every job advertisement, soon realizing that for most of the positions which appealed I was under qualified. But one day I read that the confectionery and soft drinks giant Cadbury Schweppes wanted sales people.

The interviews took place at the Post House Hotel in Manchester, which seemed a very exotic location. I had bought a new suit and travelled down the M62 motorway in my old Vauxhall Viva. I somehow seemed to impress. A few days later, when I arrived home from work there was a letter waiting for me with the Cadbury emblem on the envelope. I had been appointed to the 'Commando Sales Force'. Our team were stationed in the Granada TV region in the north-west of England. The marketing department at the company's headquarters in Bournville, Birmingham would produce TV campaigns for products like Soya Choice, a disgusting textured vegetable protein, and 'we commandos' would follow up by loading our cars from a cash-and-carry with hundreds of tins, and go out onto the mean streets to sell them. We each had a little receipt book to keep a tally of our sales victories.

I would pitch whatever that month's campaign was – chocolate, tea or jam – to anyone. I would stop at garages, cafés, street markets.

I became the most successful member of the entire UK Commando Sales Force. It was a very pure form of selling, where you can precisely measure success or failure.

I do not have a textbook technique. I certainly do not believe in people being manipulative or Machiavellian in trying to sell. Deceit rarely works. Sales is in large part pure hard work; in simple terms getting what you have to show in front of people. It's a numbers game. The more people you show, the more you will sell. And just be pleasant, natural, honest, and listen. We all sell ourselves, all the time. I went on some sales training courses and found them ridiculous. I could sell from the moment I joined Cadbury's because I had been knocking on doors, selling blackberries, as a child.

My next move allowed me at last to leave Thingwall Road and go to London. It was 1978 and I was eighteen. Just old enough to legally drink in a pub, I had applied and gained a job as a salesman for Schweppes, selling soft drinks around the London postal district SE1. My territory spanned underworld pubs in the Old Kent Road to the National Theatre. When visiting the National I had breakfast in the staff restaurant and I was surprised to sit opposite the famous actress Felicity Kendal. I felt part of this thrilling new world. Of course I was just a soft-drinks salesman, but I was mixing in the company of those my father would approve of. I was chastised by the other salesmen because I was working too hard – for me, it was pub after pub after pub.

One of my most likeable customers, a kind drinks wholesaler on the Old Kent Road who originally came from Cyprus, would always make me a latte and give me the *Daily Mail* to read. One morning as I was sitting in his back room I noticed an advertisement for a company called KeyMed, along the classic lines of, 'Have you got what it takes?' It didn't ask for a degree, and I applied and got an interview at the Russell Hotel in London. I was twenty years old.

I interested Bernard Clark, the sales director, sufficiently for him to send me for a second interview in Southend, a seaside resort on the north bank of the Thames estuary. This was to be conducted by Albert Reddihough, one of the founders of this rapidly growing medical and industrial company. After talking with him for half an hour, I was worried I hadn't impressed enough to get the job, but he supported Clark's recommendation that I join. I came down and stayed at the Airport Hotel for six weeks, learned all about the gastrointestinal tract, what endoscopes could do, who our competitors were and what the strengths of our products were.

The business fascinated me and it was growing rapidly. The technology behind an endoscope, which makes it possible for doctors to look inside the body without an invasive surgical procedure, was in itself enough to excite me.

At KeyMed I worked hard and a lot of my business values came from Albert Reddihough. He had tremendous charm, but could be quite ruthless. On more than one occasion I saw him make grown men cry. Although he was already a multimillionaire and drove a Bentley, he was in no way standoffish. And he liked young people with drive and energy. He had a tremendous influence on me and I will always be grateful for the opportunity he gave me to prove myself. He retired from KeyMed twenty-one years ago and is now in his eighties, but we still meet regularly for lunch and joke that he has become my surrogate father.

Aside from the main flexible endoscope business, the surgical rigid endoscopy arena (metal tubes with optics) was potentially a much larger market. In 1979 Olympus acquired a German company, Winter & Ibe. It was exceptionally strong in engineering and fine mechanics, but its optics were not the best. Olympus shared its own optical expertise with the new arrival. Olympus now had superb products, but in this sector, we had no history, no reputation.

I went to see Albert and told him that the basic problem was that our salesmen would always gravitate towards selling the flexible product. In flexible endoscopes everyone knew us and our salesmen were welcomed by doctors almost as partners. In the surgical business we were poor relatives. But if we could get clinicians to use our surgical products, then we would be successful. I said, 'I think we should split the sales force, and create a new dedicated surgical sales force.' I also proposed that the salespeople in the new team should earn more money, because it was harder to sell the rigid endoscope. Albert tested my conviction by asking me some questions, and then said, 'Right, okay, you set it up.' So I formed the new surgical sales force. I was twenty-one. I had been with the company less than eighteen months and this would turn out to be my big break.

We all want to find a soul mate. In the summer of 1980, six months or so before I joined KeyMed, I received a call from a friend who wanted to come down to London and stay in my room. I was unenthusiastic until he explained that he was accompanying a Spanish girl who needed to take an early morning train to Gatwick Airport. I met them at Euston Station and was enthralled by this dark, effervescent arrival. That girl was Nuncy, who seven years later would become my wife.

Her parents were both loving and warm. Her mother, Anuncia, was a saintly woman whom I worshipped. I haven't met anyone who would look more pleased to see me. In the thirty years I knew her before her death, in September 2010, she gave me more love than I could ever have dreamt of.

When I first visited Nuncy's family home, her father, Ignacio, was worried that I was an impoverished salesman, selling Pepsi Cola. I was twenty-nine when I became KeyMed's managing director. By then I had proved to him I was a responsible and respectable husband for his daughter.

To be confirmed as MD, I had to go to Japan and present my plans for the company to Shimoyama, the then president. He was less than enthusiastic about having a twenty-nine-year-old in such a senior role, but my presentation won him over. That night he agreed to my promotion and took me to the Chinese restaurant at the Hilton in Shinjuku to celebrate. I was on top of the world.

6.

Homecoming

With the toilet at last having fallen silent, we made our approach from the east, tracing the path of the Thames, performing a long, slow glide in an attempt not to wake up the eight million slumbering Londoners below.

We landed at Heathrow shortly before dawn, in that rare moment when all is still and quiet *except* at major airports. The throng of the bleary-eyed crowds reminded me of last-minute Christmas shoppers. Once through a seemingly endless queue at passport control, I felt that profound relief at being home, a feeling compounded the moment I made it through customs and into Nuncy's waiting arms.

She hugged me long, wordlessly. From her shoulder bag she took out a copy of that morning's *Financial Times*. I stared at my photograph.

Sacked Olympus chief had sought answers to over $1bn in payments. As Jonathan had promised, my story had made the front page, and also the famous Lex column, together with a major feature in the centre pages. Seeing the words on the pink paper starkly brought home that I was now an ex-chief executive and unemployed. Soble also revealed that the Olympus share price had collapsed by 18 per cent the previous day, when the world had thought my departure was due to 'management differences'. Analysts and stockholders, believing that the *gaijin* president's revival of the famous company would not now take place, aggressively sold the stock, with the company's market capitalization falling by well over $1 billion. Trying to cheer me up, a journalist later told me that in the view of the markets, I was clearly a 'Billion-Dollar Man', and I was flattered for a moment until realizing the reality of my new situation.

The stock price had gone into a nosedive as I had been hot-footing it to Haneda and it continued its fall for many weeks. If Kikukawa thought that this was a disappointing market reaction, he had seen nothing yet.

In that moment, as I stood there in Terminal Three, at barely six o'clock in the morning, my life was changed for ever. I was now a whistleblower. A wolf that had clashed with the pack. An outcast who had done what he felt he had to do, and been soundly punished for it.

Habitually travelling with only hand luggage, and my mind foggy with fatigue, I had forgotten my large grey suitcase, which was still going round and round on the airside carousel. I had to contact the airline staff and go back through a special security channel. It was over an hour before I emerged for a second time. 'Let's go home,' Nuncy said.

We took a lift to the multi-storey car park. London in October was several degrees cooler than Tokyo and I suddenly felt the cold. When we reached the car, the radio was on and the Olympus story was headline news. As the driver negotiated the early morning traffic, I searched around inside my briefcase for my iPhone and turned it on. Immediately, it buzzed, clicked and pinged with missed calls, texts and voicemails. Before I even had time to read the first one, the phone rang – it was the *Wall Street Journal*. It would keep on ringing, day and night, in the months to come.

We decided to take a route directly through the centre of London. It was reassuring to see the familiar streets and the normality of life continuing. Knowing that I should sleep but still finding it impossible to do so, I read the *FT*'s Lex column:

STORMS ON OLYMPUS

It is appropriate that a maker of endoscopes – Olympus – should expose some ugly innards. The board of the 92-year-old Japanese company has accused its ex-president, Michael Woodford, of failing to respect the strict hierarchy of management. The Liverpool-born executive, 30 years with the company, tells the FT he was fired after raising questions over more than $1bn in payments made during a series of acquisitions.

Whatever happens from here, Mr Woodford should look back on his brief spell at the top with some satisfaction. Nominated in February to succeed Tsuyoshi Kikukawa as president in April, and backed by shareholders in June with a higher approval rating than any of the other 14 directors, he made a strong start, in very diffi-cult circumstances. Supply chains were knocked out completely in several areas affected by the earthquake and tsunami. Even so, dis-counted sales of digital cameras offered compensation.

Had the yen remained constant, net revenues in the three months to June would have been only 0.2 per cent lower than the year before, rather than 3.6 per cent. Achieving any operating profit at all in that kind of environment was an achievement: it fell 60 per cent, to Y4.5bn, thanks largely to a strong grip on selling, general and administrative expenses. Investors saw that a transition was under way. From the day of Mr Woodford's appointment to the day before his removal, shares in Olympus beat the broad Topix index by a fifth, and the precision-instruments sector by 7 per cent.

The board, too, seemed to recognise some leadership qualities, promoting the president to chief executive just two weeks ago. That investors decided to send the shares down 18 per cent when they heard of his dismissal – the most in four decades – suggests that they felt they lacked the whole story.

Waiting for me at home was Edward, who had only just started at university. Hearing what had happened, he immediately returned to our home in Essex. I was jet-lagged and edgy. But Edward is per-ennially calm and thoughtful; probably the person who soothes my anxieties more than anyone else. He's able to do so because he understands his father inside out. He is a genuine friend. Not that I want to go out with him to nightclubs, but we are very close. He has good judgement and an instinctive understanding of people's motivations. We can and do talk about almost anything.

Nuncy, Edward and I were sitting together drinking tea on the two red leather settees in the glass-roofed open-plan kitchen and dining area, where the family always congregate. Edward started to play through a series of scenarios, giving reassurance to his mother throughout. Nuncy's instincts were to adopt a bunker mentality and keep confrontation to the minimum. Mine were to attack. Nuncy was sounding increasingly anxious and, looking into her troubled eyes, I said, 'My love, we have to go on the offensive, to get the truth out, to tell the story, to galvanize the authorities to do something.' She gave me that resigned shrug I've seen so many times in our marriage – neither disagreeing nor agreeing.

Ever practical, Edward suggested we go into Southend town centre and buy a new mobile phone, as I had to give back the company iPhone, which I had been shaking only the day before in the face of Kawamata. I had never been in a phone shop in my life – the IT and telecoms people at Olympus did all that for me. But they were now a historical luxury, as were my chauffeur-driven Lexus and Jaguar.

Later that afternoon Isabel arrived back from boarding school. She has the same single-minded determination as me, which can at times cause us to clash, but I adore her. I had finally fallen asleep watching an old war film, and she bounded in wearing her blue school hockey outfit, full of energy. 'Hi, Papsy,' she greeted me with that affectionate term usually reserved for when she wants something. 'Are you okay?' she asked with the warmest of smiles and gave me the biggest and tightest of hugs, knowing that I was suffering, but not fully understanding the reasons why.

That evening the four of us went out to the nearby Mr Ping for a Chinese meal. I explained what had happened the day before in Tokyo, but didn't want to alarm Isabel, so held back a little with my fears as to what the coming weeks would bring.

That first night back in the UK I woke up anxious about the security of my email system. If those people who had been involved in or facilitated a fraud were now trying to cover their tracks, they might well attempt to hack into my private AOL account. With this thought nagging at my subconscious, at 3 a.m. I clambered out of bed without switching the lights on and went to the study. I powered up the home computer, changed my AOL password, and rather than going back to bed carried on sending emails around the world. Numerous journalists had approached me after the *Financial Times* story had broken the day before, and it had been immediately picked up by the main global media organizations. I furnished them all with the information I had given Jonathan Soble, but this time in electronic form.

It was still dark outside and at 6 a.m. I went downstairs to the kitchen to make tea – a very English habit. While waiting for the water to boil, I went over to the table where I had left my laptop. I noticed the screen was frozen and that I had forgotten to log off the night before. In trying to open my email I was horrified to find that AOL had locked me out. Was someone toying with me? Every time I tried to go into my email account, a message came up saying, *This account has been closed.* The security systems were such that it wasn't possible to recover the account and I felt depressed and frustrated. It was my own fault, as in my tired state I had left my AOL account open on the laptop and then changed the password on the PC during the night. Presumably this had led to something going wrong. I realized the dangers of trying to do things when in a state of exhaustion.

I opened a new email account and contacted Jonathan Soble in Tokyo, explaining what had happened. I asked him to forward me the PDFs of all the documents that I had originally given him. Recovering this information was critically important, as in the days ahead an ever-increasing list of journalists would seek information on just what had taken place at Olympus.

That Sunday, having had a few hours to reflect, the realization dawned that it was now just me against a huge corporation. I suddenly felt vulnerable, and losing my email account could have easily been the straw which broke the camel's back. It was one of the few times when I asked myself just what I'd done to deserve this. I knew self-pity was always the greatest danger in distracting me from what needed to be done, but I did feel during those hours that everything was conspiring against me. I'm not religious, but in a state of desperation I looked upwards and asked, 'Why are the gods doing this to me?' I was on the verge of tears and wished I could have cried, to let the emotion out rather than have it welling up behind a dam inside me. If only I could experience the relief of weeping, but I hadn't done so since the loss of Nuncy's mother the previous year, and before that the loss of my own father a decade earlier.

When you hit rock bottom something often comes along to lift you up. On that Sunday morning it was two emails from the daughters of my closest friend, Long Tran. The first was from his youngest, Mai-Lan. As usual, she addressed me as *tonton* (uncle):

Dear Tonton Michael,

I'm very sad to learn the news about Olympus. But don't worry tonton Michael, be happy you are always the best! :) You have your Family and us, your friends FOREVER!

Mai-Lan

The tears which I had held back earlier came easily. And then I read the elder sister Mai-Anh's message:

Hello Tonton Michael!

I consider you as a member of my family! If you are sad, I'll be sad! I know that you are the strongest tonton Michael of the world! Fighting!!!

I hope that listening to those songs will make you smile a little bit!

A noodle soup, a delicious Duck Confit and Us, are waiting for you in Paris. So come quickly with a big smile on your face!

Mai-Anh

Mai-Anh had embedded YouTube links for a series of songs she felt would lift my mood: Gloria Gaynor singing 'I Will Survive', Bobby McFerrin doing his 'Don't Worry, Be Happy', the 'Eye Of The Tiger' theme from *Rocky* and finally Celine Dion, Carole King and friends singing 'You've Got A Friend'.

I clicked to watch the videos of the songs she had so carefully chosen. Listening to the lyrics, I understood Mai-Anh was telling me in her our own special way that Tonton Michael had friends, would survive with the aid of a few well-chosen uppercuts and that I needed to do my level best not to worry.

Later that morning, Edward and I found a small and slightly dubious computer shop. I needed my two laptops forensically wiped to protect the many colleagues who had helped me. The owner, who had a strong Eastern European accent, was proud of his work, 'Bruv, this is the same software used by the military and there is no fucking risk of anything [sly wink] bein' left on the machines.' I had a feeling that he thought I was equally dodgy in asking such specific questions about removing data. 'How much?' I asked. 'As ya need it done so quick, let's call it one fifty.' I felt this was a lot for simply running a program but I couldn't take any risks. Ironically, some of those individuals I was going to such great lengths to protect would very soon turn their backs on me.

They have to live with their own consciences.

I had been back in the UK for just over twenty-four hours and I realized that shock can be a gradual thing. When I reflected on the enormity of what had taken place, that coldness of hands and feet which I had first experienced on Friday in the Monolith building came back at regular intervals. I was in a very agitated state and was grateful when one of our dearest friends, Lesley, phoned to enquire how we were coping and to invite us for a late lunch. I had first met Lesley in 1989 when she started working at KeyMed. A friendship quickly developed between us, and our partners, Nuncy and Watson, also immediately got on. We shared the joy of the birth of Edward in 1993 and barely a month later the birth of their daughter Rhiannon, known as Nonny. The same occurred in 1995 when Isabel was born just a few weeks after Lesley and Watson's son Evan.

Watson was one of the most intelligent and sensitive men I've ever known. A plumber by trade, he would turn up on a building site with a broadsheet newspaper folded under his arm. Sometimes on Sunday mornings we would find bagels from the local Jewish bakery on our doorstep, with a note from Watson telling us to enjoy the day ahead.

At that time I was already the managing director of KeyMed, which in the small town of Southend made me a local personality. But Watson wasn't bothered about me having a grand title or living in a big house. He judged people for who they were.

When we returned from a New Year holiday in Spain on 4 January 1997, there was a message on our answer machine. Watson had been admitted to hospital and wanted to see me. He told Lesley that I ran a medical company and would understand what was going on. Without unpacking, Nuncy and I went to the hospital, but Watson was already in a coma. He had been diagnosed with a routine streptococcal infection, but unknown to all, he was particularly vulnerable to opportunistic infections, a condition he may have had since birth. In just over a week this strong and healthy man would be dead. We visited the Intensive Care Unit every day, and at just past midnight on 9 January there came an anguished call from Lesley, who had reluctantly accepted the clinical advice that the life-support machines be switched off. In those final minutes I was able to say goodbye. I

kissed his forehead with tears running down my face. I have missed
him ever since.

We have remained the closest of friends with Lesley, and Evan,
Nonny, Edward and Isabel have formed a strong circle which I know
will not be broken throughout their lifetimes. Out of all the people
I've met, if I could aspire to live my life by the purest of human values, Watson would be my role model.

On that Sunday afternoon Lesley wanted to spoil me and had
cooked her slow-roast beef casserole. Her advice was: *Michael you
will get over this and there will be an end. Life will return to normal.* She
was, of course, right – I could find a way through.

That night, although only the security staff would be there, I
couldn't face visiting the KeyMed offices to return the computers.
Nuncy offered to go. She took the two laptops, the iPhone, the keys
to my Tokyo apartment, €200 (an unused expense advance) and the
American Express corporate card, leaving them in a plastic bag at
the security gatehouse. It felt degrading, and I imagined it was
rather like giving back your police warrant card after being found
guilty of a misdemeanour.

The following morning, Nuncy drove me up to London to meet
officers from the Serious Fraud Office (SFO), which investigates and
prosecutes serious cases of corruption in Britain. I knew the SFO
would be interested in what I had to say. At the time of the acquisition by Olympus, Gyrus had been a British company and hundreds
of millions of dollars in relation to the payment of the so called
'fees' had flowed through London en route to the Cayman Islands.
We stopped at the Southend branch of Waitrose to buy a new laptop; ironically paid for in gift vouchers presented to me a few
months earlier when I was part of a group of employees celebrating
their thirtieth anniversary with KeyMed. Before visiting the SFO,
I had arranged a meeting with several of the partners of Bates
Wells and Braithwaite, my London lawyers, at their smart offices
directly facing St Paul's Cathedral. They were courteous and helpful,

but as they had also acted for Olympus, they were conflicted, so I had to find a new firm. I was directed to Lewis Silkin in Chancery Lane and an appointment was made to see them at 6 p.m., following my visit to the SFO.

I took a black cab to the SFO's headquarters, housed in an anonymous grey 1960s office block in Elm Street, Bloomsbury. Photographers and television crews were waiting on the steps of the building. With the media forming a semicircle around me, I stopped for a few moments and said that I simply wanted the world to know what had happened at Olympus . . . I knew it was not the time to give a full press conference, which would have alienated those inside the building. After signing in and being given a security pass, I was shown into a sparsely decorated, functional office and offered tea and biscuits from the vending machine. (The FBI, I was later to discover, smile less and only give you water.) Two investigating officers were involved. The more senior was in his late forties, the second several years older and, I imagined, approaching retirement. I gave them all the files and they remarked on how meticulously the material had been indexed and cross-referenced. The SFO has not enjoyed too successful a hit rate over recent years, but they showed concern and interest in what I had to say.

As the meeting neared its conclusion, I was advised that caution should be shown in raising publicly what we had talked about, as it could undermine any possible future criminal prosecution. I reassured the officers that I wouldn't mention the content of the meeting to the media.

The older investigating officer was ex-Metropolitan Police, with a dark suit worn shiny through use. Just before I left the room, I raised my worry that those involved with the fraud might try to harm me. He looked at me in a fatherly way and said, 'I can see just how anxious you are, but the SFO are not the police and we can't offer you any advice on protection. What you really need to do is visit Scotland Yard and explain things to them.'

The problem for me was that it was already five in the afternoon and I knew that in relation to my safety, even more important than seeing the police, was getting my story out as quickly as possible to a global audience. If people were trying to silence me, there would be little point if I had already created an unstoppable momentum for an investigation. That evening I committed to giving my first two television interviews – visiting the police would have to wait until the next day.

On the steps of the SFO I had been approached by Jon Snow of Channel 4 News, and I agreed to a studio interview for his programme that evening. I had already met and got to know Jon through our shared support of Reprieve, the human rights charity. It seemed right that my first television interview (I would go on to give over 200 in the months ahead) was with a man I trusted.

The Channel 4 News studios in Gray's Inn Road are just a five-minute walk from the SFO's offices. I entered the Norman Foster-designed building and the minimalist reception area with monitors playing the channel's programmes. Jon came down to collect me. His first words were, 'How terrible for you and poor Nuncy.' His sympathy and concern were not contrived. He had met Nuncy at some of the charitable events and we had also dined with Jon and his wife.

Jon wanted to understand the detail of the story and I took him through the events leading up to my dismissal. As we sat down to begin recording the interview, he looked me in the eyes and said: 'I can't give you an easy time. I have to ask the uncomfortable questions, too.'

I didn't expect or want any favours. It was a probing exchange. I gave everything of myself. Afterwards I saw the pleased reaction of the programme's editor in the newsroom – Channel 4 knew they had a scoop.

Jon had the human kindness to walk me down to the street, where one of Channel 4's cars was waiting to take me to my appointment at Lewis Silkin. I met Jonathan Coad, a young, confident

partner of the firm. The second television interview that night was
to be at Bloomberg's studios at 9 p.m., so we had three hours
together. I was impressed that he was more than willing to work
late. That night Jonathan sent a three-page letter to Kikukawa accus-
ing him of defaming me and warning that he would soon be in
receipt of a letter from my Japanese lawyers dealing with his unlaw-
ful breach of my contract by summarily dismissing me. As I read
the letter, I was somehow comforted to see Article 8 of the European Convention on Human Rights being put to good use in my
time of need.

Just before 9 p.m. Bloomberg's limousine arrived to take me to their
London studios. I had a live interview with Lisa Murphy in New
York on their prime-time show *Street Smart*. I would be interviewed
many times by Lisa in the months ahead and in an innocent way fell
a little in love with her. Now my story was out in the US too.

Aware that I had no media training, I had simply decided to be
honest and sincere in both interviews. The message seemed to get
through. The media was my conduit to the world: the way to get
the truth out. The vital new people in my life for the next half year
were to be journalists and lawyers.

Olympus appeared to be mute. Lamenting Olympus's PR disaster – the share price was now in free fall – the acerbic William Pesek
of Bloomberg was typical. *Really*, he wrote, *I'd feel better investing
with Bernie Madoff or the Marx Brothers than Olympus's board.*

Pesek's commentary went from Olympus in particular to Japan
in general:

> When I travel and speak overseas, there is a troubling lack of inter-
> est in Japan. Audiences are at full attention when talk turns to
> China or India. Mention Japan, and out come the BlackBerrys . . .
> Japan's corporate culture of denial, of ignoring problems and let-
> ting them fester, keeps running up against a globalized world that

values agility, innovation and transparency. Olympus demonstrates all too painfully how much Old Japan tolerates a lack of accountability among senior executives; inadequate disclosure; a disinclination to challenge authority and absolute deference to corporate boards regardless of share performance. Tough questions are rarely asked.

It didn't please me to read these words about a country I cared for, but I knew Pesek's analysis was accurate.

My Channel 4 appearance that evening created immediate waves and I began receiving phone calls from concerned UK employees, including Emma, one of my two KeyMed PAs. It was so good to hear from her. 'Michael, I watched your interview with Jon Snow and it made me quite emotional. Things are tense at the moment, but I had to phone you and let you know that I can feel your pain and am worried for you.' I told her I would always be there for her. It had been an incredibly long day – the lawyers, the SFO, continual calls and emails, and the two TV interviews. Buying the computer that morning with Nuncy seemed a world away, but it hadn't finished yet. Bloomberg dropped me at the Pont de la Tour restaurant near Tower Bridge, where I had a late dinner booked with Josh Shores, a senior analyst and principal for Southeastern Asset Management, which was Olympus's largest foreign shareholder.

Josh was always impeccably correct in emphasizing that our discussion must not reveal any privileged information and I was equally careful not to forget my continuing duties as an Olympus director. Olympus's board had been willing and prepared to destroy me, but I still knew my responsibilities. I was careful only to explain to him what had appeared in the *Financial Times* and what I had said on-air to Channel 4 News and Bloomberg.

In the weeks ahead Shores would make a series of public statements demanding the contaminated directors step down. He demonstrated shareholder activism in the most positive sense, and shamed the Japanese institutional shareholders. Those are mostly banks and insurance companies, household names in Japan, and throughout the scandal they failed to utter a single word of public criticism of the board. Conversely, they never spoke one word in support for my own actions in revealing the massive fraud. My view is that corporate Japan can often seem like a large and perverted golf club in which the overwhelming priority is to protect the club's members whatever they may have done.

Josh was shocked and concerned, not least because he was watching the value of his firm's investment slide. His only advice to me was: 'Don't resign your directorship.'

During the meal I started receiving text messages from Stefan Kaufmann, a managing director at Olympus's Hamburg headquarters, who within a few days of my dismissal would go on to assume my old position as head of the European business. He was harshly berating me for going to the media. This really threw me because he had been so supportive in the weeks beforehand. Indeed, we'd had dinner together at the Sgroi Italian restaurant in Hamburg just a week before my return to Japan for the final showdown. It was a delightful place with incredibly attentive staff and this shouldn't have been a surprise as Stefan had a known penchant for expensive restaurants. Stefan Schultz, the journalist who published an article in *Der Spiegel* on this story of Kaufmann's betrayal, in his research spoke with the restaurant management and serving staff who remembered us.

We were certainly a memorable couple that night: before ordering any food Kaufmann spent over an hour reading and re-reading from my laptop the five letters which I had sent to the Olympus board. Coming to the end of the these, he looked up and said, 'It must be the Mafia.' Only then did we order from the menu. The following day Kaufmann wrote an email, thanking me for the trust that I had shown in him and saying: *I wish you supernatural strength,*

to dry out this snake pit . . . You are definitely crusading for the right thing,
but also for all of us who want Olympus to be a successful and respected
company and if I can support you, please let me know.

Just when I needed a loyal ally on the inside, Kaufmann completely changed tack and decided to run with the pack, telling me
that I should have tried to change things internally. Was he blind to
what he had seen himself? Trying to change things internally was
exactly what I'd done in writing the six letters to the board, literally
begging them to act, and for this they fired me.

I suppose it shows the turmoil I had created and how Tokyo was
doing such an appalling job communicating to the staff who were
now fearful for their futures. But some people have no courage.
Kaufmann suddenly seemed to have forgotten about the snake pit
and would leave me to crusade alone.

It was almost midnight when I walked back along the river to our
apartment feeling despondent. Worse was to come. That night
marked the start of Nuncy's nightmares. She woke up about an
hour into her sleep screaming: 'Michael, Michael, they've taken everything. They're going to get us.' She continued repeating those
two phrases, in a trance, her eyes wide open. The first, I think,
meant Olympus was going to sue us, and the other was the threat
of violence. I kept saying, 'Calm down, you're safe.' It took several
minutes to bring her back to the surface.

This went on night after night. Nuncy was traumatized and I was
scared about her troubled state of mind. I was also increasingly
concerned about my own lack of sleep as I had to keep focused,
keep applying pressure. If I cracked, the family would go down with
me. I took sleeping pills but found that I couldn't function properly
in the daytime – they made me too groggy.

Eventually, that first night back in our London apartment, as the
Thames eased by silently outside, we both fell asleep and hoped for
a better tomorrow.

The next day I went to New Scotland Yard. I had difficulty finding the entrance and approached an officer in a high-visibility yellow jacket and cradling a machine gun. In a wonderfully understated English way, he gently pointed out, 'Sir, Scotland Yard does not have a desk for the public. I suggest you go to Belgravia police station on Buckingham Palace Road and I'm sure they will be of assistance.'

As Belgravia is one of London's most expensive areas, I thought it would have a somewhat luxurious police station, so was surprised to find glaring neon lighting and worn carpets, the officers on duty positioned behind thick screens of, I presumed, bullet-proof plastic.

The officer manning the front desk appraised me as he must do everybody that comes in. Being a desk officer at Belgravia means dealing with more than your fair share of time-wasters, drunks and disturbed individuals. I saw him take in my suit and my frown, his likely thoughts: *Mobile phone robbed, possibly wallet.* He sighed, 'Yes sir, how can I help you today?' I began my tale about multibillion-dollar fraud, the possible involvement of organized crime and how I was concerned that the Yakuza might attempt to assassinate me.

As I spoke, his eyebrows scaled ever further up his forehead: *A crazy, another one.* Irritated by his disbelief, I said, 'Please just go and Google my name and you'll understand.' A few minutes later he returned with a different expression. He took me into an eight-by-six-foot interview room and offered me one of the two chairs. His interest now growing, he requested some ID.

I had gone from a 'fruitcake in a suit' to a high priority. I was told the commissioner had been contacted, and the seriousness with which the matter was being treated led me to believe that my fears might have some justification. The Metropolitan Police was edgy about foreign organized crime operating on the streets of London. In recent memory, the Russian dissident Alexander Litvinenko had been fatally poisoned with radioactive polonium while dining in an Itsu sushi bar in Piccadilly.

Within a few hours, two diplomatic protection officers, with responsibility for the safety of the royal family and foreign dignitaries, visited us at our apartment overlooking the Thames. I felt relatively secure there, due to the building's special entry codes which we needed to access doors and lifts, a multitude of CCTV cameras and the 24-hour concierge. But, with Nuncy standing next to me, their assessment was not what I expected. In an almost routine way they pointed out that the front door needed to be reinforced and special hinges fitted. They said the letterbox should be sealed, otherwise combustible materials could be passed through it.

This all had a terrible effect on Nuncy. She was a schoolteacher and, like me, had found herself in a completely different world, and one where she didn't want to be. Her screams were even worse that night.

We then went to meet the senior officer at the local police station. He asked our feelings on having armed guards outside our flat twenty-four hours a day. We both thought the effect of this on our children and neighbours would be too traumatic, and so we asked if we could think about it. London's police had so far not had to deal with the Yakuza assassinating people on their territory, but they still did not want to take risks. If the Yakuza *were* about to break with tradition, they didn't want it happening on their watch.

With the children away at university and boarding school, we chose to base ourselves in our London apartment, rather than our home in Southend. The Butlers Wharf enclave to the south-east of Tower Bridge has seen many crimes over the centuries. Dickens loved strolling through the squalor – in the company of the river police – to make notes. Arch-villain Bill Sikes from *Oliver Twist* lived here and *Our Mutual Friend* begins in the mist and murk of its creeks, where a lighterman tries to fish corpses out of the river. The warehouses that once stored cardamom, coffee and caraway seeds are now office suites and luxury flats.

There was no easy access to our apartment, which is many floors up. Having declined the suggestion of policemen with machine guns standing sentry, we were told that our telephone numbers were flagged for priority response – if we dialled 999 an armed response team would be with us in a few minutes. Knowing this provided a lot of comfort.

There were also moments of black comedy. One night our neighbours went away leaving behind their teenage children – who threw an impromptu party. It had migrated outside and they were jumping on the adjoining metal balcony. The noise was unbearable. After several polite requests were ignored, at 2.30 a.m. I reached for the phone. 'What are you doing?' Nuncy demanded. 'Calling the police.' She quickly made me see sense. Did a few drunk teenagers really deserve to have their party broken up by police bearing machine guns? Come to think of it, they wouldn't upset their neighbours again.

7.

The Three Musketeers

Whistleblowers are often isolated. In the school playground whistle-blowing is known as snitching, and snitches are no longer trusted by the other children. They are lonely and contemptible.

Once I had been ousted from Olympus, my relationship with many of those left on the inside became strained. Former close colleagues whom I'd known for years suddenly treated me like some sort of leper and studiously avoided all contact with me. There seemed to be an insidious pressure on some to have nothing to do with me. I had been deemed a contaminant. I was suddenly persona non grata and couldn't understand just what I had done wrong.

I was not totally alone. In London I had Nuncy, my family and friends. But I urgently needed support, especially to help deal with the Japanese media and authorities. My inability to understand the Japanese language would have made it almost impossible to bring those responsible to account. Luckily, in Tokyo I had my two musketeers: Koji and Waku. The pair would stand beside me during the long months of struggle ahead, never protesting at the unreasonable demands I placed upon them and their families.

I had met Koji Miyata way back in 1986, while at the Caesar Park Hotel in São Paulo for the World Congress of Gastroenterology. Koji was a general manager working for Mr Kawahara, the head of Olympus's medical division; I was the sales director at KeyMed. Albert Reddihough, KeyMed's founder, held Koji in high regard and they had known each other for many years. And in turn Albert had been so effusive in his description of my talents that I was nervous I would not live up to Koji's expectations. That first meeting was memorable – we talked for over three hours in my hotel room.

There was an immediate empathy and warmth between us and we have been close friends for the twenty-six years since.

We bonded by talking about Albert and the business. Older than Koji by a generation, Albert was a highly unusual businessman and an especially demanding person to work for. But he was an inspiration in the workplace, somebody who created things and made things happen. He was also unconventional, for example in making me the sales director at twenty-six. Giving a person so much responsibility at such a young age was unheard of in Japan, where the ascent of the corporate ladder is usually slow and methodical.

Over the years Koji and I got to know each other on a much deeper level than colleagues usually do, always sharing ideas and observations about the business but also about life. We had much in common, including being close to an exceptionally talented man called Todd Mori who should have made it all the way to the top of Olympus. But he tragically died of a heart attack when he was just fifty-four. Koji and I shared many life events, including the births of my children, his many grandchildren and the loss of my father and both his parents.

We are an odd couple. I am tall, he is short. I am loud and he quiet and intensely thoughtful, with a dry humour. I tease him because he bears an uncanny resemblance to Yoda from *Star Wars*, not only in stature but in the way he's filled with wisdom. I'm sure if he put his mind to it, he could make objects levitate. At any rate, in the struggle against the inhabitants of the Death Star in the Monolith, he was invaluable.

Koji is one of the most selfless people I've met and he is buoyed and strengthened by an extraordinarily loving marriage. The relationship between Koji and his wife Akiko is very gentle but strong. Together they behave like a pair of love-struck teenagers. The complete reverse of the stereotypical Japanese husband, he is attentive and engaged but not in a syrupy way. He's no angel, being dryly cheeky and mischievous.

Our home in Southend was the first Western house Koji and

Akiko ever slept in. We took them sailing on the nearby River Crouch on a terrible day with strong winds. But they accepted with politeness, without saying anything. It was not until we were bobbing up and down in the choppy waters that Koji quietly told me that he and Akiko could not swim. And Koji can tell if I can do something well. He had a high confidence that I could run the company, but he didn't have much faith in my sailing skills. They both looked petrified.

We have history. Koji was the person who went to Kikukawa back in 2004 and told him I should take responsibility both for the American surgical and industrial business and for the medical company in Europe. Kikukawa agreed. Koji would have been even more radical and given me responsibility for the entire global medical business outside of Japan, but at the time that would have been a step too far. Six years later no one was happier than Koji when I was made president. He told me that, whatever faults Kikukawa had, choosing me was his moment of supreme judgement. I was hugely flattered.

To those who don't know Koji, he may appear more conservative than he actually is. We share the same values of right and wrong, and when he found out what Kikukawa and his entourage had been up to, he was deeply concerned for both me and the company. Koji had worked for Olympus for forty-five years, just as his late father had. With ninety years' combined service between them, his loyalty to the company was beyond question. He retired in 2006 at the age of sixty-four, I suspect because Kikukawa found him too strong a character and a potential adversary. Kikukawa didn't even allow him the dignity of helping decide his successor as head of the global medical business. Kikukawa's choice was a man called Haruhito Morishima, who would later be one of the main board's 'yes-men' and who would remain silent to my repeated appeals to investigate what had gone on.

Koji is the polar opposite of a 'yes-man'. He always has a view, quietly expressed but strongly principled. He knew the strengths and weaknesses of individuals and he would know whether a person in the West would be stronger than another in Japan, and vice versa. When he came to a decision, he carefully analysed it from every angle, but would then act decisively upon it. Unlike many of his contemporaries, he wouldn't go along with a comfortable consensus just for the sake of it.

Koji, having shared a boardroom with Kikukawa, well knew of the chairman's vanity and bullying ways, but he didn't anticipate he would turn out to be a fraudster. Just after the first *Facta* article appeared, in early August, Koji came over to my apartment for dinner. It was the first meal I had cooked for him in Tokyo and I wanted to impress. I made my legendary cheese-encrusted tuna pasta bake, complete with three different cheeses and my favourite pasta sauce that I had brought over from England. Re-enacting my days as a chef in Liverpool, and trying to appear professional, I came to the pièce de résistance: the seasoning, complete with flamboyant hand gestures. It was the first opportunity to use my new Porsche electric peppercorn grinder, which I had picked up on a shopping trip with Michiko. But I couldn't figure out how to make it work, and the bottom came away, releasing hundreds of black peppercorns across the kitchen floor. As I stood dejected, holding the empty grinder, Koji broke down in laughter for a solid ten minutes.

The conversation turned more sober later that evening when I told him about my suspicions of fraud. His reply was immediate and unequivocal: 'I will always be here for you, any time of the day or night.' And he meant it, going on to fulfil his promise in the months ahead. I know 999 people out of 1,000 wouldn't have done what he did for me.

In a strange sort of way I think the scandal and ordeal revitalized him. Sharing the experience with Waku and Nuncy, it was like suddenly finding yourself in one of those snow globes you shake up and the calm becomes a storm. Sometimes it can make you feel alive, to be shaken up, to be pulled sideways, to be involved.

Waku Miller couldn't be more different from Koji. They broke the mould after he was created. His birth name is Brian, an American from Lincoln, Nebraska who was three when he moved to

Arizona with his family. That's where he grew up and where he went on to study at the state's university before transferring to the American Conservatory of Music in Chicago. Here he attained a master's degree in Music. He also studied contemporary music at the California Institute of the Arts.

His plan was to become a classical trombonist, but he claims he 'wasn't very good at it'. I doubt this because Waku seems to be good at everything. Leaving a musical career behind him, he got the travel bug and flew to Japan for a job teaching English. The language school's receptionist Kazuko became his wife, and he raised a family in Tokyo.

We met at the turn of the century when Waku visited KeyMed with his company Lapisworks, which produced a magazine for the British embassy to promote UK business in Japan. When he came to KeyMed he was surprised by the scope of the company's Corporate Social Responsibility agenda, which supported a wide range of good causes. That awakened a curiosity in him, and we became friends.

Japanese is a notoriously difficult language for Westerners to master. Speaking it is tricky, writing and reading nigh on impossible for the faint-hearted foreign student. I never even considered taking it on in any serious way. Waku, however, persevered.

After spending only a year in Japan, he started translating professionally. He has since translated about half a dozen Japanese books into English – everything from the history of Japanese calligraphy to an analysis of productivity in automobile plants around the world.

He received his Buddhist name from Waju Murata, a monk at Ryushoji Temple on the Noto Peninsula in Ishikawa. 'Wa' was taken from Waju and *ku* means 'air' or 'nothing'. Waku says he took the idea from a Zen concept he likes – *muichimotsu*, which means 'humans don't possess anything originally, so there's no need to cling on to anything'. I clung to him like a limpet for many months through the tempest. He became my voice in Japan when explaining my protests, actions and proposals to the Japanese media.

Everywhere I went in Tokyo he would be at my shoulder, listening and interpreting.

You cannot miss Waku because, as a *shugyo-so* (trainee monk), he chooses to wear only *samue* or traditional simple workers' clothing. The arresting image is topped off by a pair of the most severe round tortoiseshell-framed glasses.

Waku is the person who opened up Japan for me and showed me the depth and richness of its culture, way beyond the world of business. He revealed to me how the country is filled with complexity and contradiction, with unimaginable subtlety you would never appreciate if your exposure was only to the one-dimensional salary-man image. Waku moves in circles of artists and writers and uses the lessons he learns from them to make business less dogmatic, sycophantic and structured.

Whenever I spoke to Waku, whether it was six o'clock in the morning or late at night, he was always warm and friendly. He is able to find the humour in any situation and has an endearing ability to defuse tension. When the reports came about possible Yakuza involvement, he was dismissive: 'Well, Mr Abe [of *Facta*] hasn't been bumped off yet.'

In July 2007 he took me on a three-day hike on a heritage trail where we had to wear bells to frighten away the wild bears. We spent the first night in the old temple town of Koyasan and then hiked for two and a half days across the hills of southern Nara Prefecture to Kumano Hongu, the site of an ancient temple. Thanks to Waku I experienced a side of Japan most foreigners never encounter.

Such was Waku's commitment to my cause that he even bought a hundred shares in Olympus so that he could attend shareholder meetings with me.

So there we were. The Three Musketeers: Woodford, Koji and Waku. An odd trio, but in our 'all for one and one for all' approach we were more than a match for the mightiest of corporations.

*

On the subject of which, over in Tokyo, Kikukawa was leading the assault against me. In attempting to explain to the company's shareholders why I had been fired, at 10 a.m. on the Friday morning, less than an hour after my boardroom showdown, Olympus held a press conference. Kikukawa opened this by saying:

> 'Mr Woodford was selected to lead our effort to strengthen Olympus's global competitiveness. However, he couldn't understand Japanese style management and was acting arbitrarily and peremptorily. I was afraid the situation, if left unchanged, would cause considerable damage to our customers and shareholders, and therefore, I had to act decisively and quickly. I am really sorry for his dismissal.'

It was hard to know where to start. If 'Japanese-style management' meant not questioning what Kikukawa and his cohorts had been up to, then his message was easily understood by me. But it was not one I would quietly accept.

His meaningless answers to the journalists' questions were typical, but one in particular made me smile. Kikukawa was asked, 'What about your own responsibility of having appointed Mr Woodford a president?' His response: 'I acknowledge my responsibility, but we must accomplish our Basic Management Plan established in 2010. I will continue to lead assuming the dual duties. I don't plan to impose a salary cut on myself or anything like that.' Imposing a salary cut on himself – what an outrageous thought that would be.

Mori had his fun, too, at the press conference. His question: 'After the announcement of Mr Woodford's dismissal, the stock price of Olympus plunged sharply. Is there any concern your globalization efforts will be interrupted?' His insightful reply: 'Our Basic Management Plan of 2010 had been in action before Mr Woodford's appointment. All the necessary gears will keep running.' Little did he know that within a few weeks those gears would be well and truly jammed.

On that Friday of my dismissal, 14 October, Olympus also issued a News Release which was posted on the company's website for all to see:

REASON FOR THE CHANGE

Michael C. Woodford has largely diverted from the rest of the management team in regard to the management direction and method, and it is now causing problems for decision making by the management team. Hence, judging that realisation of the 2010 Corporate Strategic Plan with its slogan of 'Advancing to the Next Stage of Globalisation' would be difficult to achieve by the management team led by Woodford, all the board directors attending today, except for Woodford himself who could not participate in the voting due to special interest, unanimously resolved the dismissal from his office of the representative director, President and Chief Executive Officer. Along with this, it was also resolved that the representative director, Chairman Tsuyoshi Kikukawa double as the representative director, President and Chief Executive Officer.

Global management that Olympus aims is to implement management rules, information management and operation that are common throughout the world in order to establish a business infrastructure that is more efficient and quick to respond while making the most of a Japanese style management that sets a high value on people, technology and pride of monozukuri or manufacturing. To this end, all our employees will head for the same direction as we will urgently start establishing a new structure to go towards the same goal with the entire staff as one.

It was the sort of empty and bizarre rhetoric with which I had become all too familiar. More disturbing, however, was that publishing this type of nonsense, and showing bravado at the press conference, suggested that Kikukawa and Mori really thought they could stonewall the world and business would continue as usual.

The weekend passed but the attack against me resumed in earnest on the Monday morning, when Mori gave a conference call to investors and analysts. He threatened that the company might take legal action against me.

That same night in London, in my interview with Bloomberg's Lisa Murphy, I was asked my reaction: 'I would be delighted to meet Mr Kikukawa and Mr Mori in the High Court,' I said. 'There is an obvious public interest in this story . . . let all the facts come out.' Let Kikukawa and Mori come to London or New York and explain to an independent judge why the company had paid $1 billion for three companies with no turnover, as well as $700 million in fees to unknown advisors. I knew the evidence was compelling and they would never step out of Japan for fear of arrest by the SFO or FBI.

On the Monday morning the media had published my claim that the fees paid for the Gyrus acquisition amounted to $687 million, or 35 per cent of the transaction price. Questioned about this in his conference call, Mori countered by saying that the real figure was less than half this, but tellingly declined to give the exact amount. What planet was he on – so that's all right, then – $350 million paid for nothing.

That effort to reassure investors backfired spectacularly. By the close of trading that day, Olympus's stock had plummeted by 24 per cent, extending Friday's 18 per cent fall. A cool $3.2 billion in market value had been wiped out.

Olympus was losing the communications fight. By stubbornly refusing to answer direct questions, they came across as evasive and anything but transparent. Not a good day for Kikukawa and his gang. The next day, as pressure mounted, Kikukawa agreed to an interview with Japan's *Nikkei* newspaper, in which he acknowledged the acquisitions but flatly denied any wrongdoing. He admitted paying advisors about ¥30 billion ($390 million).

So Kikukawa and Mori were trying to get their stories straight about the extortionate fees, and in the process confused everyone. Even in talking with Nikkei Inc., in my experience the most benign of inquisitors, Kikukawa could not hide that his acquisitions had hardly set the world alight with their commercial success. 'The firms we bought continue to be unprofitable, which is my fault, but the moves were necessary to help foster new businesses,' he told them. At least he was confessing to one failing.

After Mori's efforts the previous day, Kikukawa's statement made a bad situation worse. On Tuesday, at the close of trading in Tokyo, Olympus shares had plunged another 8.9 per cent. The stock had fallen 43 per cent since my dismissal on Friday and the downward slide would only continue.

In London that Tuesday night, I wrote to the head of Japan's Securities and Exchange Surveillance Commission in Tokyo providing him with everything I had given to the press. My letter was sent by air courier, so it would arrive quickly and I knew it couldn't be ignored.

On Wednesday everything started to fall apart for Olympus. Under pressure from the Tokyo Stock Exchange it was forced to issue a statement confirming my claim that $687 million had in fact been paid in fees to unnamed advisors in relation to the Gyrus deal. After the public statements Mori and Kikukawa had made in the preceding two days, publicly disputing the amount, I simply released to the media the emails Mori himself had sent me only a few weeks before, which detailed the amounts and precise details of the payments.

Olympus could not go on denying. Revealingly, the company did not explain how it came to pay such a large fee or why, the day before, Kikukawa had claimed it paid only ¥30 billion. Their statement said Mr Woodford had been fired over 'differences in management direction and method'. Olympus's credibility was shot to pieces and it was crystal clear who the liars were and who was telling the truth.

While in Tokyo Olympus was going into meltdown, in London I was getting into my stride as a professional whistleblower. My mobile phone was ringing non-stop. I was continuing to give interviews to any media source that got in touch. Even if my old colleagues did not want to talk to me, plenty of journalists did. Over the months that followed I became close to some of them; in return they got hundreds of compelling column inches. Journalists interest me. Although I had come across them intermittently during my career, this was the first time I had encountered international print and television news hounds en masse. True, they wanted something from me, but their energy and good humour often kept my spirits up during what was to prove a long autumn and winter. I learned how to pick and choose the right journalist to present with a scoop. I always returned the call. I was always available morning, noon and night.

That Thursday, Jonathan Russell from Britain's *Daily Telegraph* visited our apartment for an interview. He remarked with some surprise that 'Team Woodford' appeared to be just me and Nuncy.

'I had assumed with the wall-to-wall coverage you are getting that you had a team of about fifteen people managing your PR,' he said. 'No, it's just little me and Sir,' Nuncy replied, as she pointed to me. I was pleased to see she was in good spirits for the first time since my return. Hearing Jonathan's favourable analysis that we were getting the message through, and that people believed me, had clearly lifted her mood.

It was only the fourth day of that first week in London but having been successful in getting the message out, overseas shareholders were now starting to mobilize. The Chicago-based Harris Associates, the second largest foreign shareholder of Olympus, sent a letter to the company's board and to the Tokyo Stock Exchange seeking an independent probe into the 2008 acquisitions. It was from David Herro, Harris's chief investment officer of international equities, a man I would come to know and gain great respect for in

the months ahead. The Tokyo bourse spokesman, Naoya Taka-
hashi, commented: 'Generally, we urge companies to disclose
information on a matter that affects investors' judgments. We cannot comment whether we took such action on Olympus.' The
world was full of platitudes.

As the Tokyo Stock Exchange closed on Thursday, the company's
market value had fallen by $4 billion in the five trading days since I
was fired. David Herro went on to say: 'There are serious issues surrounding the massive destruction of stakeholder value and there
needs to be accountability. I stress stakeholders because the damage
is not just to the shareholders, but the employees, suppliers and customers whom also deserve answers.' And, I could have added, one
ex-president.

Since our dinner on the Monday night, Josh Shores had not been
idle. Southeastern Asset Management wrote to Kikukawa, formally
copying the board, Ernst & Young, Japan's Securities and Exchange
Surveillance Commission and Financial Services Agency, together
with Britain's Serious Fraud Office. The letter, made public a few
weeks after it was sent, was forensic in its questioning:

> *Dear Sirs,*
> *Southeastern Asset Management has been a supportive shareholder*
> *invested in Olympus since 2004. Currently we hold approximately 5% of*
> *shares outstanding. We are long term investors focused on high quality*
> *businesses with good people and good corporate governance. We are very*
> *concerned with the detailed allegations raised by your former CEO,*
> *Michael Woodford, over the last week. The questions that have been raised*
> *cannot go unanswered. Olympus has a storied history in imaging and a*
> *high quality medical franchise that is worth significantly more than the*
> *share price of ¥2,482 on the Thursday before the news of Mr. Michael*
> *Woodford's removal was released. Your duty to the company and all*
> *stakeholders requires that corporate governance and management match*

this quality and history. In that interest, we require answers to the questions detailed below. We request a reputable, third party accounting firm unaffiliated with Olympus or Gyrus be brought in to carry out a detailed audit. We request a third party, independent special committee to oversee this process and report its results.

Related to the Gyrus acquisition:
Was the Financial Advisor (FA) Axes America LLC (Axes)? What is the relationship between Axes and AXAM Investments Ltd (Axam)? Are any parties related to Olympus affiliated with Axes and/or Axam in any way? Who were the principals? Who did Olympus deal with at Axes and Axam?

What services provided by the FA merited a deal fee of $50 million in warrants and $176.98 million in options on a $2 billion deal, 11.4% of the deal price? Why did the FA remuneration change from $176.98 million to $620 million ($176.98+$443.02) between September 30th, 2008 and March 31st, 2010?

What were the formulas used to determine these two figures? Why did the formula change? Was professional advice sought in determining the reasonableness of the formulas that determined these payments? If yes please provide details. How does Olympus management justify a total of $670 million in payments on a $2 billion acquisition, 33.5% of the price? In an email exchange with Olympus investor relations dated May 28th of 2010 why was Southeastern told that the payment for preferred stock in the 2009 Annual Report was 'one of the financing for Gyrus acquisition' when in fact it was payment to an FA?

Relating to the acquisitions of Altis, Humalabo and News Chef:
Respectively from whom did Olympus buy these three companies? Are any parties related to Olympus affiliated with the prior owners of Altis, Humalabo and News Chef in any way?

The Corporate value of Altis, Humalabo and News Chef was carried out using the DCF [Discounted cash flow] method. What third party accounting firm carried out this calculation? Did this accounting firm supply their own analysis of the companies or determine value using

Olympus assumptions? Did the board approve these corporate values and the acquisitions of Altis, Humalabo and News Chef?

Who was held accountable for the dramatic impairment of value totalling ¥55.7 billion a mere nine months after the deals were completed? Why is this classified as Amortization of Goodwill and not an impairment charge? Why was no mention of Altis, Humalabo or News Chef made in the English 2009 Annual Report given the negative impact?

Relating to Mr Michael Woodford's firing:
As representative director why was Mr Woodford not allowed a hearing at the final board meeting?

Who will be held accountable for the dramatic collapse in the share price following his removal which has resulted in hundreds of billions of yen in market losses to shareholders?

Furthermore, Southeastern requests that we be provided voluntary access to, and allowed to make copies of, certain board minutes. We request access to the minutes of meetings related to the discussion and approval of the acquisitions of Gyrus, Altis, Humalabo and News Chef and any payments made to an FA for these transactions. To avoid any misunderstanding Southeastern does not wish to obtain material, non-public information which would affect Olympus business and/or limit Southeastern's activities. We would like this access immediately.
We await the response to these questions as furnished by an independent third party auditor no later than November 16th, 2011.

The letter was signed by Mason Hawkins, Southeastern's chairman and CEO, Andrew McCarroll, their general counsel and principal, and Josh. In a world where shareholders are regularly criticized for being passive and failing to hold management to account, this extraordinary communication shows how it should be done. They were calling the board to account in the most direct and explicit terms. Comparing the actions of Southeastern and Harris Associates to the total silence of the Japanese institutional shareholders is evidence to my opinion that the country, if it can't change itself, is on the road to ruin.

It was Friday, 21 October, seven days since my dismissal. As I woke at the end of that first week back in London, Olympus bowed to the immense pressure and issued a terse statement saying it was agreeing to a third-party probe into its acquisition activity over the previous years. A panel including lawyers and accountants would be formed.

So within a week of my firing, Olympus had been forced to set up a panel to investigate just what had gone on. But overseas, confidence in the board was now almost entirely lost. This was demonstrated that day when Olympus's third largest overseas shareholder, Baillie Gifford, joined the outcry for answers and an investigative process which was credible and transparent. Gifford is one of the UK's leading investment managers, based in Edinburgh with over £66 billion of funds under its control. Its statement showed a candour of language which would be totally alien to their Japanese counterparts:

> Baillie Gifford is extremely concerned by the recent unexpected management changes and allegations of financial impropriety at Olympus. Baillie Gifford encourages the company to make public without delay the composition of the body that will conduct the independent third party review into Olympus' M&A activity and payment of advisory fees, and to ensure the full and transparent disclosure of the findings of this review.

In retrospect, Olympus's greatest mistake was believing it could manage the scandal according to the *Alice in Wonderland* rules of Japan, where you can bow deeply, say sorry, and the problem goes away. This time it was different, with the world's media, investors and overseas law-enforcement agencies all wanting the truth. It was now a story where the facts would dictate the ending, not the language of obfuscation. I knew my role was to act as a lightning rod to draw attention to the scandal, and not let the world get bored and move on to another story.

But the world was not moving on. In fact it became ever more absorbed by the Olympus scandal and the insight it gave into the strange workings of Japan's capital markets. That day the problems piled up for the beleaguered Kikukawa and his chums when Goldman Sachs joined Nomura and JP Morgan Chase in suspending its rating and analysis on Olympus, saying the 'adequacy' of the company's accounting practices regarding past acquisitions had 'become unclear'. Effectively this meant they had little idea what had been going on behind the scenes and no longer felt able to offer any opinion about the integrity of the company's accounts. They, like everyone else, were in the dark – and they didn't like it.

On Saturday I went back to Southend, and that afternoon took a long run along the shore to clear my head. When I returned an email was waiting for me which took me completely by surprise. I had often wondered who the source for the *Facta* article was and had speculated to myself whether I knew him or her. Then, out of the blue, that person had made contact. As with most Japanese communications it began, quite unnecessarily, with an apology:

I am an Olympus employee. I am sorry to say that I have not had the pleasure of meeting you directly, but I have the highest regard for the way that you have responded to what you have learned recently about our company.

I feel horrible about having furnished outside journalists with incriminating information that I should have channelled through an internal corporate hotline. Unfortunately, Olympus does not have a hotline adequate for the information in question. I look forward to the opportunity to apologize to you for this indiscretion when you have resumed the post of CEO.

I am worried about the danger from gangsters. That worry has compelled me to act anonymously. Please know, however, that I am with you in spirit. Thank you for anything and everything that you can do for our company.

PS Michael, Please convey the following message to Olympus employees through the media: 'Don't discard any data, no matter what your bosses might say. Destroying evidence is a crime. Let's tackle this together. Let's do the right thing.' Conveying this message to your employees will contribute greatly to preserving and restoring Olympus's corporate value.

This communication both encouraged and humbled me. So there was a truly heroic person still inside Olympus. They didn't have a British passport and an exit opportunity. They had to fight quietly on. I wrote back to them in admiration and said that I wished we might meet one day.

On the Sunday morning I was really struggling with the unfamiliar software on my computer. I can't type properly and did not know one end of Microsoft Outlook from the other. An executive without back-up is truly a fish on a bicycle. At KeyMed I'd had two supremely competent PAs, plus one in Tokyo, all of whom could second guess my every move and thought. You never realize how your life is reliant on such people until they are no longer there.

I waited till eight o'clock (it was a Sunday morning, after all!) and in desperation I phoned a close friend from Southend, Peter Thompson. He took pity on me and half an hour later arrived with his business partner Ian Homan. Ian had read the *Sunday Times* that morning – which under the headline *The Southend Samurai* had a cartoon-like illustration of me as a judo black belt delivering a blow with my foot to an Olympus logo – and was clearly intrigued. I was in a ragged state and the introduction proved a life-saver.

Ian, I'm sure has an IQ double that of most normal people. Although he never bothered to tell me himself, he had been a technology supremo at the investment bank UBS and then Barclays, finally becoming head of technology at the London Stock Exchange. At the age of forty-four he decided there was more to life than high finance and retired to look after his bee colonies. (His home is on the seafront in Southend, and you can taste the seaside in that sticky amber nectar.) He was wryly amused by my technical illiteracy and decided to make me a project. He set me up with PCs, printers, software packages and Google alerts so I could keep pace with my own story. We also bought some amazing voice recognition software called Dragon – I sat with a headset barking out emails, like a 1960s office telephonist. He warned me about the insecurity of certain email systems and persuaded me to switch to one less vulnerable to hacking.

'I've seen your type a few times before in my career but never anyone who was so tortured by it,' he told me one day in his kitchen over tea. 'You're the golden boy who has been the recipient of "The Shaft". But you are a bit different because, as far as I can see, you're squeaky clean.' I took that as a compliment. And his verdict on what had gone wrong at Olympus? 'Exposure and leverage. Terrible combination. Obviously holding massive unrealized losses. Couldn't unwind 'em. They had to wash it out somehow but they do seem to have done it in an incredibly stupid way.' Typically, Ian had managed to reduce a complex problem into just a few sentences.

That afternoon the four of us had been invited for a late Sunday lunch with our friends Maggie and Brett Hollick, who live nearby but on the other side of the 'tracks'. They have a lovely home, but according to them, the railway line which divides our neighbourhood means we are much posher! Shortly after we arrived, something happened that I will always remember.

News about the *Sunday Times*' 'Southend Samurai' article had quickly spread and led to the paper being sold out in many shops in the town. Brett had gone to several different newsagents looking for it and was delighted when he eventually found a copy. We first met when attending National Childbirth Trust antenatal classes before the births of Edward and their first child, Emily. Both their daughters are charming. The youngest, Alice, a year after she was born was diagnosed with a condition known as global development delay, and is considered to have special educational needs.

With all the uncertainties created by my sudden and unexpected dismissal I was sensitive to how emotional shocks can put enormous strains on your relationships. This left me even more filled with admiration of how Maggie and Brett coped with the unforeseen challenges of having a daughter who was different from other children. They learned to adapt and have a nurturing and loving relationship. Alice recognized the large picture of me in the paper and, having only limited speech, came up and gave me the biggest hug I had ever had in my life. It was touching how she could sense the pain I was feeling and in her own way wanted to let me know that she cared.

The next day, Monday, 24 October, we learned a little more about what had been going on through a superb piece of investigative reporting by Hiroko Tabuchi, a *New York Times* correspondent in Tokyo. The article concentrated on the three 'Mickey Mouse' companies. It looked at the role of two brothers: Nobumasa and Akinobu Yokoo. The *NYT* traced Nobumasa's involvement back to 1998, when he had been employed by the Japanese investment bank Nomura and headed the prestigious Shinjuku branch. Olympus was one of his clients. (Nobumasa had also previously worked at the Wall Street investment bank Wasserstein Perella.) In June of that year he and others at the firm had left after a scandal involving payoffs to Yakuza gangs. A number of arrests were made, although Nobumasa was not implicated. He made his exit commenting to the *Nikkei Business Daily* that he wanted 'to be able to cook the rice I live on'.

Then, according to the *NYT*, Nobumasa Yokoo formed a management consultancy called Global Company, and gained back Olympus as his client. At a board meeting in 2000 Olympus decided to invest ¥30 billion in a fund known as GC venture capital, overseen by Yokoo. The strategy was to invest in new business areas via acquisition. And who was in charge of overseeing the fund on the Olympus side? None other than Kikukawa, a director at the time.

The crucial three deals had not taken place until 2006–8, when $773 million was splashed out on Humalabo, a face-cream maker, News Chef, a microwave-plate manufacturer and Altis, a medical-waste recycler. They were all new companies and had never made profits. The *NYT* could find no evidence that any due diligence had taken place before the purchases that Global was urging it to make.

If anyone had been concerned at Olympus and looked more care-fully, they would have seen that Global itself had put ¥10 million into Altis in 2005. They would also have discovered that Yokoo had been CEO of a predecessor company to Humalabo, called LEM Hanbai. Yokoo had also been a director of a predecessor to News Chef, called News. All three companies had at least one temporarily listed HQ at the same address as Global. These expensively acquired companies only brought losses; from 2006 to 2009 Altis lost ¥760 million and Humalabo lost ¥462 million. No figure was available for News Chef.

The younger Mr. Yokoo still heads Global Company, according to its lat-est filing, the *NYT* article continued. *But that filing lists no telephone number and none could be found in any public directories. A reporter who visited Global Company's address in central Tokyo found an unlocked door leading to an empty, unfurnished office. The building caretaker said the company had moved out this month*, it concluded.

The bird appeared to have flown the nest.

During these first weeks following my dismissal, I developed a great respect for investigative journalists, who so often seemed to be ahead of the authorities. Three days before the *New York Times* rev-elations appeared, Reuters journalists, as they diligently endeavoured to interlock the jigsaw pieces and find out where the money had gone, got a scoop. They had managed to track down the 'veteran banker', Hajime 'Jim' Sagawa to a waterfront duplex in Boca Raton, Florida. Sagawa was a banker who had previously worked for Drexel Burnham and PaineWebber before setting up Axes America, a company which had been intimately connected to the Gyrus element of the 'Tobashi'.

The recent history was enlightening. Beginning in 2006, Axes America served as adviser to Olympus in its acquisition of Gyrus. The advice had not come cheaply. While Olympus agreed to pay Axes 5 per cent of the deal's value, the contract was not truly capped at 5 per cent. The fee also included an unusual option for Axes to buy shares of Gyrus. *An arrangement whereby a financial adviser received a mixture of cash, share options and warrants is surprising,* PwC's report had noted, as advisers tend to be paid solely in cash.

The law firm Weil, Gotshal & Manges had told Olympus, in a 2008 document, that cash payouts were preferable, but that an unnamed financial adviser *strongly resisted the cash payment on the grounds that this will crystallize an immediate tax liability.* Weil Gotshal had only reviewed the options for paying the fee, not the legality of the fee itself. The *New York Times* reported that the unnamed adviser was apparently Axes.

'This is such an extraordinary deviation from normal fees,' said Jeffrey Manns, an associate professor at George Washington University Law School who is an expert in securities law. 'No one would have entered into this transaction if they were showing good business judgment,' he added, as most countries prohibit corporate boards from 'rubber-stamping' such large fees.

On 1 February 2008, the $2 billion-plus Gyrus deal was officially concluded. Just a few weeks later, on 5 March, Axes notified American regulators it was shutting down, and with that, the eleven-year-old firm disappeared. Axes had assigned its Gyrus shares to a new Cayman Islands operation with a somewhat similar name, Axam Investments, where PwC had identified that Sagawa had signed documents as a director.

Axam drew little notice for two years until, in early 2010, the company moved to unload its Gyrus shares, selling them to Olympus for $620 million. (This was the largest element of the $687 million total consideration, paid in the so-called fees to Axes and Axam.) After the enormous payout in March 2010, Sagawa quickly shut down his various businesses one by one. In June 2010, Axam was removed from the Cayman Islands company registry for the non-payment of licence fees.

But the Reuters reporters could not now find Sagawa. He had, however, left his wife behind as an unusually loquacious spokeswoman. She wasn't having any accusations that he'd done anything wrong. 'My husband was on Wall Street for many years and was well-respected,' she said after answering the door. 'He's as clean as a whistle, I assure you,' she said when asked about Sagawa's connection with the scandal.

Mrs Sagawa was sufficiently obliging to give Reuters her husband's cell phone. It turned out all was not well with the Sagawa marriage. Reuters remained on his tail and three months later confronted him in the Florida divorce court where he and his wife had petitioned for divorce in October citing 'irreconcilable differences'.

Interestingly the couple listed a mere $11 million in combined assets and Sagawa reported a monthly income of $2,500 with $1,800 coming from social security and $700 from interest and dividend payments. According to their settlement agreement, Ellen Sagawa was going to receive nearly $9.9 million in assets, including their Boca Raton home valued at $2.5 million. Also among the assets was $6.7 million held in a savings account.

Sagawa kept nearly $1.5 million in assets that included $1.3 million in several retirement plans, $100,000 in a savings account and $100,000 in a brokerage account. No mention was made of the $620 million Cayman Islands payment or where it may have ended up. Veteran Jim had no comment to make to Reuters.

As I followed events back in the UK, I willed the journalists and law enforcers on the trail not to give up. I would continue to campaign but I was neither a detective nor an investigative journalist. Someone on the ground needed to get to the bottom of this fiendishly complex money trail.

Later that Monday I learned Kikukawa had issued a rambling Gaddafi-like diatribe to Olympus's employees in Japan. Bloomberg had translated this into English and it was titled: *What employees should know: On MCW's behaviour.*

It was a straightforward character assassination:

> Michael C. Woodward's ('MCW') aberrant behaviour hasn't stopped. Although he has been dismissed from his post as president, he used his position as a member of the board to leak internal company secrets. Such behaviour gives the appearance that he is trying to ruin the creditability of Olympus. This is hard to forgive, and we are naturally considering legal action. I feel pain for our employees, who are fighting back complex emotions while at work, and would like to thank them from the bottom of my heart.

He went on to accuse me of running the company with a *cabal or gang*, disregarding chains of command and organizational hierarchies, and castigated me for the use of a private jet. Warming to his theme, he continued: *The expression 'delegation of authority' doesn't seem to be in his dictionary.*

Nowhere did Kikukawa attempt to explain what he had been up to, or mention the advisory payment for Gyrus, which had just been revealed by Reuters to be the largest advisory fee in global business history, tripling the previous record of $217 million for the €70 billion takeover in 2007 of the Dutch bank ABN AMRO by the Royal Bank of Scotland.

Reading his words made me feel even more like I was Alice in Wonderland. Kikukawa was the Mad Hatter.

8.

The Big Apple

The *New York Times* broke the news that the FBI was investigating Olympus on Sunday, 23 October.

Knowing how Japan operates, I had been worried that the Japanese authorities would lack the vigour and motivation to hold Olympus to account, but now that US and UK law-enforcement agencies were involved, the pressure upon the Japanese establishment to act would be overwhelming. This story was now about how the world viewed corporate Japan as a whole.

A busy day lay ahead on Tuesday the 25th, with a string of media interviews, including my first with Charles Hodson of CNN. That evening I was off to New York, where I was to be interviewed by the FBI. The *New York Times* scoop on Sunday night had been written by Ben Protess, a New York City-based correspondent, who had provided me with the name and contact details of the FBI agent who was dealing with the case. On Monday morning, I had phoned his number at FBI headquarters but there was only an answer machine. I left a message. Later that day the agent returned my call. He sounded interested in my story and we agreed to meet two days later in New York.

The afternoon interview with Charles Hodson, beamed around the world, went well. In response to a particularly pointed question I replied, 'Come on, Charles, the company has paid nearly three-quarters of a billion dollars to unknown parties in the Cayman Islands, and for what?' That sound bite said everything that needed to be said about the strange goings-on at Olympus.

My last interview that afternoon was with Bloomberg's Lisa Murphy: news that the FBI was investigating had given the story renewed momentum. There had been other corporate scandals in Japan, with lingering doubts over whether they had been satisfactorily investigated. This time it was more likely that all the stones would be turned. No one knew what would be found under them.

Bloomberg had arranged for a car to take me from their studios to Heathrow. I picked up Nuncy from the apartment and as we headed to the airport, I felt troubled. Earlier that day, I had learned that I would have to change my British firm of lawyers. Eight days after accepting me as a client, Lewis Silkin had contacted me to say they were sorry but they could no longer act on my behalf. This was because part of their worldwide alliance (Ius Laboris) had carried out work for Olympus in Germany. Sorry wasn't good enough. They had accepted me as a client, but more than a week had passed before they had discovered they were conflicted and couldn't act for me after all. They still sent their invoice, however, and I felt the least they could have done was to waive this. It is experiences like this that give lawyers a bad name.

Olympus, similar to other large global corporations, uses numerous legal firms around the world and anyone challenging these Goliaths can have real problems in finding a firm to represent them. I was becoming increasingly worried that I wouldn't find a major London practice to represent me. You feel very anxious and vulnerable without a lawyer by your side. It is like losing your flak jacket while under incoming fire.

Jonathan Coad, the partner from Lewis Silkin whom I had met the week before, had at least suggested an alternative firm, Simmons & Simmons. The proposed lawyer was an employment specialist called Mark Hewland, and an arrangement had been made for an initial call at 6 p.m. that evening, while I would be en route to Heathrow.

At exactly 6 p.m., as the car cruised along the M4, my mobile rang. From the moment I spoke to Mark, I liked him. He gave me all the signs of energetic support and belief in my case.

It was a tremendous emotional relief to learn his firm were most definitely not conflicted and were prepared to go into battle for me. I had done some research. The *Chambers UK* legal directory praised Mark for his 'extremely pragmatic approach and real gravitas'. That, combined with the fact that he had experience dealing with whistle-blower cases, was good enough for me.

Nuncy and I took the last British Airways flight out of Terminal Five. As a now unemployed businessman, I was starting to worry about money. More precisely I feared a marked lack of inward cash flow. My salary had been stopped and although we were comfortably off, we were not going to be able to survive for long on Nuncy's wages as a part-time Spanish teacher. Most of our assets were tied up in pensions and long-term investments, and consequently we did not have piles of cash sitting idly around.

Our savings were starting to diminish rapidly, as the cost of funding lawyers on three continents was considerable. I was already thinking about how long this battle might last.

The Woodford profile may have been high, but I was a one-man band taking on a multibillion-dollar corporation with almost limitless resources and a very negative attitude towards me. I knew we needed to limit our spending to the minimum, but since I had lived a lifestyle rather like George Clooney's in the movie *Up in the Air*, I was sufficiently rich in frequent flyer miles for us still to travel in business class. As the 747 left the runway, heading towards my rendezvous with the FBI, it all seemed like a scene from a John Grisham novel. I picked away at the salmon on the plate, my mind preoccupied and elsewhere. We crossed the Scottish coast and headed out over the Atlantic. At least I had Nuncy at my side.

I had been in New York only the month before, for the US board meeting, when I had been met by the presidential limousine. This time, Nuncy and I rode into Manhattan from JFK in a battered old yellow cab with a driver who lived up to all the unflattering stereotypes. How life's twists can humble us all. Driving through Wall

Street to my hotel was sweet with its own irony. This was Gordon Gekko territory, and there I was in the thick of another story of power, wrongdoing and delusion, with people convincing themselves that they were invincible.

Our late dinner consisted of the hotel's complimentary nuts and pretzels. We drifted off to sleep but in the middle of the night were woken up by text messages and emails bleeping on my phone. Nuncy got up to check, and screamed, 'Kikukawa has resigned.' Up I leapt. It was around 3 a.m. I looked out from our window, and all was quiet – nothing but deserted streets and that familiar orange NYC glare.

I called room service for orange juice and coffee, and we got working in our dressing gowns. With all the Japanese media going into overdrive, we put in some very active hours before dawn. Nuncy was in fine form: clear-headed and pragmatic, pacing herself and dealing with the ever-growing lists of requests for media interviews, while I prepared for my afternoon meeting with the FBI. We made a good team.

Olympus's announcement was typically terse and, although filled with the customary apologies, explained very little: *As we have troubled our customers, business partners and shareholders over a series of press reports and a slump in share prices, chairman and president Tsuyoshi Kikukawa today returned his titles, as well as his right to representation.* 'Returned' was an interesting choice of word.

Cracks were appearing in the pillars of the Olympus edifice. Like me, Kikukawa remained a director, despite the allegations against him. I subsequently learned that, bizarrely, even after his resignation he still came to the office each day, behaving as if it was business as usual. He had continued to have access to the internal email system, while I had been immediately locked out.

As the sun came up over the East River, I felt for the first time that we were going to win. Kikukawa, the man who had been trying to destroy me, was in retreat. He would pay the price for what he had done.

Kikukawa was replaced as president by Shuichi Takayama, whom I knew quite well. I had always found him likeable and felt more warmth towards him than any other member of the board. He was a modest company lifer who had been president of the imaging and audio business. He must have been bewildered to find himself suddenly propelled into the top job. 'Is he just one of Kikukawa's puppets?' asked one journalist in an email from Tokyo. At that stage I did not know what strategy Takayama would adopt. But within a few hours he continued the inept and evasive behaviour of his predecessor. I was not surprised, but nonetheless disappointed, as he had an opportunity to put Olympus back on the right track.

At a Tokyo news conference in front of more than a hundred reporters, Takayama calmly defended the deals (the acquisition of the three 'Mickey Mouse' companies, and the payment of nearly $700 million in fees to unknown parties in the Cayman Islands), claiming that it was my fault the share price had fallen off a cliff.

'If this secret information hadn't been leaked there would have been no change in our corporate value,' he declared. 'It was our strategy to find new growth areas to reduce our over-reliance on the endoscope business. The three acquisitions were part of that strategy.'

Nobody was buying this story any more. Both the investment community and the Japanese media, usually so passive, were beginning to tire of the charade. 'This was not an adequate explanation of whether the fundamental values of the acquisitions were reasonable and likely will not win back the trust of investors,' said Shigeo Sugawara, a senior investment manager at Sompo Japan Nipponkoa Asset Management. 'Today's explanation was meaningless because it's limited to a disclosure of information from within the company, when a third-party investigation is what's needed.'

Even after a hundred minutes of heated questions directed at Takayama, the restless reporters were demanding more time, which was denied to them. 'We have more questions and you haven't cleared up all our doubts,' one Japanese journalist called out. The market reaction to the press conference: the shares fell another 7.6 per cent. There seemed to be no bottom as to how far down they could go. Reuters pointed out that the scandal was now the biggest in Japan since the 2006 Livedoor scandal. 'It's going to be like an onion – things will come out in layers,' said Darrel Whitten, managing director of investor relations consultancy Investor Networks.

By accepting the role and then continuing to evade questions, Takayama merely made the onion de-layering worse. Kikukawa remaining as an active director was the beginning of my realization that things are very different in Japan from elsewhere in the world of business. It was, however, the beginning of the end – the sharks were circling and everyone could smell blood in the water.

With the sun now up in New York, and with Kikukawa's demise, I was feeling remarkably re-energized and making the most of my morning to speak to the media. 'The board has to go, they're all toxic, they are all contaminated,' I told Bloomberg Television, adding that I would not step down as a director of the company. 'Shareholders have contacted me and their basic message is "please don't resign". I would go back if the majority of shareholders choose that.'

That day I experienced one of those situations which can literally drive you mad with frustration. I was trying to arrange to meet Ben Protess, only to learn from my network provider that I had reached the credit limit on my mobile phone. I needed to be in touch with the world and this was a nightmare. Ironically, as an anti-fraud measure, new customers are only allowed a maximum of £400 credit in any rolling four-week period. 'Look I'll pay with my credit card!' I was desperately appealing to the call centre operative. 'What do you mean you are sorry but that's not possible?' How I suddenly yearned to be back in the corporate fold with no worries about mobile phone company small print.

With the news of Kikukawa's resignation, that morning in New

York I gave numerous television interviews including a live transmission to Jon Snow from Channel 4 News, who was in Brussels covering the summit of leaders to coordinate a response to the Eurozone crisis. Critically important were the interviews with the Japanese networks, including Fuji TV and Nippon TV. I gave an interview to the latter in a minivan en route to the FBI building, where their cameraman filmed my arrival. I thought: when these images are screened in a few hours on breakfast news in Japan, Kikukawa and his allies must realize that the game is up.

It was nearly 2 p.m., the time of my appointment with the FBI at 26 Federal Plaza. I jumped out of Nippon TV's New York van in front of the imposing building, and was met by a pair of agents straight out of Central Casting. Neat dark suits and few smiles. 'Eliot Ness' and his number two. They told me we were going over to the courthouse, where two Federal Prosecutors would join us.

So the three of us walked through the crowded square. I expected the discussion to last for about an hour. Three hours of close questioning then ensued. Halfway through, my voice had started to crack up and fade. They fetched me a cup of water from the fountain, as opposed to the tea and biscuits I had received at the London SFO. I answered all their questions. They were immensely courteous but extremely probing. I got the feeling they knew far more about what had been going on than I did. I left encouraged.

I came out from FBI headquarters and looked for Ben Protess. We had agreed he would wait for me until I came out, but after three hours I thought he must have given up. With no phone allowance, I walked into the drugstore across the street. 'Excuse me,' I asked a friendly looking store assistant, 'I'm desperate. Would you mind if I borrowed your phone? I have to make a really important call.' He could not have been more charming in dealing with this highly agitated Brit, hot-foot from being grilled by the Feds.

Protess had actually been patiently waiting round the corner. We jumped into a yellow cab and picked Nuncy up from the lobby at the hotel, where she had been trying to handle the ever-increasing media clamour for interviews. She was relieved at my return after not having heard from me for several hours.

It had started to rain hard. We were running late and the cab driver sped recklessly to JFK. Nuncy in the front and me in the back giving Ben his patiently awaited interview, we bowled and bounced through Queens. We just made our flight on the little twin-engined Airbus that puts you down seven hours later at City Airport, a stone's throw from the centre of London. We had barely enough time to return to our apartment, shower and leave for Simmons & Simmons and my first face-to-face meeting with Mark Hewland and his team.

Hewland has a calm, authoritative manner and is unhindered by being a dead ringer for the actor Colin Firth. 'Listen, Mark,' I would jest with him in the dark hours of document-drafting in the months that followed, 'when the movie about my story gets made, I promise I'll do what I can to ensure Firth is approached with a generous offer to play you. Now just take it easy on the billing.'

We were joined in a teleconference by a lawyer in Tokyo from TMI Associates, the firm with whom Simmons & Simmons have an alliance in Japan. Disturbingly, despite joining the two-hour meeting where I had been completely open in expressing all my concerns, the very next day TMI now also claimed they had a client conflict. Mark immediately set about trying to find a replacement to represent me in Japan. I had been told Nagashima Ohno & Tsunematsu (NO&T), the second largest practice in the country, were a superb firm. Just as I had been lucky in finding Mark, and his associate Liz Wake, I was extremely fortunate to meet Arai-san and his colleague Shiozaki-san at NO&T.

These two individuals were another reminder that there are many men and women of integrity in Japan. They were certainly part of the establishment, but were still prepared to do everything possible to defend my interests. They too want Japan to change.

Nuncy and I spent that weekend in Southend, but every day now felt the same as I continued, without pause, the relentless work of managing the ongoing dialogue with journalists around the world. On the Saturday night, however, I switched off the laptop as we had been invited for dinner by our caring neighbours Karen and Mike Nevin. They wanted to let us know that they were there for us. Mike is a chartered accountant and has a senior position in finance and would go on to provide me with valuable advice and ideas in the weeks that would follow.

On Sunday we escaped to have lunch with our close friends Jim and Françoise Gardiner. She is French, very warm and the best cook I know. He is English and cerebral – a retired headmaster. They were the perfect tonic. They could not have been more calm and supportive, listening and asking the occasional question over my favourite duck confit with braised leeks and potatoes. A quiet few hours in the middle of a cyclone.

The next morning, Monday, 31 October, the scent of political trouble reached the highest echelons of the Japanese government. Prime Minister Noda had expressed his disquiet about Olympus in an exclusive interview with the *Financial Times*. 'What worries me is that it will be a problem if people take the events at this one Japanese company and generalize from that to say Japan is a country that [does not follow] the rules of capitalism.' He went on to emphasize, 'Japanese society is not that kind of society.'

His remarks were unprecedented as it is highly unusual for Japanese premiers to comment on individual cases. They showed the scandal had reached the point where it was proving harmful for Japanese capital markets as a whole. His objective was to try to reassure the international investment community that Japanese markets operate in the same way as elsewhere.

Unfortunately, and with due respect, he is wrong. Japan has a unique system of cross-shareholding, and more significantly there's an incestuous relationship between companies, suppliers and the banks. Those who are members of 'the club' would argue that it ensures stability and continuity. But the result is a complete absence of hostile takeovers, and the 'creative destruction' this brings. As a result, many Japanese companies have boards of directors who are mediocre or worse, yet they stay in position until they retire. This culture only serves to undermine corporate Japan. It weakens the country.

You would never see Western company directors doggedly remaining in their positions in the way the Olympus board did. On the first two working days following my dismissal, when Mori and Kikukawa deliberately misstated the level of so called payments to advisors, they would have been gone within hours. The media's scrutiny of such behaviour in other countries would not have been survivable.

The murk grew thicker when on 3 November the *Wall Street Journal*, following leads in all directions, discovered a bizarre link between a Nobel prize-winning economist and the company. Robert Mundell had been on the Olympus board in 2007 when it approved the contract for the advisor Axes America LLC, which, with an affiliate (Axam), went on to receive the near $700 million payment for 'advising' on the Gyrus acquisition. The *Journal* had found that before Mundell took a seat on Olympus's board, he had given a series of lectures, sponsored by Axes Japan, whose largest shareholders are listed as Akio Nakagawa and Axes America's founder, none other than Hajime Sagawa.

The paper reported that *efforts to reach Axes Japan and Messrs. Nakagawa and Sagawa have been unsuccessful. The firm's current website contains only a message saying that Axes Japan stopped dealing in financial products as of Nov. 30, 2010.* Everyone was suddenly so hard to reach. *Mr. Mundell, who is on leave from his position as a professor at Columbia University in New York, didn't reply to requests for comment. His assistant says he is traveling and unavailable*, the article continued.

The seventy-nine-year-old Mundell certainly sounded like an interesting character and had once bought a sixteenth-century Italian castle to offset the effects of inflation. He had been Olympus's first ever outside director and a celebrated catch. The article went on to quote the CEO of a company on whose board Mundell sat. When the CEO had asked him about his thoughts on the Olympus situation, 'He [Mundell] said he's lucky he's not on the board right now, there's a lot of turmoil there.'

The following day Olympus said it had been forced to delay announcement of its earnings, pending the report by the Third-Party Committee, a panel of experts which had been commissioned by the company the previous month to independently investigate the allegations. Even louder groans emanated from the financial community. 'Everyone except the person who was sacked is speaking with one voice, saying something completely different from what he's saying and not explaining things,' Nicholas Benes, the head of the Board Director Training Institute of Japan, told Bloomberg. 'The perceptional aspects of this are absolutely hideous.'

Olympus announced a board meeting in Tokyo on 8 November. I was entitled to attend, but was given only a single day's notice, making it impossible for me to do so as I was 6,000 miles away. It soon became obvious why they did not want me there – it was confession time.

The formal admittance of the 'Tobashi' came that day. The company finally acknowledged that the world's largest ever advisory fee of $687 million (related to its $2.2 billion purchase of Gyrus), as well as the payment of $773 million for the three 'Mickey Mouse' companies, had been used to hide losses on securities investments.

Olympus issued a statement:

It has been discovered that the company had been engaged in deferring the posting of losses on investment securities, etc. since around the 1990s and that both the fees paid to the advisors and funds used to buy back preferred stock in relation to the Gyrus PLC acquisition, as well as the purchase funds for the acquisition of the three domestic new business companies . . . had been by means such as going through multiple funds, used in part to resolve unrealised losses on investment securities.

It ended by the board once more commenting on how sorry they were for the inconvenience caused.

When the news came out in Tokyo it was the early hours of the morning in London but a journalist in Japan made the right decision in waking me to let me know of the extraordinary developments. I could hardly believe it. I read the company's News Release and there it was, in black and white. I had finally been vindicated.

The admission after weeks of denials shocked investors and the share price collapse gathered even more momentum, falling almost 30 per cent to its lowest level in sixteen years. As the largest overseas shareholder, Josh Shores of Southeastern spoke out demanding the replacement of the entire board.

'Ignorance is no defence,' he told Reuters in London. 'If you were there and not aware of it, then you were incompetent. If you were there, and aware of it without asking tough questions, then you were negligent. Either way, you need to leave.'

At the crowded news conference in Tokyo with some 200 journalists present, a subdued Takayama spoke: 'I was absolutely unaware of the facts I am now explaining to you.' This was despite him having staunchly defended the glaringly illogical transactions when he had taken over from Kikukawa the month before. 'The previous presentations were mistaken,' he said.

All that day and those which followed were filled with interviews – the Japanese media were insatiable. Now I was seen as the hero, and Kikukawa the villain.

The next morning in London I saw that overnight Olympus's shares had slumped by their daily limit for a second day running. Bloomberg reported that Josh Shores of Southeastern was now demanding investor relations head Akihiro Nambu should go too, *because of his role as a director of Gyrus Group Plc, the U.K. takeover target used to funnel more than $600 million in inflated advisory fees to a Cayman Islands fund. After Nambu, the rest of the board must follow, said Shores.*

'*Even if they didn't know the specific details around where payments were going and exactly why, they knew that cash was going out the door and they also failed to raise their hands to ask questions,' Shores said. 'I don't know who else is involved, but somebody else is. There is a third party somewhere who received this money.'*

The Bloomberg article reminded readers that *Kikukawa, Mori and Nambu became the three directors of Gyrus in June 2008 following the $2 billion acquisition of the U.K. medical equipment maker in February that year.*

Southeastern, as Olympus's largest overseas shareholder, was certainly prepared to confront issues head-on. It issued an unusually candid press release: . . . *it is essential that Tsuyoshi Kikukawa and Hisashi Mori resign as directors, that Hideo Yamada resigns as corporate auditor, and that Akihiro Nambu resigns as General Manager of the PR and IR department, and director of Gyrus immediately, and that all of these persons fully disassociate themselves from the company with immediate effect.*

I reflected that since my dismissal less than a month before, when night and day I had been fighting to get the truth out, Nambu was heading the vigorous PR campaign against me. Only in Japan could such an individual remain in position.

Nambu's name was to come up again the following April, just before the extraordinary general meeting, when ISS, the influential shareholder advisory firm, commented that the decision to promote someone with Mr Nambu's background (extraordinarily, to manager of the accounting and financial division!) *seems to demonstrate a business-as-usual attitude in the wake of the accounting scandal,* and gave the impression that *the company is not really committed to making a clean break.*

*

Exhausted, late on the evening of Friday, 11 November I returned to Southend for the weekend.

I woke on the Sunday morning to find an unexpected and alarming email nestling in my inbox. It was from Jake Adelstein, the famous crime journalist who had written *Tokyo Vice*.

Mr. Woodford,

I'm fairly certain you know who I am but if you don't, I've been a reporter in Japan for 17 years, starting with the Yomiuri Shimbun in 1993. I've been covering organized crime for almost 17 years. I greatly admire your courage and foresight in exposing the problems at Olympus. I've written a long piece for The Atlantic Wire about some of the darker aspects attached as a PDF.

Jake went on to explain much about the Yakuza and its increasing links to mainline businesses. There has never been any evidence that the Yakuza were involved in the Olympus scandal, but after the October issue of *Facta* and now Jake's commentary, I was growing increasingly paranoid. Maybe that was not a bad thing: in the opaque world of Japan, one should always remember the saying that 'only the paranoid survive'.

Jake ended the email warmly:

I have a great admiration for whistle-blowers. My father was one; his good deeds were not rewarded but he played his cards right and did well.

Good luck.

Jake

This message, while supportive, disheartened me. Since my dismissal, Nuncy was running my office, and was therefore reading all my emails. She was already weighed down by anxiety, and Jake's warning sent her over the edge. Fearing for everyone's safety and the toll the saga was having on the family, she asked, 'Please, Michael, why can't you just drop it? What are you trying to achieve?' But I was resolute. 'Look. There's no point in me lying curled up in my basket, licking my wounds. That's never going to get us anywhere. What I need to do – with or without your help – is to get Olympus on the right road.' I felt there was no choice but to continue what I had been doing since 14 October. Talking to the media and working with the regulatory and law-enforcement agencies.

But that Sunday Nuncy was digging her heels in. The four of us were supposed to be going to lunch but, at the last minute, she backed out. 'Just take the children and go without me,' she insisted. I left the house with Edward and Isabel, but then something snapped inside me. The anger, the tiredness, the weight on my shoulders suddenly came out. I would go back to London alone – I couldn't risk being dragged down by this negative atmosphere. So I knocked on the door and started to open it. But Nuncy was pushing the other way. 'Let go of it!' I yelled. One of the leaded glass panes shattered. It was our lowest moment.

I went into the house and collected my bag. 'That's it,' I said. 'I can't stand this for another minute. I'm off to London.' And away I went down the road to the station. Edward called me, 'Come back now, Dad. Please,' he implored. 'I can't, Edward,' I replied. 'Because if I go down, then we will all be destroyed.' A few hours later he followed me up to the capital, and we went to a local French bistro on the Thames to mull things over. It was almost as if there was a reversal of roles, with my son doing the caring and advising. I realized he was my equal. 'You have to fight, Dad. Otherwise, if you leave it where it is, it's the wrong place for you, it's the wrong place for the company; it's the wrong place for the truth.'

I came back to the flat and gazed out of the window at the ever-flowing river. Then I phoned Nuncy. 'Hello,' I said in muted tones.

'Are you all right?' She was calmer and we exchanged tentative pleasantries, trying to build bridges. Call me harsh but sometimes I feel that when you are not getting on with someone, the best thing to do is just to be in different places. Make a bit of space for a time-out. After I hung up I went back to a miserable window-gaze again. Edward returned to his reading. I was convinced the whole vile business could lead to the break-up of our marriage.

Nuncy felt the same intense pressure as me, but at least I had an outlet. I was more in control of events; I was stimulated and focused on what I was doing, meeting people, receiving lots of endorsements and encouragement. Nuncy was largely helpless to influence events.

But that is the way I have always been – problems are there to be solved. What do I need to do to get from A to Z? I work out the route, surmount the obstacles and I get there. So it did put an immense strain on our marriage. I did not have enough energy to cope with her outbursts and be nurturing and caring of her.

The effect on our everyday lives was brought home to us a few days later. I had returned from London because our friends Louise and John Gloyne wanted to take us out for dinner at the Shagor, a local Indian restaurant. Halfway through the meal a large group from KeyMed came in. They were nice people, many of whom I had known for years as colleagues. Once they would have all come over, shaken hands and greeted me. We would have chatted and laughed. Maybe the odd hug. But not now.

I didn't blame them at all but it left me feeling strange and sad. This was the first time I had felt that way. Behind their guarded expressions, some of them gave quick smiles in my direction and had sympathy in their eyes. But paradoxically that just made it worse. They looked like they wanted to say something, but didn't – or couldn't. I wanted to engage with them but knew that would only cause embarrassment. Olympus had now publicly confessed that a massive fraud had taken place. Why was it therefore so difficult for the good honest people within the organization to express their empathy? The incident ruined our evening. 'Let's go home,' suggested Nuncy quietly. As I was walking back to the car, the penny finally dropped that I was no longer one of them. The organization of which I had been a part for thirty years no longer had any place for me.

I remained worried for the future of my colleagues. Investors drew back in horror as the trickle of revelations swelled into a torrent. 'This is very serious. Olympus admitted it has made false entries to cover its losses for 20 years. All people involved in this over 20 years would be responsible,' said Ryosuke Okazaki, chief investment officer at ITC Investment Partners. 'There is a serious danger that Olympus shares will be delisted. The future of the company is extremely dark.'

Olympus was officially placed on a watch list for delisting from the Tokyo Stock Exchange; a fate which would automatically result if the company did not resubmit five years' worth of corrected statements by 14 December. Olympus became a plaything for speculators shorting its stock. On 11 November – 11/11/11 is an inauspicious date in Japan – the share price had plunged to ¥460, the lowest for almost forty years. This was a staggering 81.5 per cent drop from the day before my dismissal, when it had stood at ¥2,482. Over $7 billion had been wiped off the value of the company.

But the 11th had also been a day of hope. It was the day that Koji Miyata had launched the 'Grassroots' website to enable Olympus people to talk freely. Waku's son Doug had single-handedly created this digital forum which was to prove so important. With an obvious pent-up need to communicate, it immediately proved such a success that, overwhelmed by traffic, the site crashed the server.

The following day, Koji wrote and posted on the site an extraordinary letter in both Japanese and English, explaining what Grassroots was about and its objectives.

Takayama and Morishima both begged Koji to take the site

down, but he refused. He had written that Michael Woodford was 'an inconvenient truth' for Olympus, and he was not going to stand by and watch me destroyed. *I am unwilling to sit passively and witness the demise of a company that I love . . . Friends, the good ship Olympus is listing and is in real danger of sinking. Don't think for a moment that our endoscope business is somehow indestructible. Nobody wants to buy products from a company regarded as corrupt. Winning people's trust will depend on reinstating Michael Woodford as president.*

My old friends did me proud. Koji Miyata and Waku: *Semper fidelis.*

9.

Return

With the leaves fallen, the nights drawing in and winter coming on, I was feeling the effects of having endured months with little sleep. Knowing that I had to get at least some rest at night, I began to self-medicate. I would drink a strong gin and tonic and half a bottle of wine before bed, but would still wake after only three or four hours with the gloom of the room pressing in and suffocating me.

It was like living in a bunker, my only comfort being that the more public this story became, the less likely it became that my family or I would be attacked – what difference would it make? Any vengeful act against me would surely now be counter-productive. My face had appeared on the front pages of newspapers and television screens around the world. It was too late for this story to be buried.

An association with the Mob is not the best of adverts for any business. But potential links to the Yakuza were again suggested on Thursday, 17 November when the *New York Times* published an article headlined *Billions Lost by Olympus May Be Tied to Criminals*. It referred to a memo purportedly *prepared by investigators and circulated at a recent meeting of officials from Japan's Securities and Exchange Surveillance Commission, the Tokyo prosecutor's office and the Tokyo Metropolitan Police Department*. It went on to state: *Officials say they are trying to determine whether Olympus worked with organized crime syndicates to obscure billions of dollars in past investment losses and then paid them exorbitant sums for their services*.

The article was by Hiroko Tabuchi. With her earlier writing on the scandal, she had already established herself as a courageous investigative journalist who wanted to get to the bottom of the story. She wrote that a copy of the memo had been obtained by the

New York Times from a person close to the official investigation. If it was genuine, it appeared for the first time to link the Olympus losses to organized crime groups.

Hiroko's feature went on to explain that *Olympus paid a total of 481 billion yen, or $6.25 billion, through questionable acquisition payments, investments and advisory fees from 2000 to 2009, according to the memo, but only 105 billion yen has been written down or otherwise accounted for in its financial statements. That leaves 376 billion yen, or $4.9 billion, unaccounted for.*

Its revelations grew more dramatic. *The memo says investigators believe that over half of that amount has been channelled to organized crime syndicates, including the country's largest, the Yamaguchi Gumi. The memo does not make clear whether Olympus knew about those links. But if confirmed by investigators, an association with organized crime could prompt a delisting of Olympus shares from the Tokyo Stock Exchange, under the exchange's rules.*

The *New York Times* is one of the world's most respected newspapers. It is not a frivolous publisher, and would have carried out its usual stringent due diligence and legal checks. Hiroko Tabuchi is a journalist of impeccable credentials. But the authenticity of the memo has never been proven.

I didn't know what to believe any more, and reading the constant developments from 6,000 miles away was frustrating. There was a limit to what I could achieve from London. I knew I had to return to Tokyo and, as a director, I was entitled to attend the board meeting, which was scheduled to take place in eight days, on Friday, 25 November. I booked a ticket.

On the morning I was to leave, a colleague in Tokyo emailed to warn me about rumours circulating in the Monolith that I had sold my shares at the time I had appointed PwC, back in September. The purpose of any such smear was clear: I had known the revelations would have a devastating effect on the company's share price, and selling my shares in those circumstances would constitute insider dealing. This was an outrageous allegation but it disturbed me that there were people who wanted to undermine me in such a way. I immediately emailed my colleague back:

> IT'S NOT TRUE!!! If it was they would have already used it. The amount of shares I own is modest and selling them was and remains the very last thing on my mind. I have nothing to hide. I come back to Tokyo tonight and it will be good to come home and be close to my friends and colleagues – I'm even attending the board meeting on Friday.

Could somebody pretending to be me have sold my shares behind my back? My broker was Nomura, who was also the house broker for Olympus. This was worrying and I talked with my lawyer Aki Shiozaki in Tokyo. He agreed that we urgently needed to find out the facts before this story gained traction and damaged my credibility.

My flight was leaving in four hours, so Nuncy had to rush back to Southend to retrieve my Japanese stamp and the paperwork relating to the original share purchase. My stamp was needed to give power of attorney to my lawyers, Nagashima Ohno & Tsunematsu, who could go to Nomura's offices on my behalf. It was essential to establish quickly if my shares had been sold without my knowledge. If they had, we would immediately contact the police. (The day after my arrival my lawyers visited Nomura, who confirmed my shares had not been sold. Nevertheless, it appeared there were some people who clearly didn't want me back in Japan.)

As I headed through the early evening winter darkness towards Heathrow, all manner of thoughts were spinning through my mind, but I had to retain a calm exterior as I had a Bloomberg television crew with me in the car. If my adversaries were willing to play dirty tricks like this, they would do anything to blacken my name and remove me as a threat.

As the car pulled into Terminal Three, I was spotted by a large group of waiting Japanese journalists, who collectively started to run towards me. Suddenly the bright lights of TV cameras came on and dazzled me. If I had any doubts about just how big the story had become back in Japan they were instantly dispelled. I had no idea TV crews were allowed to film in the airport but there they were, tailing me and asking questions. I walked up to the ANA desk with the media posse circling me. I thought the airline's ground staff would ask for the filming to be stopped, perhaps not wanting their brand associated with the 'Southend Samurai'! But not at all. Unfazed, the pretty ANA check-in agent spoke loudly in a voice everyone could hear: 'Good evening, Mr Woodford. How nice to see you again. We are so pleased you are flying ANA.'

It soon became quite a spectacle. As I ascended on the escalator to the fast-track security check, I was hardly able to contain my laughter. Journalists were stumbling off the moving staircase backwards against a firework-like display of camera flashes, while passing members of the public looked puzzled as to who this 'celebrity' was. I made it through security to the Singapore Airlines Lounge, which ANA used in London, for what I assumed would be a little peace and quiet, a moment to collect myself. Disaster. I had agreed to rendezvous with the driver to whom Nuncy had given my name stamp, but in wanting to escape my role as the Pied Piper of journalists, I'd forgotten all about it. I was now airside, meaning there were all sorts of security complications. I had to beg the airline lounge receptionist to go and collect it. A middle-aged woman with kind eyes, she saw my anguish and managed to return with my stamp just three minutes before the gate closed.

In the lounge I met my Japanese lawyer from Simmons & Simmons, Kenichi 'Ken' Kinukawa, a former prosecutor in Tokyo. I would grow close to him in the days ahead. As his surname was very similar to Kikukawa, I started to call him that as a deliberate slip of the tongue. He knew I was teasing and always laughed. Ken had lived in London for some years and had clearly developed an English sense of humour, where sarcasm and irony are at the fore.

Once on the plane, with my slippers on, I discovered I had an inquisitive neighbour. A canny Japanese journalist had somehow managed to book a seat next to mine. I couldn't help respecting his initiative and agreed to give him an interview. We talked for forty-five minutes and it made me happy to think of the praise he would receive from his editor. A short while later, one of the ANA stewardesses came up to me and quietly said, 'Japan needs you.' These spontaneous and unguarded few words touched me with their sincerity.

Eleven and a half hours later, as I walked up the jet bridge into the terminal building, I was met by a wall of journalists: some twenty TV crews and seventy reporters airside. A designated spokesman for the group came up and asked me to speak to this well-ordered 'welcoming committee'. The front rows were even crouching down to allow unobstructed visibility for the TV cameras and photographers. There was no way I could decline the request and anyway I very much wanted to speak from the heart.

'I wanted to come back to Japan, to be close to my colleagues, and talk with you through the camera lens,' I said. 'I have also returned as the truth needs to come out and this week I will be meeting with the Tokyo Prosecutor's Office, the Tokyo Metropolitan Police and the Securities and Exchange Surveillance Commission.' I was asked whether Olympus would survive. Slowly, but with force, I said: 'Olympus can get over this and be a successful global company which Japan can once again be proud of. We have exceptional products and people. The only thing wrong with this company is the sickness in the boardroom.'

I talked for about twenty minutes. As I stood on the moving walkway heading towards immigration and customs, I was followed by the whole media entourage. It was a surreal experience, but one I quickly became accustomed to.

I then noticed a number of men with discreet earpieces. I

remembered that Ken in the preceding days had been liaising with the British embassy and the Tokyo authorities to ensure my safety on returning to Japan. The men with earpieces and dark suits were from the Tokyo Metropolitan Police.

As I came through the arrivals gate Waku was waiting for me. We hugged and he said, 'It's good to have you back home.' I replied with a simple 'thank you' and never have I meant these two words more. Again the media circus continued and we were surrounded by more TV cameras as we walked towards the car. Waku was making me laugh by shouting out in a deliberately loud and high-pitched voice 'Michael, Michael, Michael!' as if I were Michael Jackson. It was wonderful to see him and have a moment of levity in the midst of so much turmoil. From then on, whenever I returned to Japan it was always the next leg of the Moonwalk Tour. All I needed was that single, sequinned glove. And the ability to dance.

We were driven to the Park Hyatt in a limousine organized by Toshihiro 'Toshi' Okuyama, senior staff reporter from the *Asahi Shimbun*, the world's second-largest selling newspaper with a morning circulation of over eight million copies. Toshi is an interesting man. He has investigated a number of financial scandals and written several acclaimed books including (in Japanese) *Power of Whistleblowing: What Would Whistleblower Protection Act Protect?* He takes a more probing approach than is typical in Japan, perhaps influenced from his time at the Investigative Reporting Workshop at Washington's American University.

Toshi had previously come all the way to London to see me on 3 November and, in recognition of his long journey, I had given him a three-hour interview at my apartment. Initially he was a little defensive about my caustic views of the Japanese media, namely being self-censoring and deferential to powerful forces including corporations. In the months which followed, I think it is fair to say that Toshi moved closer to my own position. He went on to write some of the best pieces in Japan on the Olympus scandal, including a feature on the dialogue between us as to how the Japanese media had conducted itself in comparison to their Western counterparts.

When we drew up in front of the Park Hyatt, I felt I was home again. The general manager and the senior management team were there to greet me. Although I had booked a standard room they upgraded me to a large suite. As always, I experienced a level of service which I have not found anywhere else in the world. Late on that first night, I phoned up for some mouthwash: it arrived in less than a minute and the chambermaid apologized profusely for the delay. I love that hotel.

On my arrival in Japan, I released a message to my colleagues in Japanese through the Grassroots site:

> *My dear fellow Olympus employees*
> *This is Michael Woodford. Olympus has been exposed to a crisis that threatens the existence of the company. Due to the acts of a few directors past and present that has gone beyond the bounds of common sense, 92 years of great history, our pride in its name and shareholders value of Olympus, together with the trust and love that our users of our products and services throughout the world have given us, has been critically damaged.*
>
> *I am sure you are aware of the nature and the scope of this unbelievable saga Olympus is facing now, and desperately wanting to know what is required to recover from it. The very first task that we all have to accomplish, is to make sure we fully cooperate with relevant authorities and expose the full details of this unfortunate incident. If we fail in this first task, we have no future. We hide nothing. We will try and make sure that those who are criminally responsible are punished, we as the company pay whatever penalty the rules require, and say to the world that we are clean once again. If the world believes us, then we have a chance.*
>
> *I know that Koji Miyata, the retired former director of Olympus and*

one of my good friends in Japan, has initiated a website 'Olympus grassroots.com' calling for action to reinstate me as the President/CEO of Olympus, and during the first week, more than 300 colleagues registered to express their support. I was genuinely touched to know that some of you have the courage to put your true identity when registering. I am also truly grateful that the site has been overwhelmed by the messages coming from all over the world, including those from Olympus shareholders and users of our products, expressing their support for us.

It is the shareholders of Olympus who can reinstate me as the President/CEO. If the majority of them want me back to where I was as of 13 October 2011, I want to come back and work with you to put the company on the right track for recovery. However, the situation at Olympus could be far worse than you and I comprehend, and our options may be quite limited. My return alone won't suddenly make everything fine. It will be a long, painful and difficult road ahead of us which requires the firm resolution and commitment of every one of us. If the majority of our shareholders support my leadership again, and if you are willing to accept this difficult task of recovery, and if I am convinced there is a practical scenario for the company's survival and recovery, then I will return to the company that I love.

Michael Woodford

I had just enough time to shower, and at 7 p.m. gave an interview in my room to NHK, Japan's government-owned national public broadcasting organization. What was revealing was that, during the interview, I repeatedly named *Facta* magazine as the original source of the information which had allowed me expose the scandal. I subsequently learned that NHK edited out all my mentions of the magazine. It troubled me that the mainline media seemed reluctant to acknowledge the role *Facta* had played.

After reading Hiroko Tabuchi's daring reports in the *New York Times*, I wanted to meet her. Together with Waku, we met for dinner in a private room in Kozue, the Park Hyatt's contemporary

Japanese restaurant, with its clean lines and wood-and-glass interior. Petite and attractive with a formidable intellect, Hiroko was someone I knew I could trust. She and the *NYT* continued to be relentless in their incisive coverage. We discussed every aspect of the story and, most interestingly, her own angles on where it could go. At the end of the night I was happy to pay the bill but Hiroko insisted on paying her third, not wanting to do anything to undermine her impartiality.

I realized how little I knew about American journalism, and from my experience throughout those difficult months, in observing the resources they dedicated to the story, I was left with a profound respect for both the *New York Times* and the *Wall Street Journal*.

That night, I struggled to get to sleep, not just due to the time difference, but because I had been unsettled by a rumour NO&T had heard that Friday's board-meeting venue was to be changed to Hachioji in the suburbs of Tokyo, where Olympus had various facilities. I was only going to be in the country for two days and if the board meeting was not to be held at the Monolith in Shinjuku, it would wreck my plans. In the end there was no change of venue but my lawyers spent wasted hours trying to verify this.

The following morning, 24 November, began a crucially important day. It started with a breakfast meeting in the hotel's forty-first floor Girandole restaurant, where we had reserved a private area by the window, looking out across Tokyo. Waku, Ken, Jason Daniel (a Simmons & Simmons colleague based in Tokyo) and my two Japanese lawyers, Shiozaki-san and Arai-san. Listening to the wise counsel around that table made me feel confident we would be able to take things forward in the right way. I have received many accolades for what I did, but the truth is that it was my good fortune to have had the support of a small number of extraordinary individuals. Without these people at my side, I would have been destroyed.

We left the hotel in good time for our first meeting in Chiyoda-ku with the Special Investigation Department of the Tokyo District

Public Prosecutor's Office (TDPPO). Trying to avoid the waiting press, we asked the taxi driver to drop us in front of the Hibiya Park side of the Japan Bar Association, which was less than a minute's walk away, but a much more discreet means of making our entrance. The TDPPO building had that anonymous Orwellian feeling of government premises everywhere. But the two prosecutors impressed me. They seemed genuine in their assurances that their investigation would be comprehensive. Of course, getting to the whole truth would never be easy, as so much of the money had passed through the Cayman Islands. At the end of the meeting, they kindly agreed to let us stay in the room for lunch and we sent out for sandwiches. During this period, Ken, an ex-prosecutor himself, had a short private meeting with the two investigators. He came back and said they were serious and committed. I left feeling buoyed.

After lunch, the TDPPO provided a car to take us over to the nearby Securities and Exchange Surveillance Commission, and to avoid the press we left by the rear entrance. We accessed the SESC building via an underground car park. My Japanese lawyers had counselled that such discretion would be appreciated by the enforcement and regulatory agencies and I was happy to oblige.

The commission, which is under the authority of the Financial Services Agency (FSA), has a mandate to ensure fair transactions in both the securities and financial futures markets. Unlike the US Securities and Exchange Commission (SEC), the SESC does not have any direct power to punish those who violate the law or regulations. Instead it reports its findings to the cabinet, the TDPPO, and the FSA. It was therefore seen by some to be a toothless body. While it had not been scheduled for them to do so, both the SESC's secretary-general, Mr Mario Takeno, and deputy secretary-general, Kazumi Okamura, joined the meeting. I was impressed with their tone, although whether they could deliver was another matter. I sensed that the SESC knew the eyes of the world were on them.

I was told the meeting could not have gone better and my mood was sunnier still as we left the SESC in a taxi. Conveniently, our third appointment of the day was also in Chiyoda-ku. We drove down the ramp into the basement entrance at the Tokyo Metropolitan Police (TMP) headquarters. As I got out of the car, there was a blitz of camera flashes from photographers who had guessed we would enter that way, and had strategically positioned themselves at the top of the ramp. We were escorted into a lift and then along a short corridor into a large but shabby office where we were warmly greeted by the director and assistant director of Investigation Division 2. With their large silver badges hanging prominently around their necks and listening to Waku's translation of what they were saying, we could easily have been meeting with NYPD officers. I liked them and had confidence they would round up the bad guys . . . or at least some of them.

Just before the meeting ended, Aki called me outside the room for a private word. Jiji Press (a large Japanese wire service, comparable to Associated Press) had run a story, leaked by sources close to Olympus, that I had accepted the CEO title in return for my silence. This is what was published:

EXCLUSIVE: WOODFORD OFFERED TO KEEP QUIET OVER OLYMPUS SCANDAL

Tokyo, Nov. 24 (Jiji Press) – Former Olympus Corp. President Michael Woodford has offered to ignore questionable corporate acquisition deals, including hefty advisory fee payments, by the optical equipment maker, company sources told Jiji Press on Thursday.

Woodford took office as Olympus president in April. Soon after, he grilled then Chairman Tsuyoshi Kikukawa by e-mail and other methods over the questionable acquisitions in response to a media report on suspicious flows of money related to the deals, the sources said.

On Sept. 29, Woodford requested the resignation of six top

Olympus executives, including Kikukawa and then Executive Vice President Hisashi Mori, the sources said.

He is believed to have demanded the post of chief executive officer in return for not seeking the resignation of the six.

The Olympus board decided at a meeting held on Sept. 30 to give Woodford the CEO post.

At the meeting, Woodford said he is convinced that no Olympus executive has profited personally and expressed an intention to stop questioning the acquisition deals, according to the sources.

He also promised not to make inside information public, saying his e-mails that have raised questions about the deals would remain between the parties concerned even if the issue is taken up by major media and shareholders, the sources said.

But he grew dissatisfied after he was unable to take full control of the company as CEO, the sources said, adding that this resulted in a rift opening up between him and the other executives.

Olympus dismissed him as president and CEO on Oct. 14. At the time, the company said he was significantly out of step with other executives and was an obstacle to corporate decision-making.

In early November, Olympus admitted covering up latent securities investment losses by using inflated payments it made in connection with the corporate acquisitions, reversing its repeated defense of the deals.

I was incandescent. Jiji had not even asked me about the allegations before publishing. So that was how it worked in Japan, one-sided stories based on 'sources close to'. I was glad that I had Aki by my side as his diligent monitoring of events had allowed me to prepare myself before we left the building. We said goodbye to the director and his colleagues with smiles, bows and handshakes.

On the pavement outside the TMP building a large group of journalists and camera crews had gathered. As I approached them,

I was greeted by the now familiar sensation of camera flashes creating a strobe-like effect. The reporters wanted to know about my three meetings with the authorities that day and my answers were much more positive than the journalist anticipated, as I expressed confidence that they would investigate and get to the facts. Then a journalist asked: 'Did you agree to accept the CEO role and keep quiet?' Prepared, and with a touch of anger in my voice, I replied: 'You're referring to the Jiji article which is completely untrue – it is disgraceful they would publish something like that.'

I went on to explain:

'There are two simple facts as to why what they have written is utter nonsense and the allegations can be reputed here and now.

'1. I was made CEO on Friday 29th September when the alleged deal was supposedly made yet the very next working day, Monday 3rd October, I commissioned PwC to report.

'2. My fourth letter raising my concerns with the board was dated and sent on 26th September and my fifth letter was dated 27 September. Both these letters had been formally copied, not just to the Ernst & Young senior partner in Japan, but to the partners responsible for Asia, Europe, the Americas and finally the worldwide Chairman and Chief Executive of Ernst & Young.'

The journalists understood that, if I had accepted the CEO position in a deal to keep silent, I would not then have gone back to London and immediately commissioned PricewaterhouseCoopers to report. Even more significantly, before the alleged deal was made, I had written two letters formally copying the worldwide senior management team of Ernst & Young and unless one believed in a global conspiracy, which I didn't, my actions demonstrated that the story could never be put back in the box.

I had originally copied Ernst & Young's senior partners because I had feared for my life and if something had happened to me, then the truth would have still come out. But this action now also protected me against any accusations that I had accepted inducements to keep my mouth shut.

That night I had been asked to speak at the Economist Forum at the Diamond Hall in the Aoyama district of Tokyo. I was on a panel with Shigeo Abe, the proprietor of *Facta*, Ken Cukier of *The Economist* and Jonathan Soble of the *FT*. The large ballroom was completely filled and at the back there was a line of twelve television cameras. I spoke for around forty minutes. A question-and-answer session followed. Several people praised me in the most effusive terms for what I had done. Then a female journalist stood up: 'Mr Woodford, did you really agree to keep quiet about the whole Tobashi if you were made CEO?' The hairs on my neck rose. I asked, 'Is anyone here from Jiji Press?' In the corner of the room, a man meekly put his hand up. I asked him, 'Can you please repeat your paper's accusations? You should be aware that my lawyers are in the room. Because that's lousy journalism, a story you've just been drip-fed and is absolutely not true.' I went on to repeat the points I had made a few hours earlier on the pavement outside the Tokyo Metropolitan Police building.

'Hang on, Michael,' Ken Cukier interrupted. 'Jiji is a large organization, please be fair. This is just one man who may have no knowledge of it. In the spirit of transparency and fairness, would the journalist want to answer Michael's question?' The Jiji journalist quietly uttered, 'No comment.' To which I replied, 'Well you'd better start reading the *Financial Times* then' (the *FT*'s legendary slogan had once been 'No *FT*, no comment'). That provoked much laughter.

That afternoon NO&T had sent a strong letter of complaint to Jiji Press, who responded by expressing their regret and admitting that the article was inappropriate for not having sought my comments before publishing. While I was still talking at the Diamond Hall, Jiji published an update that I had denied the allegation, and subsequently withdrew the original article.

Just as we were leaving the venue, a group of excited journalists came up to me and said, 'Have you heard, Kikukawa, Mori and Yamada have resigned their directorships?' This meant they would not be appearing at the board meeting the following day. While there was a reassuring finality that these three men would no longer be linked to the company, part of me was disappointed. I had been waiting a long time to look them in the eye and let them know that what they had tried to do to me and my family was shameful. But, cowards that they were, they had denied me that opportunity.

Early on the morning of Friday I had an appointment with Chikako Ishiguro from *Nikkei Business*. She is an outstanding journalist and was the first Japanese reporter to visit me in London. I learned quickly she had the courage to pick up the story and really run with it. I had not gone to sleep the night before until after 3 a.m. and now regretted having agreed to a 7 a.m. interview. I had risen at 6.40, showered, and was edging around the hotel room doing my familiar zombie impersonation. The previous night I had reluctantly taken a sleeping pill, as with the adrenaline pumping around my system and the time difference, I just wouldn't have slept. These tablets may force sleep on you, but their after effects the following morning can be grim.

At seven o'clock sharp, while I was still in my bathrobe, there was a knock at the door. I was feeling like death but there was Chikako, and I knew she would not take no for an answer. She reminded me of my commitment to give her a one-hour interview and hurried me to get dressed. One does not argue with Chikako in full flow.

Following the interview I went down to Girandole for a working breakfast. Waku had cycled over to the hotel to join me, Aki and Ken. This was one of the few occasions I could tell Waku was an American: he ordered two portions of hash browns to go alongside his scrambled eggs. I had a café latte and hard-boiled eggs. We talked through how I should conduct myself at the board meeting.

We were transported the half mile in a TV Tokyo van. The channel was filming a documentary about me called *Sayonara Gaijin*. It
was a beautiful sunny morning and I had really wanted to walk and
get some fresh air. That was deemed ill-advised, as with the press
watching our every move, we would have made painfully slow progress along the pavement. In less than five minutes we arrived at
Olympus's headquarters from where I had been so rudely ejected
on 14 October. I stepped out of the van.

The scene outside the Monolith was bedlam. The huge media
presence was encouraging a crowd of onlookers to assemble. I had
to make the thirty yards between the van and the building. The
Monolith's security men were trying to get me through the crowd.
I noticed several representatives of Olympus whose role was to
escort me to the fifteenth floor. Right at the centre of the mêlée I
suddenly felt serene. It was as if I was curiously removed from this
yelling madness of pushing and shoving, and watching from above.
Like being in the still, quiet eye of a hurricane. Maybe this is how
real rock stars feel. Who knows? It was not something I was remotely
accustomed to.

But I was making no forward progress so a security guard decided
to take matters, and me, into his own hands. My instant reaction at
being rudely accosted from behind was, 'Sod that, he's going to tear
my trousers off and show my boxer shorts. What does he think he's
up to?' Like one of those legendary men who used to force passen-
gers in through the doors of the Tokyo metro, with a hoik, a shove
and a shoulder, he got me through.

In the lift, the doors closed, and there I was up on the fifteenth
floor and in the executive suite. I recognized several faces but no one
spoke to me. It was disorientating seeing these people and my old
surrounds for the first time since I had been dismissed because it
seemed very familiar and comfortable. I had been coming here for all
those years, most recently as president. And yet it was so different.
Was I one of them any more? Were they with me or against me?

I was not alone. I had my two lawyers – Ken and Aki – flanking me. My old secretary Michiko came out to take us through to a waiting room. She could not have been more courteous, smiling warmly. I was happy to see her looking at ease. 'Tea?' she asked. 'No,' I replied with a grin. 'I'm not touching the tea. It might be poisoned.' She started laughing, but I was only half joking. When entering the executive floor, I had been given a half-smile by Masanori, the old head of the secretaries' office who had been drafted back to the corporate floor due to the crisis. He was someone I had felt tender towards; he was a gentle and kind man. He had been so supportive in helping me settle into my new role as president, attending to numerous practical issues such as organizing suitably sized furniture for my office and all the arrangements to do with my apartment. After four months, he had explained that he felt inadequate in serving me because of his inability to speak English. If anyone felt inadequate because of the language, it was me. But I respected his decision and reluctantly agreed to his transfer. I really wanted him to stay because I knew he was a decent person. On this morning it was nice to see his face.

We sat patiently for about ten minutes. The door opened and I was politely asked to go through to the boardroom. Ken and Aki couldn't accompany me, for only I as a director had a legal right to attend. There, in the same room where I had been fired the month before, were my fellow board members. What was left of them.

The meeting played out like a black comedy. No one shook my hand, indeed they barely acknowledged me. I greeted them with '*Ohayou gozaimasu*' because I was not going to be discourteous. Takayama replied with a neutral, 'Oh, hello.' We went through the agenda. The first part was routine; the main issue was how to ensure that the company should remain listed. We discussed what had to be done to ensure the 14 December deadline was met for representing the company's restated accounts for the last five years.

As I had said repeatedly in public, I believed strongly that it was important that Olympus remained listed. There were legitimate arguments the company should be delisted on the grounds of fraud on such a scale. It had failed to live up to the standards expected of a publicly listed Japanese corporation, and some said it should be delisted as an example to others. But I never accepted that logic. If individuals had acted wrongly they should be held to account. It would seem counter-productive to damage the corporation itself, because innocent employees and shareholders would suffer. On that issue there was a consensus.

As the meeting drew to a close, two directors spoke to me. First, my 'old friend' from Europe, Suzuki: 'You had the resources to do these things, but I didn't.' I had no idea what he was getting at. As a recipient of the six letters, Suzuki could have supported me at any time. He could have phoned me, asked to meet with me. He seemed to be trying in a tangled fashion to make excuses for his own conduct. I had no interest in listening to him.

Then it was the turn of Yanagisawa, the fancy-shirted Corporate R&D director: 'What you did by speaking critically in public of the Third-Party Committee was despicable.' In the weeks before, I had expressed concern that there would be some obvious questions on the investigation's efficacy, as the committee did not have any judicial authority or the resources of a large number of forensic accountants. Yanagisawa's comment had riled me. 'What has been despicable,' I pointed out through gritted teeth, 'is what's been done to my family and me. That's what's despicable.'

The room was filled with tension but I tried hard to be civilized in my demeanour. It was clear they were afraid of me. They had no idea what my next move might be. What mystified me was how they could just continue with business as usual and live with their shame. Maybe they felt no shame.

Looking at them, I was managing my emotions, but part of me just wanted to blurt out: *You all had six letters and the PwC report. Don't try to rewrite history. Not one of you had the courage to stand up.*

You are weak and do not deserve to be here. Yet you still carry on with your self-serving nonsense. However, I knew this was not the time or the place.

The meeting came to an end with no shaking of hands. I just got up and left. It had not lasted very long.

That evening over in Hong Kong my efforts to publicize what had gone on led to an important breakthrough. KPMG LLP's global chairman Michael Andrew spoke out on the Olympus scandal. He said fraud was evident at Olympus but emphasized that his firm had met all legal obligations to pass on information related to Olympus's 2008 acquisition of Gyrus before it was replaced as the company's auditor. 'We were displaced as a result of doing our job,' Andrew told reporters. 'It's pretty evident to me there was very, very significant fraud and that a number of parties had been complicit.'

To which I had two thoughts. First, having parted company, why did they not shout longer and louder? Second, if KPMG had been so concerned, how could they have signed off Olympus's 2009 accounts without qualification?

On the same day Toshiro Shimoyama, an ex-president of Olympus, gave an interview to the Gendai Business website. 'It was a mistake to bring a foreigner in to be president,' he said. I cannot say this mean-spirited outburst came as much surprise to me. Shimoyama was classic old school in the worst sense.

Despite the fact that he'd agreed to my promotion to head Olympus's UK subsidiary at the age of twenty-nine, I had sensed his barely concealed prejudice towards me. President from 1984 to 1993, he was unable to let go of power and had made himself the company's 'Lifetime Supreme Advisor', which enabled him to come into the office and make a nuisance of himself. The result was a rather sad and tragic figure.

Reading this slight took me back to a Saturday afternoon nine months before, and the 'Annual Olympus Old Boys' Reunion'. It was held in the ballroom of the Keio Plaza Hotel where I gave my first speech as president elect. The sky had been a perfect blue with clear visibility across the city and I had been struck by the inspiring sight of Mount Fuji. I spoke without notes to the assembled audience of retired Olympus employees. I described how looking at this magnificent mountain had reminded me of the history and heritage of Japan. I talked about how when I had jogged around Shinjuku Park that morning, I had seen young couples in love, old people doing morning exercises, children playing. I said Tokyo didn't feel alien, that this was my second home. I was proud to be there and proud to be running a Japanese company. I was really reaching out. I was told my speech moved a lot of people, and I meant the words. At the reception, it was uplifting to see the kind smiling faces of old engineers, many of whom came up to introduce themselves.

On the way out, Kikukawa had turned to me and said: 'So many have praised me for making the right choice in choosing you.' Then he added, 'Except for one.' 'Who would that have been?' I asked. 'Shimoyama,' he said. 'But pay no attention. His vanity blinds him.'

That was not the only thing to which Shimoyama had been blind. When quizzed by the *Nikkei Business Daily* about whether he had been able to recall any attempt to conceal losses during his leadership of the company, he replied, 'As president it wasn't the case where all financial reports would come to me, so I have no memory. During that time Masatoshi Kishimoto [Olympus's president from 1993 to 2001] was the treasurer . . . I wouldn't have heard financial details.'

My two days in Tokyo seemed like two months but everything was moving in my favour. On Friday lunchtime I was due to give an address to the Foreign Correspondents Club of Japan. I was subsequently told I had captivated the filled room of normally jaundiced and cynical hacks. My words were reported around the world, including a feature in *The Economist* titled *Banyan – Tribal Japan*. This picked up on my theme that Japan's cherished loyalty system was part of the problem.

The unnamed author captured the mood: *The venerable Foreign Correspondents' Club of Japan experienced a volley of camera flashes, jostling television crews and shouts of 'heads down at the front!' – the sort of attention it has rarely enjoyed since the country began its gentle slide down the world's news agenda. The occasion was the return to Japan of Michael Woodford.* I smiled when I read: *His subject, in a nutshell, was corporate governance – not something that, in the abstract, usually sets reporters' hearts aflutter. But as the club pointed out, not even the Dalai Lama had drawn such a crowd.* The rest of the afternoon I gave interview after interview, including one with Lucy Craft of CBS and a set-piece televised interview with the main anchor of TBS (Tokyo Broadcast System).

The whirlwind two days finished with dinner with Waku, Koji and friends at Robata Honten. Owned by a wise old sage called Inoue-san, the restaurant is an old wooden building laid out on three floors. It nestles among a line of modern buildings in a frenetic part of Tokyo. It is an oasis of civilization and good food and despite being frequented by literary types and filmmakers, it somehow remains unpretentious.

The following morning I was invited for a traditional English breakfast at the embassy with David Warren, the British ambassador. I must have caused him no end of diplomatic difficulty but he was never less than charming. He shook my hand and wished me well. I was on my way to Narita, this time heading for America for further meetings with the FBI and Federal Prosecutors.

As I walked through the airport concourse, several people approached me to let me know of their appreciation for what I was doing to help change Japan. It was becoming normal for me to be stopped in the street or in restaurants, with unknown strangers expressing solidarity. I left Japan feeling more enthralled by the country than ever.

10

Rotten to the Core

The long flight from Narita to JFK gave me space for reflection. It was growing clear that there was no point in continuing the charade of being an Olympus board member while being unable to influence its actions. If I was going to change the future of Olympus, I needed to be free of the legal constraints imposed upon me by remaining a director. I needed to talk to large shareholders and other potential investors about an alternative way of moving ahead. I needed to orchestrate a new slate of directors who would have the confidence of investors and employees.

The only way Olympus could start to rebuild itself was with an entirely new board, uncontaminated by the past. The remaining directors, all of whom had done nothing despite overwhelming evidence of wrongdoing, had to leave. I started to think through the practicalities and implications of resigning.

As I walked towards immigration, I checked my emails on my iPhone. In my inbox was a message from Kenzie Delaine, a shooting producer with Bloomberg Television in the United States. He said he'd be waiting at the arrivals gate at JFK and would escort me to the hotel so he could film me while I was in the city.

I walked out of the terminal building at Kennedy into a clear autumnal morning. Among the waiting journalists and camera crews from the Japanese networks I spotted Kenzie, who had described himself to me in his email. We drove into Manhattan in a large black MPV, and en route I learned about his unusual way of garnering information – by hanging around outside high-end nightclubs at two in the morning to catch those who could fill in the blanks in his stories. It was enlightening to learn what people were prepared to say after drinking the night away.

Kenzie passed me a copy of that morning's *New York Times*. My face stared out of the front page of the business section, above an article co-authored by Hiroko Tabuchi and Ben Protess. The scope of the Olympus story was broadening: a number of European banks were now under investigation by Japanese authorities to determine whether they had helped the management of Olympus hide irregular payments. Ripples in a pond.

Kenzie suggested an alfresco breakfast at a trendy spot downtown. Watching the Manhattan elite at play on a Saturday morning made my showdown in Tokyo with the Olympus board only the day before seem a world away. After eating, Kenzie wanted an interview and so as not to draw attention to ourselves, he filmed at the table, using the movie function on an SLR camera, propped up by the sugar bowl. As we talked, a well-groomed man at the next table leaned over: 'I apologize for interrupting but I work in the finance industry and have followed your story. I believe what you have done is awesome.' To be recognized everywhere as a sort of hero was strange. I felt somewhat uncomfortable with how the world saw me.

Nuncy flew in that afternoon from London and we spent the weekend in Long Island with friends. After resting for a few hours, we walked to the nearby Oceana fish restaurant on 49th Street and on the way we went past the Rockefeller Center, where the Christmas tree (without its lights) was already in place. We asked a tourist to take our picture and that image with both of us smiling in front of the Christmas tree is still the screensaver on my iPhone. Over dinner I told Nuncy about my adventures in Tokyo. We were picked up the following morning by Jeff Cronen, a wonderful American friend who with his wife Ann had invited us to spend the weekend with them at their home in Long Island. We were spoiled and made to feel right at home. American hospitality at its best. On the Monday evening, Jeff drove the four of us back into Manhattan. It had been a blissful slice of normality.

On the Tuesday morning my American attorney, Homer Moyer of Miller & Chevalier in Washington, had breakfast in my hotel suite before my second encounter with the FBI, the Federal Prosecutors from the Department of Justice and representatives from the SEC. Lots more questions from Eliot Ness and his colleagues.

I spent the rest of Tuesday giving interviews. The reporters were speculating on what the Japanese authorities would do following my meetings with them the week before. Everyone wanted to know if and when they would act. The resignations of Messrs Kikukawa, Mori and Yamada had created an almost unstoppable momentum for accountability.

On the Wednesday morning I woke up early but alert and thinking clearly. I was now certain that I should resign my directorship of Olympus. I would then seek the support of shareholders for my return to the company at the head of an entirely new board. I talked at length to my lawyers in London and Tokyo. And of course my two fellow Musketeers, Waku and Koji. It was important that things were done right. As my resignation would be considered market sensitive, I needed to make it public before the Tokyo market opened on the Thursday morning and also when the New York market was closed, since Olympus trades in the US as an ADR (an American depositary receipt).

NO&T agreed with me the following precise schedule:

Time Japan/NY	Events
6.50 a.m. / 4.50 p.m.	NO&T sends Resignation Letter (English) to Olympus's lawyers
7.00 a.m. / 5.00 p.m.	NHK 7 a.m. news to break story 'Mr. Woodford has announced his resignation this morning in protest to Olympus's management'

7.30 a.m./5.30 p.m.	Michael sends out invitation to press conference to be held at 7 p.m.
	All media inquiries to be pointed to Michael's press conference
9.00 a.m./7.00 p.m.	Michael holds press conference in NY (Japanese and English press release to be issued at time of press conference)
?	Olympus will likely issue some statement or comment on Michael's resignation

With these timings, we would make the breakfast news programmes in Japan and the announcement would be flashed across the world by the likes of Bloomberg and Reuters. To achieve this timetable required Aki Shiozaki to work throughout the Wednesday night in Japan without sleep. As always, he delivered.

Within seconds of the story breaking I started receiving messages from seemingly every financial journalist in town. I held the press conference in my hotel suite; luckily I had received an upgrade so it was just about large enough to accommodate the journalists and numerous television crews. To ensure clarity of communication, I handed out a press release explaining my reasons:

OLYMPUS: THE WAY FORWARD

I am announcing my decision to resign from my position as a director of Olympus Corporation. I was, of course, only a director without executive authority following my removal from office on 14th October 2011.

It has been a difficult decision for me to resign from a Company that I have devoted my entire working life to, and I can assure you that it is one which has been reached by me as a last resort after reading the President of Olympus Corporation's Message dated 28 November 2011.

Following the Board Meeting that I attended last Friday in Tokyo, I was extremely concerned about the way in which the Olympus management team would be reformed in order to best position the Company to move forward. Whilst I remained hopeful that a credible solution would be formulated, it would appear from the President's Message dated 28th November that Mr Takayama and the existing board plan to preside over reform of the Company's management team with the likely outcome being that these same people will either appoint or at the very least influence the appointment of the Company's new board members.

I believe that the promise for reform or reconstruction by Mr Takayama and the current board carries little or no credibility and is continuing to harm Olympus and its long term future. I am strongly of the view that it's completely inappropriate for the current management team who are tainted by its past mistakes to make choices about the identity of new board members. Key decisions such as this should be made by the Company's shareholders, and a new management team which is entirely independent from the current management should be appointed as soon as possible.

Following my resignation, I intend to liaise with all interested stakeholders with a view to formulating a proposal for the constitution of a new board. This proposal should be considered by the Company's shareholders and, with this in mind, I formally request the current management to convene an extraordinary shareholders' meeting as soon as possible to allow the shareholders to decide who should lead the Company through these challenging times.

Let me make it explicitly clear: I am not walking away from Olympus. I believe passionately in the Company, its employees, its products and its future. It is a wonderful and successful company which has been led down the wrong path by the actions of some of its board members. Olympus has the potential to once again become a world class organization which is the envy of its competitors demonstrating the highest standards of corporate governance. I would like nothing more than to return to Olympus and lead it towards achieving this status. However, in the absence of a shareholder vote enabling me to do this, I am committed to ensuring that Olympus has the best possible opportunity to succeed going forward, starting with a new and untainted board of directors, and I believe my resignation is necessary in this context.

Finally, I hope my action will provide an opportunity for the current management team to reflect on their past mistakes and that it will encourage each of them to accept their responsibility for the Company's existing difficulties and to do what is in the Company's best interests by standing aside after an extraordinary general meeting.

I believe that this course of action is the best way possible to ensure the successful future of Olympus, a company I care so deeply about and for which I will give everything of myself to achieve the right outcome.

Michael Woodford

So here we had it. The president and CEO of an iconic Nikkei-listed company had been dismissed for exposing massive fraud, and was now challenging those who had fired him. Nothing quite like this had ever happened before.

It was 9 p.m., and at the end of a long and memorable day Lisa Murphy came over to the hotel for a one-to-one exclusive interview. While the camera crew were setting up she talked about her own life and of her family in Korea. She was prepared to show vulnerability and openness, which was endearing. Lisa was another journalist who had made an impression upon me in the most positive sense. (I was sad to learn in April 2012 that she had left the network.)

The next morning was 1 December. I now had no formal links with Olympus's board and felt a great sense of freedom and liberation. I had only contempt and antipathy towards those men. I could fight back without constraint. With my mind focused on that objective, I met with some of Olympus's American shareholders. They agreed that the position of the current directors was untenable.

That afternoon for the first time I declined requests for interviews, and went with Nuncy on a long and reflective walk in Central Park. There was a spring in her step and her sense of relief that I was no longer connected to a boardroom filled by men without principle was palpable.

That night Joel Young drove down from Connecticut to see how we were. We had a wonderful Veronese dinner at Antica Bottega del Vino on East 59th Street. Joel bought a bottle of Bollinger to celebrate what had been achieved since our last dinner together, just eleven weeks before. He presented me with a baseball cap on which was printed the word 'Victory' in Japanese characters. He tried to insist I wear it, but it seemed premature and I politely refused. Back at the hotel, as we were talking in bed about Joel, Nuncy remarked, 'I know you've always worked hard at friendships but do you know just how lucky you are with the people you have around you?' 'I am lucky,' I replied. And with that thought, I fell asleep.

We left the next day for London on a daytime British Airways flight. When we arrived at Heathrow it was nearly 10 p.m. local time and we were met by Stuart Greengrass, another person I was lucky to have around me. Stuart was one of the most able managers I have worked with and shortly after I became managing director of KeyMed, I promoted him to the board. Many people work hard to push work away but Stuart was the opposite and his support in taking the company forward was invaluable. He had joined KeyMed in 1972 and after thirty-two years' service retired in 2004. But the friendship had gone far beyond work and our two families were always in each other's houses, eating, drinking and being merry. Stuart had written to me explaining his frustration at not being able to support me at such a difficult time, but didn't know what else he could do.

Although his friendship and that of his wife Sue was more than enough, knowing I was worried about running out of money due to the ever-mounting legal costs, Stuart came up with the idea of driving me to and from the airport. He did this on numerous occasions and it was such a thoughtful and practical gesture. I still tease him about 'Stuart's Taxis'.

Tuesday, 6 December 2011 is a date that I will always remember. I was back in London at our Tower Bridge apartment and was awoken by my mobile phone. A Japanese journalist in Tokyo had conveniently forgotten the time difference and rang me just after four in the morning. I was still having trouble sleeping and had taken a sleeping tablet a few hours before, so was somewhat comatose. With an excited voice, he was asking me in broken English about my reaction to the *Nikkei* story about Kikukawa and something about where the money had gone. It was the best I could do to mumble, 'It's four o'clock in the morning here. Please phone me back later.'

With a few seconds' more thinking time I realized something big was up and almost instantly the adrenaline kicked in. I got out of bed, and before making a coffee fired up the laptop to run a Google search for the *Nikkei* article – but couldn't find it. At 4.23 a.m. an email pinged. It was from Chris Cooper, the debonair Bloomberg correspondent in Tokyo.

Michael,

Olympus's independent panel is set to release its report in a couple of hours, followed by a press conference.

So far the Nikkei has reported that losses peaked at 130 billion yen ($1.7 billion), the cover up started in fiscal 1998 and Tsuyoshi Kikukawa and his predecessor Masatoshi Kishimoto approved the cover up.

Are you free to talk after we've gone through the report? I'll send you our story on the report and give you a call around 7 am your time.

Regards,

Chris

Chris and I spoke several times that morning and as soon as the report was officially released, the media madness started again. Everyone wanted to talk to me.

I had had my doubts about the Third-Party Committee investigation. It could have been a classic Japanese whitewash that advanced the cause of the truth not one iota. But when I read the summary of the committee's 185-page report it was clear it had not pulled its punches. The work of five senior judges and lawyers, with forty-nine legal support staff, it was written in a considered forensic style, unmasking the story right back to the beginning.

The retired supreme court justice Tatsuo Kainaka, who chaired the committee, did not mince his words. Olympus's senior management was *rotten to the core . . . Olympus should remove its malignant tumour and literally renew itself.* That was promising.

The cell from which the Olympus malignancy had spread was traced back to 22 September 1985 in a hotel in New York. The finance ministers of the United States, Japan, the United Kingdom, West Germany and France agreed, under the 'Plaza Accord', to bring about a devaluation of the strong dollar, which had appreciated by 50 per cent in value against the Japanese yen between 1980 and 1985.

The knock-on effect was an immediate handicap to the export-led Japanese economy. Goods such as Olympus's cameras and endoscopes, when sold in the local currencies of the United States and Europe, were exchanged for far fewer yen, which led to a rapid slump in profitability. Olympus's profits in 1985 were ¥6.8 billion and the following year (as I was climbing the corporate ladder at KeyMed) had fallen to ¥3.1 billion.

If the Japanese government did nothing, a deep recession would inevitably result. It was then that the fatal expansionary monetary policies, mainly exceptionally low interest rates, were put into place, leading in turn to the notorious Japanese asset price bubble of the late 1980s. When this bubble burst, as all bubbles eventually do, the period thereafter became known as the 'The Lost Decade' (失われた10年・Ushinawareta Jūnen). But it wasn't like the global banking crisis of 2008, when Lehman Brothers filed for Chapter 11 bankruptcy and events moved rapidly. In contrast, the asset price bubble's collapse within the Japanese economy occurred gradually rather than with a 'big bang'. Often the whole period of the 1990s and 2000s is referred to as the 'Lost Two Decades' or the 'Lost Twenty Years' (失われた20年・Ushinawareta Nijūnen).

But this is to leap ahead. With the company unable to deliver the financial returns expected from its core medical, life science and consumer electronics businesses, the decision was made by the then Olympus president, Shimoyama, to begin relying on earnings from highly speculative investments in financial products. He effectively bet the farm to go gambling at the races. Shimoyama was not alone in taking Olympus down this perilous road – many Japanese manufacturers poured billions of yen into speculative trades that turned sour when the bubble burst.

Hideaki Kubori, a leading Tokyo lawyer specializing in corporate governance and compliance, whom I know and respect, put it well: 'This has been two lost decades for corporate accounting. It's easy to imagine companies hiding losses for years, waiting for financial markets to recover . . . But the recovery never came.'

With the continued and relentless decline in the value of Japanese assets, Shimoyama's high-risk strategy backfired spectacularly. Rather than facing up to the losses by liquidating the positions and openly recognizing them in the accounts, Shimoyama elected, in collusion with external investment advisors, to embark on a path which attempted to win them back. The gambler in him decided he had to chase and retrieve his loss. So he commenced the process of digging Olympus into an even deeper hole with even riskier potentially high-return financial products. Shimoyama entered the murky world of derivatives: interest rate swaps, currency swaps and structured investments – devices about which we were all to hear much more nearly two decades later in the great crash of 2007–8. The financial products he backed flopped, with the result that by the end of 1990 the company was looking at a loss from the speculative investments of ¥100 billion.

Shimoyama's successor in 1993, Masatoshi Kishimoto, appears to have been far less comfortable with complex financial instruments, and rightly wanted to focus attention on the company's core business as a source of increased profitability. But he didn't face up to the losses, preferring that his Portfolio Management Department dealt with the mess. Finance group leader Hideo Yamada was given the role of sitting on the time bomb hidden below Olympus's books. Yamada was so concerned he repeatedly suggested that the losses should be admitted. Kishimoto thought otherwise, noting hopefully, 'We will wait because the losses will decrease when the market recovers and then we can turn things around.'

This deception continued through the decade of the 1990s. And who became managing director in charge of finance in 1999? None other than Kikukawa. Despite his repeated denials when I was trying to bring the world's attention to the mysterious payments, the Third-Party Committee report explicitly confirmed that Kishimoto and Kikukawa were both informed by Yamada about the loss-concealment fraud scheme – and approved it. Watching Kikukawa lie so easily in those press conferences, without regard to its effect on me and my family, made me realize how utterly ruthless and selfish a man he is.

The end of the 1990s brought a tricky problem for Olympus. The decade had been one of embarrassment for Japan as these off-balance-sheet losses ballooned, and the accounting community had started to accept that the nation could no longer continue valuing assets according to what had been paid for them originally. The new accounting standard would be on a 'mark-to-market' method. This would mean the financial assets on a company's balance sheets would be based on what they were really worth, as if they had to be sold on the open market.

If such a new standard was introduced, Olympus's hidden losses would become immediately and painfully apparent in the accounts. Akio Nakagawa, president of Axes Japan Securities, and Hajime Sagawa, president of Axes America, were brought in by Yamada and Hisashi Mori to assist. Both were ex-Nomura Securities executives. They were asked to devise a scheme to 'blow off the loss' from the balance sheet. Olympus was to enter the world of 'Tobashi'. This practice was rife among struggling Japanese conglomerates, but Olympus got to it later and continued it for longer than most similar organizations. Tobashi was made infamous by Yamaichi Securities, which hid over ¥200 billion in losses. Yamaichi collapsed in 1997 and it somehow seemed appropriate that it had been Olympus's preferred broker.

In simple terms, Olympus's Tobashi was created to sell the financial instruments, all of which were carrying huge unrealized losses, to outside funds at their book value so that the unrealized losses did not appear on the company's consolidated financials. The acquiring funds of course required the cash equivalent to the book value of the financial instruments involved. So secret routes to funnel cash to these outside funds had to be established. There were three: a European route, a Singapore route and a domestic route.

THE EUROPEAN ROUTE

Olympus established two funds: Central Forest Corp. and Quick Progress Co. (How on earth did they decide on these names?) In 1998 Yamada and Mori persuaded a private banking outfit, Liechtenstein

Global Trust (LGT Bank) to loan the funds ¥30 billion, which was secured against Olympus bank deposits of Japanese government bonds.

THE SINGAPORE ROUTE

In 1999 Commerzbank provided a ¥45 billion loan, again under the pledge of bond deposits. By a variety of means, a total of ¥60 billion flowed into the Tobashi via the Singapore route between 2000 and 2005.

THE DOMESTIC ROUTE

A business capital fund called GC New Vision Ventures (GCNVV) was set up in 2000. Olympus used it to transfer around ¥30 billion to Quick Progress.

The web had been spun. Olympus had been successful in 'blowing off' a total of ¥94 billion to Central Forest Corp. and Quick Progress Co.

However, simply moving bad assets from the balance sheet was only one half of the Tobashi. Olympus had received loans that needed to be repaid. Again Yamada and Mori went to work, and this time came up with a scheme to bring the Tobashi to a conclusion. The fraud here was to buy the 'Mickey Mouse' companies from off-balance-sheet funds at inflated prices, and secondly to pay grossly inflated M&A transaction fees to these funds. The excess payments that Olympus would make would then be booked as 'goodwill', which could be amortized (written off) over a number of years.

It took two years of hunting to come up with Altis, Humalabo and News Chef as suitable targets. Incidentally, the face-cream maker Humalabo specialized in shiitake mushroom mycelium culture extract, which it claimed could activate the immune system to fight tumours. The 'Mickey Mouse' companies made some truly hocus pocus promises.

But as the Third-Party Committee discovered, two funds run by Olympus – Neo and Class Funds IT Ventures (ITV) – purchased shares in the loss-making companies of Altis, News Chef and Humalabo. Amazingly, then in turn GCNVV bought from Neo and ITV, Altis shares at ¥5.79 million per share – a cool 115.8 times the original purchase price; Humalabo shares came in at ¥14.4 million per share, 288 times; and News Chef at ¥4.45 million, a mere 22.3 times. It was all enough to make the head of the most determined forensic accountant spin.

Meanwhile other investment funds run by Olympus, with the bizarre names Dynamic Dragons II SPC and Global Targets, also bought shares in the three companies from Neo, at similarly inflated prices. In 2007 a slight hiccup occurred. A change was implemented in the accounting rules which would have forced GCNVV's and other dodgy investments to be disclosed in the financial results. This would have exposed the Tobashi in all its glory and would have been catastrophic for Kikukawa. The solution: all GCNVV's investments were transferred at book value to Olympus and GCI Cayman (a general partner of GCNVV), which kept the whole thing hidden. The termination of GCNVV thus closed and settled the domestic route.

Neo and ITV then sold its shares in the three 'Mickey Mouse' companies at grossly inflated prices to Olympus. Yamada told Kikukawa what was being done behind the scenes. 'Let's move • ahead based on this,' said Kikukawa. 'We absolutely must do something about the three domestic companies. If things go well, the losses will decrease by a large amount, won't they?'

Eventually, Olympus bought all three firms via Olympus Finance Hong Kong Ltd for ¥9.6 billion from Dynamic Dragons II and ¥4.1 billion from Global Targets. (Altis had risen in price to ¥10.5 million per share, Humalabo to ¥19.5 million and News Chef to ¥9 million.) In reality the whole lot – which had cost ¥73.4 billion – were worse than worthless. They generated no profit and had zero prospects. Their only function was to conceal the casino-type losses.

However, they were real companies, and would continue to deplete the corporation's resources in the years ahead.

The bank loans were repaid to the LGT bank and the European route was also tied up and settled. One left. The Singapore route also required settlement, but here a different approach was chosen. This time Yamada and Mori decided on large-scale acquisitions as a way to generate more cash and hide the losses. They drew up an agreement with Axes America in which share options for a stake in a big acquisition were granted to Axes. These options were a front and only created to enable Olympus to buy them back at a vastly higher price, so that the excess money made by the repurchase could be used to offset the undisclosed losses.

They identified the British firm Gyrus as a target. But this is where they bungled. Although the $2.2 billion price Olympus paid was at a considerable premium to the pre-acquisition price (and the owners of Gyrus must have thought Christmas had arrived early!), it was still materially lower than originally anticipated. Under the financial advisory agreement with Axes America it would therefore not generate the anticipated funds for the concealment project. This is why they were forced to inflate the advisory fee to Axes to such unheard-of levels. In June 2008 Axes America sold the share options and warrants to its affiliate, the shadowy Cayman vehicle Axam Investments, for $24 million.

Olympus's accounts department valued the Gyrus share options at $177 million, but Yamada and Mori needed to make more funds for the concealment. They then concocted a scheme to buy the share options in exchange for preferred shares in Gyrus rather than cash, with the plan to repurchase the preferred shares when Gyrus was bedded into Olympus and showed signs of synergy. Kikukawa asked Yamada and Mori: 'What do you think? Can it all be eliminated?' Once this clandestine discussion was over Kikukawa remarked: 'It will be nice if this were the end.' Indeed it would have been.

By November, Axam had arbitrarily decided that the value of the preferred shares was between $530 and $590 million. The Olympus board thought it would, indeed, buy them all back but ran into trouble with the company's external auditors, KPMG AZSA LLC, who pointed out that the advisory fee was far too high. This in effect led to the termination of that relationship. The new external auditors, Ernst & Young ShinNihon LLC, who were appointed in 2009, agreed that the difference between the book value of the preferred shares of $177 million and the purchase price could be put down as goodwill. (Both sets of accountants attracted criticism from the Third-Party Committee and it felt unable to deem the behaviour of either 'appropriate', which seemed to me somewhat an understatement.)

Eventually, the preferred shares were bought back from Axam for a staggering $620 million in March 2010. Using these funds, the Singapore route was also settled and the original losses from decades before disappeared into thin air. And that is how things would have remained if *Facta* and I had not come along.

When the Third-Party Committee added everything up it found that ¥96 billion in losses had been moved from the balance sheet between 1999 and 2000. But these losses inflated to ¥117.7 billion by 2003, as the figures ran away with the conspirators. This was due to the failure of new investments in funds to which the losses were transferred, losses resulting from the disposal of ITX shares, payments to Tobashi collaborators and the rising operational costs of the overall scheme. As a result, a final total of ¥134.8 billion had been used to make the 'problem' of the undisclosed losses disappear. That was a tidy $1.7 billion.

Retired supreme court judge Kainaka and his committee made five recommendations: management replacement was necessary; those responsible should be pursued by the law; specialized committees in governance and management supervision needed to be established within Olympus to prevent a recurrence; independent directors and statutory auditors must in future be elected; a change in mind-set in the new management team and the auditors was required in order to restore shareholder trust and restore transparency. I concurred with all these points. I wished that never again should such blind and unquestioning deference be shown to the company's CEO by an Olympus board.

That December day in London I gave more television interviews than ever before. At each I made a great effort to explain that it was the company's senior management who were at fault, rather than the overwhelming majority of employees. As I could give interviews to only a small number of those who approached me, I issued a statement.

December 6, 2011
Statement in Regard to the Report by the Third-Party Committee

Let us hope that the findings announced today by the Third-Party Committee will help catalyse positive change at Olympus. My overriding concern is the welfare of Olympus employees and their family members, of Olympus's long-term shareholders, and of Olympus's customers. That concern will be first in mind as I carefully evaluate the content of the report that was issued today.

The committee's report has made one thing painfully clear: the massive scale of the malfeasance from which the present directors and statutory auditors persistently averted their gaze. I sought to call attention to the wrongdoing through a series of six letters in English and Japanese, copied to all the members of the board, and through the submission of a damning report by Pricewaterhouse-Coopers. Yet not a single director stood up in support of my efforts to expose what had taken place.

Olympus and its shareholders would have incurred far less damage if the current directors had acted appropriately on the clear signs of misconduct that I had explicitly brought to their attention. Now, the work of revitalizing Olympus can proceed only under the leadership of untainted executives.

The report released today by the Third-Party Committee pro-
poses measures for preventing the recurrence of the wrongdoing
that has occurred at Olympus. Among those measures, the committee calls for a sweeping 'renewal' of the board of directors. I
interpret that call as coinciding with the kind of change that I
regard as indispensable at Olympus.

The report makes several observations with which I concur
fully. For example:

> 'The directors and statutory auditors should be keenly aware
>   of their responsibility to the company and to society and
>   should not be unduly deferential to the CEO in raising
>   issues of concern at meetings of the board of directors
>   and at other executive gatherings.'
> 'The directors and statutory auditors should possess strong
>   convictions and be prepared to place their jobs on the line
>   in examining and debating important issues. They should
>   be uncompromising in regard to proposals that they find
>   less than fully acceptable.'
> 'A candidate for CEO should be an individual who has a
>   strong sense of right and wrong and a vigorous commit-
>   ment to enforcing compliance with high standards of
>   corporate ethics.'

Today's report must be the beginning, and not the end, of our
efforts to discover what has happened at Olympus. Elucidating the
full extent of the wrongdoing cited in the committee's report will
require a wide-ranging investigation by agencies armed with
investigative authority and advanced forensic resources. I met on
November 24 with representatives of the Tokyo District Public
Prosecutor's Office, the Tokyo Metropolitan Police, and the Securities and Exchange Surveillance Commission. The authorities
impressed me with their commitment to undertaking a thorough

investigation. I am confident that they will fulfil that commitment, and I will closely follow their progress.

Olympus remains a great company that boasts a proud history, superior human resources, distinctive products, and unparalleled technology. I look forward to working with shareholders and employees to revitalize Olympus and steer the company towards realizing its tremendous potential.

Michael Woodford

The next day I was given a small measure of credit by Takayama, when he told reporters, 'Woodford did have a dogmatic style but he also shed light on the issue, and that is something not one of us could do', and went on to say, 'He deserves recognition for doing that.'

I am filled with respect for Tatsuo Kainaka and his committee's report. Yet still many questions remained unanswered. How much, for example, did the fraud-enablers outside Olympus actually make? It should be remembered that independent forensic accountants were never called into Olympus and the judge's investigation didn't have any judicial rights to access bank accounts and to 'follow the money' in the true sense of the word. I therefore feel uneasy that we may never know the full extent of the involvement of the counterparties, but compared to other scandals in Japan, at least some of the truth has come out.

Winning the Argument,
Losing the War

Now the Third-Party Committee's report was out and the fraud admitted, the question was what would happen to the stricken Olympus. It was a rudderless ship. Its reputation was in tatters. Its current captain, Takayama, was in denial. It desperately needed a new start with a new board.

After a series of private meetings, I now knew I could bring together a slate of eminent new directors – men and women – from outside and inside Olympus. They would all be Japanese.

On 11 December I flew back to Tokyo again, this time via Hong Kong. There was a need to strengthen the company's balance sheet and I had entered into exploratory discussions with a private equity firm in one of the world's financial hubs. The stopover followed up a meeting the previous week in London where we had reviewed alternative means of raising finance. With the company's deteriorating financial position there had been considerable speculation, encouraged by Takayama's statements that Olympus was endeavouring to find a preferred friendly partner. Olympus had the option to issue a third-party allocation of stock, up to an amount equating to 25 per cent of existing equity. I was firmly opposed to this approach as it would dilute existing shareholders' stakes at the worst possible time, and more significantly bring about the likely end of the company's independence.

In Hong Kong the private equity firm took a highly ethical stance. I'm not naïve but in this case it wasn't all about the money – the firm's partners wanted to help bring about change to corporate Japan. They came up with a clever alternative: a rights issue which they would underwrite at no charge. This would mean existing shareholders would have the option of maintaining their holdings at current levels, and the company wasn't selling its soul, history and heritage to an outside party. Since my resignation as a director on 1 December, I had had a series of meetings with some of the world's leading investment banks. All of these financing options would have to be considered by the Olympus board – but clearly not by the board in control at the moment.

I landed at Tokyo's Haneda Airport late on Tuesday, 13 December. As at Narita the month before, I was greeted by a reception committee of enthusiastic reporters. Once more I gave an impromptu press conference, just a hundred yards from the arrivals gate.

'I have returned to Japan because I want to help find a new way forward for Olympus and have a completely open mind,' I said. When asked by a journalist whether I would be meeting with Mr Takayama, I responded: 'I am prepared to meet with Mr Takayama any time of the day or night. If he has the company's best interests at heart, we could sit down together and discuss how we can move ahead in forming a new slate of directors, as the company desperately needs new leadership untainted by the past.' I adopted a conciliatory tone but stressed that after a transitional period, all the existing directors would have to resign.

Waku welcomed me back in his usual style. No one has a cheekier smile. Again he screamed 'Michael, Michael, Michael' and gave me my updated itinerary for 'Moonwalk 2'. We drove through the dark streets in a TV Tokyo minivan, as the channel was continuing to film material for its planned documentary. Arriving back 'home' at the Park Hyatt, I was given an even larger suite than on my previous visit. It was late, but Koji joined Waku and me for a nightcap and to go through the next day's programme, which was filled with meetings with the media, bankers and candidates for the new board.

I was genuine in my willingness to meet Takayama, but he didn't seem to want to meet me. The Third-Party Committee's damning report had presented a short window of opportunity for me and the existing board to meet and agree on an orderly transition to a new board. It would mean holding an extraordinary general meeting, but if there was a consensus about the new directors, it would avoid the uncertainties of a proxy fight – where shareholders attempted to force change.

If Takayama and I could reach an understanding, the company would start the healing process. But of course Takayama himself and his diminishing band of yes-men – on 7 December, another director, Makoto Nakatsuka, had resigned following accusations of his involvement in the fraudulent accounting practices – knew that it was a prerequisite for me that they couldn't be part of the 'New Olympus'.

This was what the overseas shareholders wanted. David Herro of Harris Investments was also in Tokyo that week, and Takayama had agreed to meet him, as well as to a conference call with Josh Shores of Southeastern in London. These were the two largest overseas investors of Olympus – both urged Takayama to bring me back.

Before flying out of the country, David sent an email telling us the meeting had gone okay: *I said my piece. He balked and then said he would consider.* David suggested to Koji I arrange to meet Takayama as soon as possible.

In response to David's request to set up a meeting between myself and Takayama, that afternoon Waku phoned the president's office to persuade him to meet me. Waku updated everyone by email:

Dear all,

We are working on a meeting. I placed a call this morning to request a one-on-one meeting between Takayama and Michael next Wednesday morning: no lawyers, no subordinates present, just the two of them and interpreters. I ended up talking with Takayama's secretary (Michael's former secretary), who pledged to get back to me this afternoon.

Koji is calling Morishima, who doesn't answer. He will try to catch Morishima at home tonight.

We will, of course, keep you posted.

Waku

That same day Koji conducted some backdoor diplomacy by contacting Morishima, the director responsible for the company's medical business, in an attempt to schedule a meeting between me and Takayama. Koji emailed me back:

Morishima said he saw no value in Takayama meeting with you since it is widely shared within Olympus that your style of leadership is not welcome. He said the majority of Olympus employees, domestic and abroad, don't want you to come back. I told him that's quite different from what I hear, but he said he was sure.

We knew from the Grassroots site just how much support I had from employees but it was easy for Olympus to state, without any evidence, that I was not wanted back. This claim was starting to be picked up by the media and we had to find a way to counter it.

The next day Waku heard back from Olympus. His email made me laugh out loud:

I just got a call from Mr. Hyakutake, the general manager of the secretarial division at Olympus. After careful consideration, they have concluded that Takayama does not have time to meet with Michael. Waku: 'Not even two minutes standing at adjacent urinals sometime during one of the days that Michael is here?' Hyakutake: 'Sorry. No.'

A chance meeting in the 'Little Boys' Room' being out of the question, what was becoming clear was that I needed to meet the person who was pulling the strings. The puppet master was not Takayama. In reality the show was now being run by Sumitomo Mitsui Banking Corporation (SMBC) – Olympus's main bank, with loans of $1.1 billion to the company, and one of its largest shareholders.

The key man was SMBC's president, Takeshi Kunibe, whom I had encountered before. I was not keen on his style and I sensed the feeling was mutual. My very first meeting with him in spring 2011 had left me shocked. I had been dragged over from the Monolith by Kikukawa to be presented as the new president, but aside from the initial greeting and the goodbyes, I was not given the opportunity to say a word. The episode had said a lot about the power structures between Japanese corporations and their bankers . . . especially one as deep in the debt hole as Olympus.

The half-hour conversation had been held in Japanese, despite the fact that both Kikukawa and Kunibe speak good English. I had to make do with a translator at my side. During the meeting Kunibe barely acknowledged me and asked no questions about my plans for Olympus. But he appeared intimate with Kikukawa; they even had a little chinwag about golf.

We returned in our separate cars to the Monolith building and on arrival I was still fuming. I called a meeting with Kikukawa and Mori (who had been present at the SMBC visit, as ever at his master's side). I went straight to the point: 'Do not ever do that to me again. It was completely degrading. It humiliates the company. I wouldn't treat a junior person in that fashion.' In hindsight, that incident should have been a clear sign of how the ground lay.

But that was water under the bridge. I had to focus on the present. My first day back in Tokyo had included secret meetings in my room with candidates for the new slate of Olympus directors: leading businessmen and senior members of the establishment in Japan. They understood and deeply cared about what I was trying to achieve, although before committing their names they wanted to know whether I believed we could really prevail in the face of staunch opposition from Japanese institutional investors. I explained my logic that if the eminent list of names was made public in early January, it would create such pressure that Olympus and the institutional shareholders would have little option but to enter into a pragmatic dialogue.

The day was not yet over and the most important event on this trip was still to come. To address Takayama's accusation that I was not wanted back by the employees of Olympus, Koji had arranged for me to appear with himself and Waku on the Nico Nico internet video site. This is a wildly popular website that bypasses conventional broadcast channels and has built a loyal following among young Japanese. When Koji had first raised it as an idea, I was nervous – it seemed completely uncontrollable. But we went ahead.

The show had been widely trailed and everyone in Olympus knew I was appearing that night. In the green room at Nico Nico's studios, Koji warned me I would be given a hard time. He told me that I had to prove Takayama wrong. Then he dropped a bombshell: at the end of the programme, viewers would vote on what they had heard.

Suddenly we were in the bright lights of the studio. On one side, behind a quiz-show-style desk, were Koji, Waku and me. Facing us was a female presenter with the whitest porcelain-like skin. She would relay the questions from the viewers. The opening captions came up on the screen and Waku quietly explained in my ear that the programme was called *Michael Woodford Answers Questions from Olympus Employees.* It was being transmitted live and would run for ninety minutes, from 9.30 to 11 p.m.

As I sat there, I realized how exhausted I was, but adrenaline kicked in. The first few questions were difficult. 'How can you run a Japanese company if you don't speak Japanese?' 'Do you care more about the overseas business than those in Japan?' They continued in this vein. After about fifteen minutes the presenter intervened and said the viewers were unhappy that the questions were overly negative and they should stop giving me such a hard time. I could see the viewers' comments on the monitors, and many were in English. I was touched by their caring and supportive words, some even telling me I was looking tired and worrying for my health. One said 'Fuck You Takayama'.

Next came the vote. I had spoken from the heart but had no idea how I had come across. There was applause in the studio as the results came through: 75 per cent of viewers supported me, with only 10 per cent against. Tears welled up in my eyes. I felt an even greater commitment and obligation to my Japanese colleagues, who, despite everything they had been told, were willing to support me and not the board of yes-men in their Monolith hideaway.

Koji ended the programme by reading a statement:

President Takayama, Vice President Morishima,
Since I first started my website Olympus Grassroots.com I have been
sending you the same message, 'Let's solve this problem internally. Admit
that Michael Woodford was right and you were wrong. Ask him to return
and, with the understanding that the current Board will all resign, build
the plan to revitalize Olympus together.' Olympus is not in a position to
waste its energy and time for a lengthy proxy fight.

Despite my plea for such a cooperative scenario, you have chosen
confrontation, saying, 'Woodford is not qualified to lead Olympus.

Majority of employees don't want him back. We don't need his coopera-
tion to revitalize Olympus.'

Mr. Woodford has accepted my request to participate in the Internet
Live Program Nico-Nico today, and answer those questions sent to my
website from Olympus employees, shareholders and customers. Questions
I have chosen are from those who seem to be more negative than positive
about his return. He has answered them in the most straightforward and
honest way. Now it's your turn, Mr. Takayama and Mr. Morishima.
With the permission of the program director of Nico-Nico, I am hereby
asking you to participate in the similar program and answer those
questions of Olympus employees and all the stakeholders in the world
who care about the future of Olympus. And if you still think you are
right and Michael Woodford is wrong, then go ahead and decide the case
in the proxy fight.

14 December 2011

Koji Miyata, Olympus Grassroots.com

Takayama and Morishima never accepted the invitation to appear on the programme. It would have been a wonderful piece of corporate democracy, if employees had been able to vote on who they wanted to run the company. Koji had been right about the power of the programme, and Olympus never again claimed that my colleagues didn't want me back. They knew that the Nico Nico results would be used against them.

When I returned to my hotel room an hour later, there was an email from Peter Virgo. Like Stuart Greengrass, he had been a direc-tor with me during the years of KeyMed's dramatic growth. Peter was an intelligent and questioning colleague – quite the opposite of a yes-man. The relationship was sometimes edgy, but there was mutual respect on both sides. I was therefore particularly touched when I read his words about the Nico Nico broadcast, knowing them to be sincere:

Exposure

From: PETER VIRGO To: MICHAEL WOODFORD
Subject: NICO NICO LIVE – MCW ADDRESSES THE OLYMPUS NATION

Phenomenal personal performance Michael – a quite superb
balancing act on the highest of high wires and all without a safety
net! – ladies and gentlemen I give you (if there's any justice in this
world) the soon to be re-instated President of the company we all
hold so dear, OLYMPUS.

Such an event was always high risk what with jet lag and the
enormous potential for interpretation/misinterpretation of words,
body language etc. but what a truly stellar performance by the
young scrapper. I really cannot praise your performance highly
enough – your responses to questions were pitched perfectly to
appeal both to hesitant Japanese shareholders and most importantly to a frightened and concerned Olympus workforce which
has, prior to this event, been subjected to a barrage of deliberate
mis-information and to highly distorted and biased scaremongering
as to your nature and intentions – well not any more old son!
BRILLIANT JOB Michael now go and have the worlds biggest G&T
and tell Koji he's looking outrageously good for a man of 70 –
Lesley thinks he looks very handsome!

Not sure what the % scores at the end of programme meant but
presume from your and Benny Hills response it was favourable to
the scrapper!

Onwards and upwards

Pedro

Koji would be pleased to be thought of as good-looking but I wondered whether Waku would know who Benny Hill was. Peter's
nickname for me throughout my battle with the Olympus board
was 'Scouse Scrapper', meaning a street fighter from Liverpool!

My presence in Tokyo and all the media attention had led to a surge in visits to the Olympus Grassroots site. Employees now had a platform outside the office or the factory to talk freely and express their unhappiness. So many of them went online, the server crashed once again, but Doug Miller was there to get it up and running within a matter of hours. The tide was turning.

We were in the middle of December and the world's media had begun the process of summing up the events of the year that was drawing to a close. When I got up on the morning of Thursday the 15th I learned that *Time* magazine, in its famous 'People Who Mattered' feature, praised me 'for challenging a tight corporate cabal that traded on loyalty above all else . . . Whatever happens, the world's corporate cronies have been duly reminded that sometimes loyalty comes at a price.'

That day I had two televised meetings with parliamentarians from the Democratic Party of Japan, who since the 2009 election had been the ruling party, and the opposition Liberal Democratic Party, previously long dominant in Japanese politics. I reflected on just how far we had come in little over three months: here I was giving advice to the respective committees which had been set up to improve corporate governance in Japan. I wondered what those on the fifteenth floor of the Monolith were thinking as they heard me talk.

I was in some ways impressed by the politicians of both parties, but I remained sceptical as to whether either would bring in meaningful legislation. There is a desperate need for the country to ensure that all listed companies have a minimum number of external (non-executive) directors, but Japan's powerful business lobby asserts tremendous influence on limiting any such reforms. (My instincts proved to be right when on 18 July 2012 Japan's Justice Ministry scrapped plans to make it mandatory for companies to appoint even one outside director.)

Late that afternoon Takayama held a press conference announcing Olympus would not be delisted – it had successfully filed corrected financial statements covering the last five years. He told reporters that the company would hold an extraordinary general meeting (EGM) in March or April the following year and, most worryingly, when pressed would not confirm that he would step down at that time. He made the meaningless statement that he would work with me but wouldn't meet me. He then went on one of his Politburo-like ramblings:

'We'll review our management structure, corporate governance and our business plans as we prepare for the shareholder meeting. We'll be reborn as new Olympus so that we can provide value to all our stakeholders including shareholders, customers, banks and our employees.'

In response, Olympus shares fell by almost 20 per cent.

A few hours later I held my own press conference at the Japan National Press Club. I became quite angry and in my frustration I asked the Japanese journalists how they could be so passive with Takayama. After all, the company's own independent investigation had deemed him to be one of a board of yes-men, and despite his announcement the preceding week that he would leave the company (which was even reported in the *Nikkei*) he was now desperately trying to hang on to office. Many of the journalists seemed almost bemused that I cared that much to feel emotional.

With such a large number of journalists in the room I decided to use the opportunity to ask publicly for a meeting with Takeshi Kunibe of SMBC. That night my lawyers sent a short letter by facsimile asking for a meeting.

But the following Monday, I was rebuffed when my Japanese lawyers NO&T received a call from the West Shinjuku branch manager of SMBC, passing on a message that Mr Kunibe could not meet me because Olympus's revitalization plan 'was going to be in the hands of the Management Reformation Committee' (MRC) and 'they did not want to interfere'. This was ludicrous as two of Olympus's contaminated 'outside' directors, Hiroshi Kuruma (the former senior executive from Nikkei Inc., who had criticized me for copying my letters to Ernst & Young) and Yasuo Hayashida, were chosen to be the two-man committee responsible for appointing the MRC chairman and its members. Neither of these independent outside directors had responded in any way to my repeated written warnings. Outside directors are there to provide oversight and scrutiny of the Executive; however, when questioned about my dismissal in November, extraordinarily Dr Hayashida had told Reuters: 'I do attend board meetings but I have no idea about their content. I only provide medical advice.' Now these two characters were to choose the members of the Management Reformation Committee. More *kabuki*.

It was clear SMBC would dictate the future but they were playing their cards close to their chest. That is the way such things are done. After all, the bank never issued one word of criticism of Olympus. What kind of fiduciary duty was that? It summed up why corporate Japan felt to me like such a busted flush. With national debt at over 200 per cent of Gross Domestic Product, the country needs a vibrant corporate sector. It needs some openness and a willingness to endure some vital creative destruction before it can rebuild. But all it gets are unedifying power games played out behind closed doors by a privileged elite.

That night I had a clandestine meeting at the New Otani Hotel with some former colleagues, the most senior of whom was prepared to stand as a director on the new slate. We drank a lot of beer and there was a close bond between us. I was humbled by their willingness to risk everything for the company. I felt a strong sense of responsibility towards them and had to be certain we could win before exposing these people to a process which could ruin the rest of their professional lives.

It was past 3 a.m., as I lay restlessly in bed at the Park Hyatt, trying to beat the jet lag. I was seething. I had exposed the fraud and given everything of myself. I was offering to fix things.

Financially, I was in a position to sue the company for many millions in compensation for the four years remaining on my contract. After the Third-Party Committee's damning report, there was no doubt I would win. I was in effect prepared to go back to work for nothing, because I would not be able to make a claim if I were reinstated as president. I couldn't sue my own company.

I didn't want to desert my colleagues. I knew that with a new group of directors around me, we could realize the potential of a wonderful business. But I was starting to see that in effect it was SMBC and the other institutional shareholders who would dictate the future.

I had been drained of nearly all my energy, but I was not just fighting with the board of Olympus; I was fighting against Kunibe, the board of SMBC, the other institutional investors and the whole Japanese system.

The following day, thoroughly disheartened, I flew back to London.

On 20 December Reuters reported that Olympus was *preparing to issue about $1.28 billion (¥100 billion) in new shares to bolster its depleted finances, with Japanese high-tech stalwarts Sony and Fujifilm seen as possible buyers.*

The financial situation was indeed desperate. Commentators had noted that after the restated accounts had been filed, the company's capital ratio had plunged to only 4.5 per cent at the end of September, from 11.9 per cent a year earlier. That compared to a 44 per cent average in the precision-engineering sector, according to Bloomberg. But to sell off a large slice of the company to a 'friendly' Japanese giant without a shareholder vote would have been a classic Japanese cross-shareholding stitch-up.

On 21 December, as Christmas approached, the authorities' present to Olympus was a raid on its offices by prosecutors, police and officials from the SESC. The press carried pictures of a long line of men in dark suits marching into the company's head-quarters. What amused me was that the raid had been known about by many in the media long in advance; and any element of surprise would have been lost. Once again it was evident that Japan operates in very strange ways.

Gerhard Fasol, of Eurotechnology Japan, commented to the BBC: 'In a way it is a good thing that this has happened, as there were fears that this affair may be brushed under the carpet. This raid will ease any such concerns.' I was not so sure.

I was cheered up when I learned on 23 December that the *Independent* had named me its Business Person of the Year, and the feature made me smile with its words: *If Michael Woodford follows through with his threat to write a book on the events leading up to his dismissal by Olympus it promises to be a real humdinger, maybe even along the lines of Too Big to Fail or Barbarians at the Gate.* All I can say, as I sit here with my two-fingered typing and voice recognition software, is that I am doing my very best.

The next day, Britain's largest circulation national daily, the *Sun*, named me its 2011 Business Cracker. I was pictured at the top of a Christmas tree above Steve Jobs. In its own unique editorial style the *Sun* told its readers: *In a brutal year for British business one man stands out – Michael Woodford . . . Promoted to chief exec of Japanese titan OLYMPUS in April, he smelt a rat over dodgy accounting, was booted out and promptly blew the whistle on the scandal. He was threatened to the point where police told him not to go out on to his balcony.* There was my story in forty-six words of hard-boiled précis.

The accolades were now coming in thick and fast, and I learned that the *Daily Telegraph*'s Britons of the Year list had me just above P. D. James, the doyenne of British crime fiction. Its headline was *Whistleblower Who Paid the Price.* The synopsis read: *Michael Woodford emerged from relative obscurity in October brandishing a folder, a laptop and a story that would lead to the near collapse of one of Japan's most famous companies.* The conclusion of the feature meant something to me: *The future for both Olympus and Mr Woodford remains uncertain, but at least one of the two has finished 2011 with their pride intact and their reputation enhanced.*

Christmas 2011 was a little flat. We went to Nuncy's Spanish home-town, Burgos, for four days and from there we would spend the New Year in La Gomera, in the Canary Islands. Christmas is emo-tional at the best of times. It can always go either way with so many expectations. I was melancholic on Christmas Day and I especially missed Nuncy's mother, a beautiful and truly remarkable woman who had passed away the year before.

To avoid confronting my demons throughout the holiday I bur-ied myself in emails and work. It was during that week in La Gomera, talking with Nuncy, that I came to a realization: I had won the argument, but was losing the war. Nuncy had been bold enough to confront me with the truth: 'You need to understand. They do not want you back.' I replied, 'But "they" are not the Japanese peo-ple in general, and certainly not the company's employees. It's SMBC and the other institutional shareholders.'

If the company had not been so indebted, it would not have mat-tered. If, if, if.

In my heart, I knew Nuncy was right. I was the lone wolf who had left the pack, and the pack had closed ranks against me. Being readmitted to the fold was never going to be easy. I had left the pack to fight for its collective well-being, its survival, but, in doing so, had made myself an outsider. My actions in exposing the fraud had at least ensured the company was purged of its most pitiful leaders and would undoubtedly survive, but it was starting to appear as if that continued existence would be without me.

And so another year turned.

12.

Rising Suns Also Set

It was 1 January 2012. A new year had begun, and I was glad to be in La Gomera. We had been coming to the state-owned *parador* (hotel) since before our children were born, and the island holds many special memories for us. It was a warm sunny morning and from the veranda I looked out across the shimmering Atlantic to the nearby island of Tenerife, some twenty miles away, dominated by the dormant Mount Teide. At 3,718 metres it's the highest point in Spain. Its familiar magnificence reminded me of Mount Fuji.

As ever, I had been the first to rise and Nuncy and the children would be asleep for several hours yet, especially after the celebrations the night before. I went back inside to collect my laptop from amid the discarded New Year's Eve party streamers and face masks. There was no Wi-Fi in the room, so I walked down to the garden courtyard to pick up a signal from the reception area.

The Andalusian-style courtyard was always tranquil, but before 8 a.m. on New Year's Day it was deserted. It is my favourite area of the hotel, and could easily be part of the Alhambra. Chairs and benches are generously spaced along two of the canopied sides, which open up onto a grassed area; among the palm trees a small fountain gurgles away reassuringly. A waitress I had known for more than twenty years passed by, and asked cheerily if I would like some coffee and orange juice. I gratefully accepted.

Following my ritual of starting the day by checking Google alerts, I discovered that in their New Year's Day edition the *Sunday Times* had named me its Business Person of the Year. The caption was *Michael Woodford was sacked by the Japanese giant for exposing a decade of deceit. He sets an example to others.* While reading the accompanying profile – favourite book *Brixton Beach* by Roma Tearne; favourite film *Brief Encounter* – it was disconcerting to see myself being talked about as the *ex*-Olympus president. It was an extensive feature stretched out over two pages and the journalist, Andrew Davidson, had done his homework, interviewing a number of people who knew me. Clive Stafford Smith, the campaigning human rights lawyer (who had written articles for the Huffington Post news website and the *Guardian* newspaper in support of me), was quoted as saying he thought I should go on to run a charity. Clive was on the right track in that charities had always been important to me as their activities have an intrinsic value beyond commerce.

Over the last two days in La Gomera I had reluctantly concluded that, while I was confident of the support of all the overseas shareholders and large numbers of private individuals in Japan, the country's institutional shareholders had made it clear by their deafening silence that they did not want me back. Those advising me believed this grouping controlled a majority of the company's stock, and it would be extremely difficult to win a proxy fight against them. It was nothing to do with what was right or wrong, but simply the unwritten rules of the 'club'.

If winning was unlikely, then I couldn't take the risk of damaging those who were prepared to go public in their support of me. Of course, with the Olympus story, new developments were unfolding on an almost daily basis – anything could happen. Nevertheless, in discussing the way ahead with Koji and Waku, there was agreement that we either had to publish the names of our slate or withdraw. After much agonizing, we decided to withdraw.

I wasn't going to make that announcement in London, 6,000 miles away. I owed it to all those who had supported me, in particular the Japanese public, to go back to Tokyo and explain my reasons. And, of course, to say goodbye in person.

This time I would not tell the press that I was coming back to

Japan. On 4 January I arrived at Heathrow to take the British Airways 005 daytime flight. I wondered how many times since my first Tokyo flight in the early 1980s (then it was via either Anchorage or Moscow) I had made this journey. As the Boeing 777 waited in a long queue for its turn to take off, my mind was vacillating wildly. While I was 90 per cent certain I was going to withdraw, I still thought something might happen to make me change my mind. You just never know.

We landed at Narita at 9 a.m. the following morning, Thursday, 5 January. Moonwalk 3. This time there were no cameras to greet me. It was good to see Waku again, although there was a sadness in his eyes.

We travelled to the Park Hyatt in a car arranged by the *Asahi Shimbun* as I had decided that news of my withdrawal from the proxy fight should be broken by a Japanese newspaper. I had chosen Toshi Okuyama, who had impressed Waku and me with his endeavours to report the story with honesty. Several times during the interview with Toshi I went quiet; gracefully, he didn't push me.

As we drove on the highway into the city I felt very sad that it was not in my power to return to the company I loved and be with my colleagues once again. I was not worried for myself. I knew I could build a new life, dedicating myself to the causes which mean most to me: human rights and road safety. I was concerned for those I had worked with and would leave behind, especially those in Japan. A company may not be a human entity, but it is made up of people. I slowly realized how many of them I would miss terribly. I ended the interview with Toshi by making clear I still wasn't certain that I would withdraw; nothing should be published until I had my meetings that evening. Toshi smiled gently and told me he understood.

That afternoon I met my lawyers to consider the legal aspects of withdrawing, followed by meetings and calls with those who were ready to stand as candidates on a new slate. They were kind, but also recognized the cold logic of my conclusion: without at least one Japanese institutional shareholder breaking ranks, we were unlikely to be successful.

At 8 p.m. I had the most difficult meeting since the start of my campaign to return to the company. In my suite we had a final 'council of war' over drinks and rice crackers. I had gathered my supporters and allies to tell them of my decision.

There was understanding and resignation, but one person didn't agree. One of my former Japanese colleagues at Olympus, who had agreed to stand as a new director, said: 'Why make this decision now? Why not just wait and watch? Things will happen. The board will change.' It was a wholly rational argument. 'I hear what you're saying,' I replied, giving myself a few seconds to think before I continued. 'But I just cannot see how we get around the obstacle presented by the banks and others. It shouldn't be this way but there has been no breaking ranks among them and that is what we had hoped for. These institutions seem impervious to public opinion and the views of those looking in from outside Japan.' I paused again. 'It would only hurt you and the others if we fight on.' If I had followed his advice the outcome might have been different. We will never know.

Looking into the earnest eyes of this man, who was prepared to risk his whole career, I felt deeply humbled. After a minute of silence I spoke again. 'I'm so sorry but I honestly believe I have done everything that I can. It's now time for others in this country to pick up and start questioning and challenging.'

There was not much more to be said and everyone tried hard to lighten the mood. They were unsuccessful. We had not achieved the happy ending of the dismissed president returning victorious to lead his company to a brighter future. However, as I have learned over the years, life is not always filled with happy endings, but the experience I shared with these people will be one of the most precious things to me until I die. At difficult times words can be clumsy, and as we said goodbye to each other I hoped those who had stood alongside me could see just how much I cared for them.

Late that night, initially on their website, the *Asahi Shimbun* broke the story of my withdrawal from attempts to return as Olympus's president. Early the following morning I sent my statement to the world's media. It had taken me hours to compose but I wanted my message to be understood:

STATEMENT BY MICHAEL WOODFORD – TOKYO, FRIDAY 6TH JANUARY 2012

The last 12 weeks have been the most emotionally demanding and challenging period in my entire life. The brutal way I was dismissed as President on 14 October, and the subsequent lies and denials, have been traumatizing for all those around me, especially my family. It's been a frightening period for my wife, who has suffered a lot and every night still wakes screaming in a trance and it takes several minutes to calm her. She finds the uncertainty and hostility of the public fight difficult to cope with and I have therefore decided for her emotional well-being that I cannot put her through any more anguish, and will today withdraw from any further action to form an alternative slate of directors.

Of course the major reason for the continuing uncertainty is that despite my having done the right thing, none of the major Japanese institutional shareholders have offered one word of support to me and conversely have in effect allowed the tainted and contaminated board to continue in office. The fact that such a situation can exist despite the explicit findings of the Third-Party Committee is depressing and totally disorientating to those looking in on Japan from the outside. The cross-shareholding system in Japan, while clearly serving the country well in the years following the Second World War, is in today's world harmful due to the unwritten convention that one must never publicly criticize another. Such a compliant approach removes one of the essential safeguards in relation to governance and also allows the boards of companies which are underperforming to remain in office. I hope this reality will be seriously debated in relation to legislative changes which would strengthen the country's corporate governance and in turn the vibrancy of the Japanese economy. I believe this issue of the weaknesses created by the cross-shareholding system is the most important single factor Japan needs to address to be successful in confronting the obvious challenges it faces, in this ever more competitive world.

In this context, throughout recent months it has been important to me not to allow the Olympus situation to be framed as a Japan vs. non-Japan issue, but to emphasize this has been a debate of importance between the reformers and the non-reformers within the country. I believe much good has come out of the on-going scrutiny by the regulatory and law-enforcement agencies in and outside of Japan and the domestic and international spotlight of publicity that the Olympus scandal has attracted. This has allowed a focus on the culture of 'yes-men' and total absence of effective corporate governance that created the organizational and cultural weaknesses of Olympus, with the result that the fraudulent acts continued to occur for so long. With this background the remaining existing directors should surely never be allowed to influence the constitution of the next board and as the Third-Party Committee recommended they should all resign, as each of them spectacularly failed to act to the most explicit warnings of concern of wrongdoing, detailed in my six letters to them and also the condemning PricewaterhouseCoopers report. If this transpires not to be the case, then the world will make its own judgement.

In assembling a slate of director candidates, I've been humbled by the individuals of impressive stature who have offered to stand alongside me as alternative directors. I hope each of you can understand that even if we had been successful in winning a proxy fight, it would have created a dichotomy between the institutional shareholders in Japan and those outside of the country and this would have been damaging and the wrong basis on which to move forward.

I would like to take this opportunity to thank those who have inspired and supported me. Firstly Waku (Brian) Miller and Koji Miyata – these two extraordinary individuals stood with me to challenge what was so clearly wrong and they've gained nothing for their tireless efforts. Their only motivation was to ensure the truth came out and that Olympus had the leadership it deserves for the future. In this time of globalization, you had a Japanese, an American and an Englishman standing shoulder by shoulder, wanting the very best for Olympus and Japan. Can I also express my sincere appreciation to the members of my legal team. I have met many lawyers during my career but I've never encountered more caring individuals, who at all times have provided me with the wisest of advice and genuinely care about the issues involved.

Most of all I would like to thank from the bottom of my heart, my colleagues at Olympus from around the world, who have encouraged me throughout but especially those in Japan and I will never forget the Nico Nico broadcast on the evening of 14 December and your hundreds of messages of support. I feel a deep sense of sadness that I've not been able to fulfil your expectations but I have given everything of myself in trying to do so. Olympus has been a huge part of my life for the last thirty years and it will always remain an essential part of me.

Lastly and most importantly may I thank the people of Japan. When I've walked in the streets or eaten at restaurants, so many individuals have come up to me to tell me that what I was doing was the right thing. While I've always loved your country, my affections have only been enhanced by the numerous acts of kindness and human warmth which have been extended to me during these difficult weeks.

Japan is a truly great nation and I will continue to come back frequently to enjoy all it has to offer and of course to see my friends.

Michael Woodford

Almost immediately after pressing 'send' I received the first of hundreds of emails and texts expressing the most generous and warm sentiments. We had touched a lot of people.

I spent all of that Friday morning talking to and emailing those who had supported me around the world. In trying to offer them some solace, I used my experience and perspective from working in road safety and the people I had met who had lost loved ones in road accidents. In comparison, this situation was not a tragedy and some good would come out of it. No one had been physically hurt and everyone involved would, as human beings do, start to move on. I will never throw away or delete the emails and letters I received from so many people and their words left me feeling optimistic about the world.

That afternoon I held a packed press conference at the Japan National Press Club. Before speaking I was asked to sign the visitors' book, where I saw the message I had written the month before: 'Long live a free press in Japan'. This time I simply wrote, 'It is good to be back!' Many of the questions from journalists were phrased to compliment me, implying that I had changed Japan for the better. Several times Japanese friends have told me that the country needs external influences to bring about change. Maybe I edged this process forward. But true change has to come from within. Japan had been sleepwalking through the latter part of the twentieth century and into the twenty-first. It needs to wake up.

On the Saturday night at their home, Waku and his wife Kazuko held an afternoon 'We Tried' party for me and everyone we knew came round. I was pleased to see that Koji's wife Akiko and Kazuko were becoming friends. We finished the evening at a nearby local restaurant and I felt that, with my friends around me, I was the luckiest man in the world.

On the flight back to London I thought about the journalist who had asked if I wanted to sever my ties with Japan completely. The answer I had given was a definite 'no'. Japan and I had a history together and I wasn't going to turn my back. The country was going through hard times – rising suns also set – but I had met people who, if given a chance, could help it find a way back to growth and prosperity.

As the flight went on I reflected on my affection for Japan. I had told very few people that my family's links to the country went back long before I was born. When I was young my father and uncle had spoken in reverential tones about Japan as a land of honour. That was because my grandfather had run a rubber plantation for Dunlop in Jasin, north of Melaka in Malaysia. During the Second World War the Japanese invaded the British colony and the Woodford family had to adapt to a new way of life. The commander of the local Japanese forces, Colonel Miura, showed them great kindness in the most difficult of circumstances. On one occasion an illegal radio was discovered at the house but Colonel Miura intervened, saving the family from a labour camp.

The colonel spoke perfect English, and my grandfather even let the children stay at his place for the night. The family kept in touch with him after they were liberated and he returned to Japan. His family had all been killed in Allied bombing attacks, and he was left destitute on the streets. In one letter he begged my grandmother for a pair of boots and some clothes; she sent him two big cases of items but we never heard from him again. The Red Cross said they couldn't contact him.

For a British child, brought up on films like *The Bridge Over the River Kwai* and *Tora! Tora! Tora!*, it's easy to forget the Japanese also suffered back in their homeland. The atomic bombs dropped on

Hiroshima and Nagasaki caused almost a quarter of a million casualties but the firebombing of Tokyo in March 1945 by American B-29s killed even more, including Miura's family.

From the ruins of war Japan had proved the most amazing industrial success story. And it wasn't just cars at which they excelled: cameras (Olympus's first was brought out in 1936, the 'Semi-Olympus I'), the video recorder, the CD player, the Walkman – all had their origins in Japan.

So by the early 1980s, when I joined KeyMed, the Japanese were the commercial and manufacturing envy of the world. They had to do something with their cash surpluses and the response was to go on a spending spree abroad. In the 1980s Japanese firms made overseas direct investments of $280 billion, then equivalent to buying the whole economy of Australia or India. Sony bought Columbia Pictures in 1989, Fujitsu bought the UK's International Computers Ltd (ICL) in 1990. They picked up Hugo Boss, the Turnberry Hotel and golf course in Scotland, and something similar in California at Pebble Beach. And, in a far smaller deal, Olympus purchased KeyMed from its founder and my mentor, Albert Reddihough.

KeyMed proved an extremely successful investment and by 1990, after Olympus had taken full control of the company, it was clear that Britain was the favourite destination for Japanese direct investment. By this stage the UK accounted for 38 per cent of Japan's $42 billion investment in Europe. Toyota moved into Derbyshire, Honda to Swindon and Nissan to the North-East. Sony made TVs in South Wales, Oki made computer printers in Glasgow, and Olympus became one of the largest employers in Essex. France, incidentally, was the recipient of a mere 7 per cent of Japan's investment – maybe this had something to do with the views of people like Jacques Calvet, boss of Peugeot-Citroën, who called Britain an offshore aircraft carrier from which the Japanese could launch their attack.

Such was the perceived threat of their success that Michael Crichton's *Rising Sun*, published in 1992, shot to the top of the bestseller lists. Its cover blurb stated that the thriller followed *a head-long chase through a maze of industrial intrigue – the Japanese versus the Americans. A no-holds-barred conflict in which control of the electronics industry is the fiercely coveted prize and the Japanese saying 'Business is War' takes on a terrifying reality.*

The underlying reality was more subtle. Japan had hidden weaknesses. In the 1970s and 80s Japan appeared to boast a superior form of capitalism and management: one that seemed more egalitarian than the 'tooth and claw' variety practised by the Americans and British.

Japan's share of world exports peaked in 1986 and then a malaise set in. Questions were asked about the real nature of the Japanese system and what its weaknesses might be. These are forcefully highlighted in Michael Porter's book *Can Japan Compete?*, which the celebrated Harvard professor co-wrote with two Japanese collaborators, Hirotaka Takeuchi and Mariko Sakakibara. It is unusually readable for a business textbook.

The strengths of Japanese business and its corporate model had for years been drummed into every MBA student: high quality and low cost; a wide array of models and features; lean production; regarding employees as assets; permanent employment; leadership by consensus; strong inter-corporate networks; long-term goals; internal diversification into high-growth industries; and staying close to a supportive government.

One by one Porter went through these attributes. He showed how they had been found wanting, as world markets changed, or perhaps, as he suggested, they were not so powerful in the first place. He found companies, including Olympus's camera business, chasing market share at the expense of profit. He found that leadership by consensus (usually with elderly men at the helm) led to conformity and lack of innovation. He found 'competitive convergence', something that occurs when, he said, *all the competitors in an industry compete on the same dimensions. The more rivals source from world class suppliers, often the same ones, the more similar they become. As rivals imitate one another's improvements in quality, cycle time, or supplier partnerships, competition becomes a series of unwinnable races down identical paths.*

What concerned Porter most was that many of the most successful Japanese companies made consistently low returns on investment. This lack of profitability was widely tolerated because nobody wanted to rock the boat. Unlike their Western counterparts, and in the absence of pressure from shareholders, large Japanese companies often maintained unprofitable divisions indefinitely. Japanese executives euphemistically called these 'healthy red divisions'. Much of corporate Japan is unable to produce a commercial return on capital. This is the most basic indicator of flaws in the system. None of this was news to Japan's near neighbours, the ultra-competitive Koreans, who were waiting for their turn in the spotlight.

Such flaws became painfully apparent in the 1980s. The country amassed so much cash that the yen grew strong, while the US dollar began its long downward slide. For a while the Japanese had never known it so good. Pumped up by the success of their exports, the asset bubble began to inflate. Then, inevitably, it burst.

The lead the Japanese had held in electronics was especially impressive. Who bought a Korean Samsung rather than a Sony or Panasonic television in the 1990s? But the lost decade took its toll and the dive since has been astonishing. Between 2000 and 2010, Japan's electronics production fell by 41 per cent and exports tumbled by 27 per cent. Japan's global market share fell by almost half to 10 per cent by 2009, whereas Korea's rose to nearly 10 per cent.

A month before I took over as president, it was confirmed that China had overtaken Japan to become the world's second largest economy after the US. It lost the number two spot after nearly five decades as runner-up to the Americans. This was what I had walked into as the new president of Olympus – a company and a country in trouble.

*

Just two days after my return to England on Monday, 9 January came the news that Olympus had decided to sue nineteen of its current and former executives, including its current president, for almost $50 million in compensation. Although all the board members subject to the lawsuit would resign in March or April, Olympus was left in the extraordinary position of continuing to employ its most senior executive, Shuichi Takayama, and several other directors that it was suing for mismanagement. The directors were in effect suing themselves.

They were like condemned men resigned to their fate. 'Essentially, everyone feels they are on death row. It does seem extremely strange to have the death-row cell inside the company,' said Nicholas Smith, head of Japanese equity strategy at CLSA in Tokyo. How on earth the directors were supposed to manage the company while suing themselves was anyone's guess. It certainly left Olympus rudderless and vulnerable. Takayama greeted the company's graduates on 1 April, as I had done a year before. I wondered what the new starters must have thought.

On the 11th, courtesy of Olympus's shipping agent, my life in Japan came back all neatly packed up in a box. Twenty-seven boxes, in fact. The haul included three toilet brushes and a boxful of metal coat hangers from the dry cleaners. Notably missing were my precious first American edition of *Animal Farm* and my print of Rudyard Kipling's poem 'If'. To this day I still do not know what happened to them. I would have been more than happy if the board had kept *Animal Farm* – they could have learned something valuable from it.

The next day, Thursday, 12 January, I went back to the Serious Fraud Office to help them with their continuing enquiries. That evening, as a supposed man of leisure, I visited the London Boat Show with my friend Peter Thompson. As we were walking around together admiring the yachts, I received a call from the Association of Certified Fraud Examiners in Dallas – an organization which has 60,000 members. I was the winner of the 2012 Cliff Robertson Sentinel award 'For Choosing Truth Over Self'.

I was starting to lead a new life. I began to travel the world and talk about the Olympus scandal and the lessons that could be learned from it. My story had to keep changing as developments linked to Olympus continued apace.

On Monday, 6 February Olympus bowed to the inevitable and announced an EGM. For Takayama and the remaining members of his board of yes-men Judgement Day was nigh.

On the theme of judgement, ten days later Kikukawa, Mori and Yamada were arrested for suspected violation of Japan's Financial Instruments and Exchange Act. The prosecutors also arrested Akio Nakagawa, the former president of Axes Japan who had been cited in the Third-Party Committee's report. Nobumasa Yokoo was also arrested by the Tokyo Metropolitan Police.

Then, on Wednesday, 7 March, prosecutors formally charged ex-chairman Tsuyoshi Kikukawa, former executive vice-president Hisashi Mori and former auditor Hideo Yamada with inflating the company's net worth in financial statements for the fiscal years ended March 2007 and 2008. Nakagawa, Yokoo and Taku Hada (on the board of Global Company and the three 'Mickey Mouse' companies) were also charged. In learning of Kikukawa's arrest I felt no sense of victory. Just very sad that it had all come to this.

The indictments had followed a global investigation involving agencies in the US and the UK and spanning jurisdictions from Florida and the Cayman Islands to London and Hong Kong. Hajime Sagawa, who had come under close scrutiny in the case, had not been charged by the Japanese authorities. Reuters had reported in December that Sagawa, a US citizen, had apparently left Florida for the Cayman Islands, a month after he divorced his wife and sold her their Boca Raton home for $10. At the time of writing Ellen Sagawa still lives in Boca Raton, Florida in the 7,217-square-foot, canal-front house that the couple co-owned until October. When Reuters sought confirmation of her ex-husband's whereabouts she declined to comment. A 32.5-foot yacht named *Snapper* registered to her was docked behind the home.

The weeks passed. After the dark and sometimes terrifying early months, life was returning to some sense of normality and many good things were happening. In late March I was chosen as the *Financial Times*'s 'Boldness in Business' Person of the Year. (It was the first time four different national newspapers had all chosen the same businessman of the year.) All the 'great and the good' from the business world were present and the grand awards evening took place in the splendid surrounds of the British Museum, where Karl Marx wrote his devastating critique of capitalism, *Das Kapital*. Over dinner, watched by huge, silent Egyptian artefacts over 4,000 years old, I was placed between Lionel Barber, the editor of the *FT*, and Lakshmi Mittal, chairman and chief executive of ArcelorMittal, the world's largest steelmaker.

I took the whole family, and the best part of the night was watching the way Edward and Isabel conducted themselves at such an august gathering. It didn't faze them one bit. They are as comfortable in the company of Britain's richest man and the waiters who served them champagne. They respect people for who they are and not their titles. This was the real reward of the evening for me and for Nuncy.

In his speech Lionel Barber said:

'If there was one person who captured the spirit of boldness in business in 2011, it was Michael Woodford. His selection was a matter of serious discussion among the judges. There were concerns that it might be misconstrued as an incitement to whistleblowers and a broader insurrection against business. But these concerns were allayed once the logic of the choice became clear. Woodford took a considerable risk in exposing wrongdoing. As chief executive, he was arguably acting against his self-interest, since his job was obviously in jeopardy. Yet he did the right thing. He campaigned for proper accounting and persuaded the Japanese authorities to act. He was a study of boldness in action. By choosing him, the judges followed suit.'

Nuncy told me afterwards that while I was visiting the washroom, Barber leaned over and said to her, 'He really is completely authentic, isn't he?'

It was all very enjoyable and flattering, but I remembered Rudyard Kipling's words: 'If you can meet with Triumph and Disaster and treat those two impostors just the same . . .' I made sure I took it easy on the champagne that night.

13.

Sayonara to All That

Over Siberia we all came, 300-ton ships of the night, into the Land of the Rising Sun. In the lead at 39,000 feet was Swissair 160, closely followed by Lufthansa 710, Air France 276, KLM 861, Finnair 73. Then me, flying the flag, on British Airways 005. SAS 983 and Virgin's 900 brought up the rear. I had looked at an upgrade to First, for old times' sake, but a recent invoice for a five-figure lawyer's bill had made me think twice.

As dawn rose on 17 April we came over Sendai province – its crippled and useless Fukushima nuclear power plant still threatening – before the long turn right over the sea and into Narita.

I was returning at a time when the outlook for Japan's massive conglomerates was growing ever bleaker. Sony had just announced 10,000 redundancies. Judged by many as a disappointment, Sony president Howard Stringer had just made his exit with record losses forecast for his last year in charge. The results transpired to be even worse than anticipated when, on 11 May, Sony announced a record annual loss of $5.7 billion, with the shares that day falling to a thirty-two-year low. This was the once-mighty corporation's fourth consecutive year in the red and Stringer had retired hurt, handing the reins back to a Japanese president. 'Sony's schism', Reuters called it.

I checked in at the Park Hyatt where the ever-supportive management rewarded my loyalty with the largest suite I have ever stayed in. Up on the fiftieth floor, it had a thousand-book library and a baby grand piano. Not even Bill Murray got pampered like that.

No sooner had I unpacked my bag than another of the small band of *gaijin* bosses threw in the towel. This time it was Craig Naylor of Nippon Sheet Glass (NSG), an American who had previously enjoyed a stellar thirty-six years at Du Pont, and had attended my own inauguration. He quit citing 'fundamental disagreements' with the board over the speed and scale of the restructuring that he deemed necessary for NSG's long-term survival. With only Carlos Ghosn of Nissan remaining, Japan seemed to be shutting the doors and I wondered how long it would be before another *gaijin* would be invited to run a large Japanese corporation.

Now I had come back to face my old boardroom adversaries publicly at the EGM, this time in my capacity as a shareholder. To handle the media's demands for interviews, Waku had filled my 'Moonwalk 4' itinerary with back-to-back meetings leading up to the EGM on Friday.

The pace was relentless. I had only just landed but my first engagement was to talk at lunchtime to the Japan Association of Corporate Directors. This may seem like a labour of love, but the very fact I had been invited to give a talk about governance standards was positive. I cared about the subject and would never decline such a request. There were a number of senior executives from leading companies: Sapporo, Fujifilm, Konica Minolta, Pioneer, Sony and Kirin were all represented. I was encouraged.

The difference on this trip was that I felt I had little to lose. I could speak entirely freely and honestly about what I saw as Japan's problems in its corporate sector and capital markets. Another difference was the absence of a feeling of threat – I no longer sensed menace and danger.

I told each journalist who filed into my suite that Japan desperately needed an economic renaissance to once again lead the world in commercial innovation. But this could not come about without a major change of attitude. Why was it, I asked, that despite everything that had been revealed about Olympus's appalling conduct, not a single Japanese institutional shareholder had uttered a word of criticism about the incumbent board, or a word of support for what I had done in exposing the fraud?

Of course social cohesion is a strength, and the unity derived from a 'we not I' approach is important and to be valued. But unquestioning tribal loyalty was crippling Japan's future. The real trouble was leadership. Leaders needed to challenge, make unpopular decisions, ruffle feathers. Yes, they even needed in extremes to fire people who were not achieving the grade. Many senior Japanese managers at Olympus had never fired anyone in their entire career. Dismissing people is horrible but sometimes necessary. Choosing the right people is important, but getting rid of the wrong people is probably even more important. From my experience of working with Japanese managers, many of them completely shied away from challenging weak individuals who reported to them.

Being unilateralist, confrontational, challenging – all of which are required to bring about progress and improvement – comes with great difficulty to a culture where harmony and cohesion are prized. Japan needs more mavericks – it needs some of those old founding engineers like Soichiro Honda who went against the grain. It requires, perish the thought, a few Steve Jobs. Why had Sony Ericsson been so decisively beaten in the mobile phone market by Apple and Samsung? Where was Sony's new Walkman?

And where were the women in Japanese business? Never mind in the boardroom, but in those vital middle-management roles? I am not a sociologist, but I'm good enough at basic maths to know that if you turn your back on 50 per cent of the talent in your population, then you're making a big mistake.

I reflected on these issues when in July 2012 the Fukushima Nuclear Accident Independent Investigation Commission delivered its long-awaited report to Parliament. Its opening message was that *this was a disaster 'made in Japan'. Its fundamental causes are to be found in the ingrained conventions of Japanese culture: our reflexive obedience; our reluctance to question authority; our devotion to 'sticking with the programme'; and our 'insularity'.* It is sadly for the same four reasons that I believe much of the country's corporate sector is doomed to failure, and that in the years ahead we will see many more stories coming out of Japan about other companies which weren't quite what they appeared.

Maybe it will take a further and rapid decline in Japan's fortunes before a great leader is thrown up. But one will arrive eventually. Maybe they will get a Margaret Thatcher, a woman whom many despised, but as I saw in those early years in Liverpool, when the country was sliding ever deeper into economic malaise and even anarchy, she did a job that needed doing.

As far as Olympus was concerned, my prognosis was relatively simple: it could again become one of the world's most successful healthcare groups. I decided that in future I would only talk about my experiences up until the EGM. The company needed to move on with its new board. I would not be one of those sad individuals harping on from the side of the stage.

In relation to the outgoing board, however, I had been appalled by their decision, announced a few weeks earlier, that Karl Watanabe and Shinichi Nishigaki, two of the tainted board of yes-men, were to continue in senior executive roles. This was wholly wrong and went against the Third-Party Committee's recommendations. I knew my concerns were shared by other shareholders who had made their feelings clear.

After three days of repeating all this to journalists, I was wearing out. Jet lag makes you vulnerable to mood swings: your heart sinks as your head slumps forward with fatigue. By Thursday afternoon I found myself day-dreaming about jogging along the beach in Southend.

On the morning of the big day, Friday, 20 April, just over a year since I'd assumed the president's job, I was up at 4.10 a.m. I flicked the switch to open the curtains, had some coffee, and then video-called Nuncy back in Southend. She said she loved me and wished me luck.

I went to the hotel's pool to swim fifty lengths, and spent a few minutes talking with an East European businessman I had been bumping into for years. In Zen-like fashion he was gliding up and down the pool, doing the three hundred lengths he completes each morning. A Japanese parliamentarian and member of the sports club came up to me in the changing room and said he was praying for me. These exchanges made me realize there were all sorts of people on my side. I put on my late father's cufflinks for good luck.

There was heightened media interest in just what would happen that day. Aside from my attendance, in the weeks preceding the EGM, in a highly unusual step, nine foreign funds, including the Florida State Board of Administration and RPMI Railpen Investments, had after the naming of the proposed new board members written an open letter to Olympus's management expressing unhappiness with the *apparent willingness to grant banking interests undue influence*. Furthermore, ISS, the leading shareholder advisory firm, had recommended a vote against the proposed new chairman and president. None of this, however, had influenced the Japanese institutional shareholders, who seemed untroubled that overseas shareholders saw things so differently.

Waku and I left the Park Hyatt with plenty of time to spare: I wasn't about to risk being late for one of the most publicized events in Japan's corporate history. We arrived at the vanilla-coloured New Otani Hotel in our little taxi, passing the serried ranks of black company limousines – one of them had, I'm sure, been previously Nick's and mine – which had deposited the Olympus top brass, probably hours earlier. The police were there in considerable numbers. There had been warnings that the EGM might be attended by professional *sokaiya*, or troublemakers. These individuals have caused immense disturbances at some Japanese shareholder meetings and even attempted to extort boards.

We took our places near the front, Koji to my right and Waku to my left. The Three Musketeers together again. Then in front of us, up on the stage, there was some movement. In filed the board, dressed in identical dark suits. As expected, President Takayama was playing master of ceremonies before taking his final bow and leaving the company.

The title would be his for only a few hours more. He began with an apology and a lecture about the robustness of the company's new compliance systems. When he finished, the board bowed collectively. A disgruntled shareholder shouted out: 'You arseholes! If you think that's going to make a difference you're wrong.'

This set the scene and things went from bad to worse. A protest came next: 'Why have none of the directors name plates in front of them? This is highly unusual.' Clearly those on stage were ashamed to be identified by name. A series of hostile questions followed. One discontented shareholder went to the microphone: 'I want Woodford-san back.' These people had seen their shareholdings, often a retirement nest egg, plunge in value. Their displeasure was in full flow and the barracking of the board was relentless.

At one point a gentleman from Kansai shouted at the directors, 'Where's the money? Why don't you take an endoscope and look in the company safe?' That received a loud and enthusiastic round of applause.

One shareholder linked me to Bushido, the 'Way of the Warrior-Knight'. This was particularly flattering: the code of warrior conduct embodies frugality, loyalty, martial-arts mastery and honour unto death. (My karate, incidentally, remains as bad as it was when, aged eleven, I was whacked over the head by my mother's wooden clog for practising it on my sister.)

A motion was then made to remove Takayama as chairman of the meeting. He protested and asked for a vote of confidence, whereupon a weak round of applause was deemed to be the majority vote. There was no show of hands.

Takayama made an error in deferring too many questions to Masataka Suzuki. This irked one member of the audience, who aggressively barracked Suzuki every time he shuffled up to the microphone. 'You bum, Suzuki!' 'Get off!' and 'You've brought shame on us in front of the world!' Suzuki had made a kidney-punch-style pop at me at the board meeting on 30 September, and after my dismissal had been the enforcer dispatched to my UK stronghold, Olympus KeyMed, to throw his weight around. So seeing him sweating and being mercilessly taunted seemed poetic justice. However, I found myself starting to feel uncomfortable for him; I don't enjoy watching people publicly humiliated to that extent, whatever they may have done.

I kept putting my hand up, signalling that I wanted to ask a question, and eventually I was invited to speak. My lawyers had submitted a prior written question requesting the specific reasons as to why I had been dismissed. At the microphone stand, with Waku at my side to translate, I repeated its content. It was important to establish that the new board accepted that sacking me had been unjust. If they didn't accept this as a point from which to start afresh, how could they lead the company forward?

As I expected, they came back with some obstructive excuse about being unable to answer the question, hiding behind the litigation back in London, where I had launched an action alleging unfair dismissal for whistleblowing and for discrimination. What I knew was, they simply couldn't do this. With the help of my lawyers I had done some homework. Japanese company law states that if the potential financial damage to the shareholders exceeds the reason for the refusal – the costs of their lawyers and coming to a settlement with me – then they had to answer. How the proposed new board viewed the scandal was critical to help the shareholders know whether to vote for them.

'Come out from behind the curtain,' I urged all the hidden lawyers typing away their answers for Takayama and his stooges. 'Because if you don't, such illegal conduct may constitute grounds for this EGM to be cancelled in court. That will mean that all the resolutions of today will be null and void. Answer this question clearly.'

Again they tried to dodge the question. This was getting me seriously riled. I hadn't come halfway round the world to be fobbed off by these tainted pen-pushers. I went for the jugular.

'Judge Kainaka did Japan a great service by describing the board of directors on this stage as tainted, contaminated men who spectacularly failed to act upon six letters from me that contained the most explicit warnings of fraud. The directors Watanabe and Nishigaki are not leaving. They are staying as executive officers. Do you not realize how that looks to the world? Today is supposed to mark a "new start". The judge said get rid of the contamination, and you keep those two gentlemen in the company. How dare you? Shame on you.'

I surprised myself. But all this pussy-footing around just got to me. My crescendo would have made Laurence Olivier proud.

'Sit down,' ordered Takayama, the ringmaster who had lost control of his circus. He looked grey and shell-shocked. But I'd made my point, so I did as I was told. I didn't hate Takayama, I almost felt sorry for him, presiding over this farce. He was a marionette having his strings pulled by the lawyers behind the curtain.

I had done what I came to do. There was no point in my staying any longer. I decided to leave before the meeting was over. When I left my seat and made for the exit, a sizeable part of the audience started chanting 'Michael, Michael, Michael', and Takayama had to stop talking at the podium. As I left the hall I was mobbed by shareholders thanking me and asking me to come back as president. Humbling, but it was never going to happen.

I went outside the hotel and spoke to the hordes of media. 'Today is the day the "New Olympus" was supposed to start. But what we've just witnessed was a mockery. It's why the world looks on and continues to think that Japan works in a completely different way. It's *Alice in Wonderland*.'

When the voting figures were released later that day, with the institutional shareholders already in their pocket, the 'club' won. They got the board they wanted, but 30 per cent of shareholders had failed to vote for the new president Hiroyuki Sasa and 35 per cent for the chairman Yasuyuki Kimoto, an almost unprecedented result for a Japanese Nikkei-listed company, where votes in support are usually nearer to 99 per cent. In coming to a voting decision, there had been a clear dichotomy between the overseas and Japanese institutional shareholders.

(Interestingly, a mere three days after the Olympus EGM came the historic announcement from Hitachi, one of Japan's largest manufacturers, that it planned for the first time in its 102-year history to buck the bad old ways and shuffle its board so that outside directors would outnumber its own executives for the first time. Even more intriguingly, one of the suggested new independent directors was George Buckley of 3M. Another *gaijin*. I wish him luck.)

I was whisked away from the EGM to the Japan National Press Club. Now in holiday spirit, I decided to give this talk the full nine yards. I told how a couple of weeks before, I had given the keynote address at the Council of Institutional Investors in Washington. The head of a pension fund responsible for billions of dollars of investment had come up to me and described Japan as a 'banana republic' in the way it manages its companies, adding that he wouldn't touch the country's capital markets until it improved its corporate governance. If something didn't get done, it would be the final shutting of the door on the international investment community and we'd be back to the days before the Black Ships arrived. (This was the name given to the four United States Navy warships which on 8 July 1853 steamed into Tokyo Bay on their mission to 'open' Japan. The well-armed Black Ships forced the end of a 250-year policy of seclusion by the Tokugawa shogunate.)

With passion I explained my belief that what needs to happen is a breaking up of the cosy corporate clubs that have dominated Japanese business for so long. Someone should stand up to the grey old men in dark suits, otherwise foreign capital will cease to come to Japan. It will return to being closed off from the outside world like in the old days. Why were the Japanese people so sedated in their tolerance of all this?

Then I had a go at them directly – the Japanese media. 'What would have happened if I had come to you rather than the *FT*?' I asked. 'Many of you, in private, have told me that the story would have been too "hot to handle" and you would have been fearful of the reaction of offending some of your largest advertisers.' I pointed out that the most candid Japanese journalists were often employed by foreign news organizations.

They all continued to smile politely, which only perturbed me more. I asked when the media 'guard dog' was finally going to start barking. 'It's not even stirring at the moment. It's lying sedated in its basket.'

This may have sounded apocalyptic but I believed it. The world is in a nervous state and investors want a degree of reassurance. Japan isn't exploiting its strengths: wonderfully educated people, an unsurpassed engineering culture and dedication to absolute quality. But its management remains weak.

I was so tired I was starting to hallucinate. But Waku wasn't finished with the day's programme. It ended after seventeen hours in a surreal fashion. I had again been booked onto the Nico Nico channel, and this time the format was a late-night talk show. I was to reveal my more personal side.

The beautiful host, Mizuho Mashiko, giggled as she set to her task of probing the real me. I can't say I minded. Flanked by Waku and Koji on the large white sofa, I talked about my family and took online questions. Before long I was advising anxious teenage boys who had never had a girlfriend about the best way to get a date. If only I had known myself . . . Several people admired my tie and I ended up giving it to Mashiko.

Only in Japan.

Epilogue: Bells and Whistles

I was never sure that the term whistleblower quite described what I was.

Whistles tend to get blown by policemen in the pursuit of a thief. Or they are sounded by referees to stop play so they can upbraid a player. The expression was made popular in the 1970s by the activist Ralph Nader, who saw it as a welcome alternative to derogatory terms such as snitch or informant. Commercial whistleblowing is usually traced back to the States as well. The first US law adopted specifically to protect whistleblowers was the 1863 US False Claims Act, which tried to combat fraud by suppliers of the government during the Civil War. The US even has its own National Whistleblower centre - motto 'Honesty Without Fear'.

In the UK we had to wait until 1998 to get a Public Interest Disclosure Act. Japan's came only in 2006, and is shaky, at best: whistleblowers may not contact outside parties such as mass media unless 'there is a strong reason to believe that notifying their employers of irregularities won't go anywhere and that the companies might even hide evidence'.

Blowing a whistle wasn't really my style. I wasn't a cop and I wasn't the referee. I was a player who saw members of his own side not following the rules.

One of my Japanese colleagues who remains at Olympus described me as someone who 'rang the bell'. I like that. When there is a fire, the bell ringer runs to the church and stirs people to action. He sounds an alarm.

*

During that week in Tokyo, there was one last thing I desperately wanted to do: meet the original whistleblower.

Although we had been in brief communication through carefully forwarded emails, I had never spoken to the person within Olympus who had taken the story to *Facta*. I had no idea what part of the organization he or she worked in. But I desperately wanted to meet them. They had done a far braver thing than I.

The journalist from *Facta* responsible for the exceptional reporting on the scandal was Yeshivas Yamaguchi. Waku explained to him how important it was to me to meet his source, and that I had clearly demonstrated that I could be trusted. To my great relief, the original whistleblower agreed to meet me.

A clandestine rendezvous was arranged late one afternoon at Waku's house. I travelled out from central Tokyo on the Chiyoda underground line to Nezu Station. Then I walked the few hundred yards past the small grocers, flower shops and restaurants. Waku and Kazuko greeted me, I took off my shoes and went up onto the tiny roof terrace and waited. A chill wind was blowing from a grey sky. The whistleblower was late and I was worried that they might have got cold feet.

Then I heard two people enter the house: Yamaguchi-san and his contact. They came up the ladder to the roof and I was so overwhelmed with emotion that I did a very un-Japanese thing and gave them a hug, which embarrassed them a little. Hugging complete strangers isn't done. Except this person who I had been so anxious to meet wasn't a stranger. We'd lived parallel existences through something momentous.

I'm not going to describe them because that would put them and their family at risk. I was reassured by my colleague's obvious basic decency. No superheroics. No airs and graces. Just another Olympus employee. Except, of course, they weren't. Their courage marked them out.

Amazingly, the whistleblower's first words to me were an apology. How Japanese.

'When you became president I really wanted to email you to tell you what was happening. But I didn't know you weren't one of them. I'm sorry.'

'Please, don't apologize,' I replied. 'You did absolutely the right thing and didn't know me or whether you could trust me. It was good that you went to *Facta*. That way I found out.'

We sat over some cans of warm Sapporo beer and Ritz crackers and just talked about the company: the good guys and the bad guys. How things might pan out. Starting to really relax, the whistleblower said, 'That Mori, what a typical Japanese yes-man. To think they probably wanted him to be the boss.' I nodded in agreement, again feeling as if I was in some sort of film. Not least because our conversation actually had a soundtrack – we could hear Dvořák's New World Symphony coming over the rooftops from a neighbouring house.

'You know,' I said, 'when Kikukawa suggested that I didn't like Japanese people, it made me more angry than anything.'

My ex-colleague smiled and asked, 'When will you be back in Japan?'

'I don't know,' I answered truthfully.

That coming Sunday I was returning to England to begin the rest of my life, unsure what direction it might take. On Monday the whistleblower would be back at work, worrying if anyone suspected they were the bell ringer and worrying too about the precarious future of their company. I thanked Yamaguchi-san and then looked at the whistleblower: 'If I can ever help you, you must always tell me.' We shook hands and the reporter and his source went downstairs. I didn't see them off; you can never be too careful and it would not have been a good idea for them to be seen in my company.

So I watched from the terrace as the pair walked off down to the end of the little lane, turned the corner and were lost from view. Anonymous on the teeming streets of Tokyo. Which is how I hope he – or she – will remain.

Afterwords

Jake Adelstein

Conquer anger with calm
Conquer evil with good
Overcome greed with generosity
Vanquish liars with the truth

The Dhammapada (teachings of the Buddha), verse 223

Michael Woodford is not just a whistleblower – he's a truth teller and a hero.

These are rare things. As a society we may laud honesty and integrity, but when someone actually stands up for those principles, we think to ourselves, 'What a nutter.' In Japan, this is all the more noticeable thanks to a culture that emphasizes decorum and keeping the status quo. But there is no such thing as a society immune to corruption and hypocrisy. Loyalty triumphs over principles, lawsuits and money muzzle the naysayers, and intimidation keeps people quiet.

I don't think Michael Woodford is a nutter. On the contrary, I think he's an honest man, and today that makes him a noble oddity. I'd call him the Buddha of Liverpool but he's still a little too angry to be a Buddha, and with good reason. It doesn't make him any less of a hero.

As a journalist I am supposed to be objective in my assessment of people. If I was writing a newspaper article on the Olympus scandal, I'd be hesitant to use the word 'hero' to describe Michael

Woodford because people would assume I was biased. But this isn't a newspaper, and I am biased. It's kind of hard to root for Tsuyoshi Kikukawa and his underlings who perpetuated a massive accounting fraud, lied about it, and then fired and tried to ruin the reputation of the man who tried to fix the problem and do the right thing.

What makes Michael Woodford a hero is that instead of going quietly, he told the world what had happened. Immediately after his dismissal from Olympus, he met with Jonathan Soble from the *Financial Times* and told him what had happened. Other people would have just left the country as soon as possible.

Forgive me. Once again I've called Michael Woodford a hero. This is a journalistic taboo. Just as we're not supposed to call anyone a hero, we're also not supposed to call liars and thieves 'liars and thieves'. We're supposed to look at both sides – at the shades of grey that colour each news story. I suppose that's the curse of being slightly colour blind and spending most of my career as a newspaper journalist in Japan – I tend to see everything in black and white. And in this case, it's very clear who the hero and the villains are.

Some may argue that Kikukawa and his board did what they did 'for the greater good of the company' – I doubt it. Some in the Japanese press have implied that Michael Woodford had a hidden agenda, that he was secretly working with other companies to plunder Olympus of its assets and pocket a load of change. I never believed it. He has no hidden agenda. His only mission was to bring the truth to light and reform the company at which he spent most of his working life. It was a brave and dangerous thing he did. He was a little lucky to have come out in one piece.

You think it's paranoid to believe that in Japan someone might be killed to hush up a $1.7 billion accounting fraud? Consider some past events.

In 1998, as the investigation of bribes paid by Japanese brokerages to banks and politicians reached its zenith, lawmaker Shokei Arai was found hanging in his hotel room. He was the key person in the investigation and parliament was scheduled to vote on his arrest the next day. The weeklies would later report that there were sounds of angry voices in his room, but his death was still labelled a suicide. It scuttled the investigation, which also involved employees at Nomura Securities, who had paid off a Yakuza-backed racketeer.

In January 2006, when the Livedoor insider trading investigation began – prompting panic selling on the Tokyo Stock Exchange – a close aide to the president, Hideaki Noguchi, soon showed up bleeding to death in a hotel bed. His wrists were cut and he had stabbed himself in the stomach several times. It was ruled a suicide.

In March of the same year, a real estate consultant, Kazuoki Nozaki, who clashed with an organized crime boss over a piece of property worth ¥2 billion ($25 million), was stabbed to death in the streets of a high-end Tokyo suburb. The police caught an accomplice and the driver – five years later. The police issued an international arrest warrant for the actual killer, Takashi Kondo, in December of 2010. Kondo was shot to death in Thailand under shady circumstances in April of 2011, and the case remained unsolved. The boss who gave the order to kill Nozaki was never prosecuted or identified.

That $25 million is a lot less than what was at stake in the Olympus affair. Certainly the Tokyo Metropolitan Police Department believed Michael Woodford was at risk. The security upon his first return to Tokyo was airtight; no chances were taken. The police are well aware that people who know too much in Japan tend to meet a bleak fate when corporate scandal erupts. And yet he never backed down.

Early on in the Olympus story, while listening to Woodford speak at a press conference about his experiences, I was reminded of Albert Einstein's expression: 'The world is a dangerous place. Not because of the people who are evil; but because of the people who don't do anything about it.'

Michael Woodford stood his ground and spoke the truth. It's

people like him who keep our society from falling into total darkness. Japan – and the world – could use more people like Michael Woodford.

In the West, Japan is often portrayed as a duplicitous society, and the country abounds with words and proverbs that seem to indicate that dishonesty is acceptable. People are expected to have both a public image (*tatemae*), and their real intentions (*honne*), but only voice the publicly acceptable *tatemae* positions.

There is a Japanese saying that I'm sure Michael Woodford felt was true at one point in his struggle: 正直者が馬鹿を見る・*Shojikimono ga baka o miru.* 'The honest man is sure to lose.' If you believe the proverb, you'd think Japanese society actually has disdain for the honest man. Maybe some of Japan does.

But as with many things in Japan, there is a contradictory viewpoint. Try another proverb: 正直の頭に神宿る・*Shojiki no koube ni kami yadoru.* 'The Gods dwell in the head of the honest man.' The metaphorical meaning is that the Gods bless an honest man. While this proverb is not as well known as the first one, there must be many who believe it, because the Japanese edition of this book became a bestseller. Rare as these qualities may be, people admire honesty and bravery in any culture.

Michael Woodford fought against the currents, the lies and betrayal of his former employers, and the fate handed down to him. He won. He did it by cataloguing the falsehood, keeping his head and not giving up. He made his own luck and he wrote the ending to his own story, just as he wrote this book.

Maybe, this time, the honest man did have the blessing of the Gods. I would like to think so.

Tokyo, July 2012

Jake Adelstein is an investigative journalist and is considered to be the foremost Western expert on Japanese organized crime. He graduated from

Sophia University (Jochi Daigaku) in 1993 and worked for the Yomiuri Shimbun, *Japan's largest newspaper, primarily as a crime reporter from 1993 to 2005. He is the author of* Tokyo Vice: An American Reporter on the Police Beat in Japan. *He is a contributing writer to* The Atlantic Wire *and manages the website japansubculture.com. His next book,* The Last Yakuza: A Life in the Japanese Underworld, *will be published in 2014.*

Koji Miyata

My first encounter with Michael Woodford remains fresh in my memory. It was in 1986 at an exhibition convened in São Paulo by the World Organization for Digestive Endoscopy. He was twenty-six. I was forty-five. He was the sales director at KeyMed, the Olympus medical operations' UK distributor. I was the general manager for overseas marketing.

KeyMed's founder and president, Albert Reddihough, was about ten years older than me and was an entrepreneur of rare genius and arresting individuality. I had acquired the habit of going out of my way on business trips to catch up with him and to bask in his insights.

Reddihough had told me that he had a young colleague whom he was eager for me to meet, and we had agreed to rendezvous in his hotel lobby before dinner. My preconceptions led me to expect a tall, blond Briton who would evince a barely concealed contempt for foreigners. So I didn't even take note of Michael until he was right beside me and thrust out a hand and declared, 'I'm Michael Woodford. I'm delighted to meet you.' The facial features betrayed something Asiatic, the skin a bit dark for a Caucasian. Although nearly twenty years my junior, he evoked a stunning presence.

The dinner conversation proved every bit as startling as the encounter in the lobby. At the time, Reddihough had confided, 'This is still confidential, but I intend for him to succeed me as president.' Olympus held an equity stake in KeyMed, which employed a few hundred people and conducted some product development and manufacturing, as well as importing sales and marketing of Olympus products. It was, in other words, an operation of strategic importance to Olympus. And Reddihough was old enough that the question of his successor had become a subject of concern at Olympus headquarters.

KeyMed had several competent managers, including an executive who had served as Reddihough's right-hand man since the company's founding. I couldn't believe that the founder would reach over the heads of all those candidates and promote a manager of twenty-six to run the whole show.

'Why?' I asked incredulously.

'Koji,' Reddihough replied, 'the world is full of managers who would make a good No. 2, but those who would make a truly good No. 1 are few and far between. And rarely does a good No. 2 ever become a good No. 1, no matter how much knowledge and experience he or she might accumulate. So finding the right successor for a CEO is a matter of finding a good No. 1 and providing him or her with the appropriate training. If management fails to find a true No. 1 and settles for a No. 2 as CEO, the organization immediately begins to decline.'

Still unconvinced, I persisted: 'And what, exactly, is the difference between a good No. 2 and a good No. 1?'

'The CEO is responsible for steering the company safely through even raging tempests. Running a company is not a job for the faint of heart. The CEO needs to be someone who can keep the company on the right course, who possesses the wisdom to recognize hazards and the fortitude to steer clear of danger. That wisdom and fortitude are the difference between a good No. 2 and a good No. 1. The good No. 1 will keep a steady hand on the wheel through any storm. That's the most important consideration in choosing a CEO.'

From that day on, I kept an eye on the young manager to whom

Reddihough was prepared to entrust KeyMed. I watched carefully to see if he really exhibited the 'good No. 1' qualities cited by his mentor. To the extent that my management authority allowed, I broadened his scope of responsibility and monitored his performance and growth. Reddihough made good on his pledge, and Michael became KeyMed's president at the age of twenty-nine.

The new president emphasized discipline and attention to detail as management fundamentals. He put in place an action plan for tackling a full range of management issues and ensuring maximal performance. And he personally oversaw activity in every nook and cranny of the organization. People elsewhere in the Olympus Group made light of what they regarded as Michael's micromanagement. But all acknowledged the results that he produced.

Michael crafted detailed models for marketing endoscopes and for managing sales personnel that have taken hold throughout the Olympus Group. His management style was demanding of all around him and, most of all, of himself. It produced results, though, and Michael's responsibility and authority increased steadily.

I became concerned about Michael's escalating workload, only to discover another crucial facet of his 'good No. 1' qualifications. We were in a car after work en route to a dinner engagement in Tokyo in autumn 2003. The car was headed down Gaien Higashi-dori Avenue. Just before we reached the crossing in front of Akasaka High School, Michael shouted out to the driver, 'Stop!' The driver complied, pulling over to the side of the road. Michael, pulling a miniature digital camera out of his pocket (an Olympus, of course), instructed the driver to wait for a couple of minutes and stepped out of the car.

Negotiating heavy traffic, Michael photographed the scene from several angles. He then got back into the car and we headed for dinner as if nothing had happened. A few days later, I received a lengthy email, attached to which were several photographs. The photographs were of the road and traffic light in front of Akasaka High

School, and the text described hazards in regard to the traffic light and outlined countermeasures. Michael was concerned about the poor visibility of the traffic light and called for installing an additional one equipped with high-visibility light-emitting diodes (LEDs).

Michael instructed me in the email to discover the municipal agency responsible for the traffic light in question, to identify the person in the agency directly responsible for the traffic light, to translate his email and send it by registered mail to that individual, and to follow up with a personal phone call. The email message was polite but unilateral, leaving no room for ifs, ands, or buts.

Olympus had invested KeyMed with management responsibility for a broad and growing range of group operations, and Michael's brief Japan visits were invariably packed to the last second. I marvelled at how he could find the time to indulge an interest in road safety. Putting my reservations aside, I complied dutifully with Michael's instructions and telephoned the police authorities responsible for the problematic section of road. The voice on the other end of the phone provided information about the higher-ups in the Metropolitan Police Agency, and I sent Michael's long message, translated into Japanese, to a bureau chief there.

I dispatched the letter to the Metropolitan Police Agency on 16 October 2003. What followed was an exchange of numerous letters, faxes and telephone calls, which finally resulted in the installation of the LED traffic light that Michael wanted in spring 2005. The project had entailed an immense investment of time and effort on the part of Michael.

'Why,' I later asked Michael about his road-safety endeavours, 'do you devote so much passion to this cause?'

He seemed almost taken aback by the question. 'This is something that I've been doing for nearly twenty-five years,' he replied. 'It's something of value, something that I can do, something that I intend to continue doing. And I want some help with this work in Japan.'

Michael, I learned, had witnessed a fatal traffic accident at the age of fourteen. On looking into the background of the accident, he discovered that simple safety measures could have prevented the tragedy and the pain suffered by the victim's loved ones. And that prompted what became a lasting involvement in road-safety activities. He began participating in an international road-safety organization that operates under the auspices of the European Union. Years of commitment to road safety would later earn royal recognition with the bestowal of the prestigious title Member of the British Empire.

Michael has tackled several road-safety projects in Japan. He has not accomplished as much here as he has in Europe, however, largely on account of the language barrier and cultural differences. We can only wonder how much more he could have accomplished here had he been able to mobilize more supporters. His efforts on behalf of road safety in my nation put me to shame, and I pledged to help as much as possible.

'I'll be far more satisfied when my time comes,' he once confided, 'with the lives I've saved through road-safety efforts than with anything I've accomplished in business.'

Nearly ten years have passed since my road-safety cooperation with Michael began with that project near Akasaka High School. Recently, I contacted a non-profit organization that he sponsors, the Safer Roads Foundation, about the number of projects that he has undertaken. A precise number is unavailable, but the foundation reports that he has been personally involved in more than 1,000 projects.

More than 1,000 – and all while shouldering an oppressive burden as a global executive. The mind fairly boggles.

Olympus's scandal has provided a stirring reaffirmation of Albert Reddihough's prescience in naming Michael his successor as Key-Med's CEO. Several knew what was going on, and all but one kept their silence, pretending to have seen nothing, waiting for the storm to pass. Michael alone took a principled and uncompromising stand.

Blessed with spectacular technology and compelling products, Olympus nonetheless left the world aghast, betraying its customers and damaging its shareholders. Its management has hewed to the ludicrous assertion that Michael was somehow unsuited as president. Numerous people inside and outside the company have longed for and called for his reinstatement. The powers that be have thwarted these hopes however, and Olympus today is little different from a bankrupt company in reorganization under the guidance of its main bank.

Reddihough was right a quarter-century ago. Olympus has capsized at the hands of 'good No. 2s'. The question now is whether anyone can right the ship in the absence of the singular good No. 1.

Tokyo, April 2012

Koji Miyata is former senior executive managing officer, Olympus Corporation, and former president, Olympus Medical Systems Corporation.

Acknowledgements

Firstly, I would like to thank those whom I'm not able to name. After my dismissal I would have undoubtedly gone under had it not been for those former colleagues at Olympus, at all levels of the organization and from around the world, who found ways of communicating with me and offering their personal encouragement. These people know who they are, and I'll always remain immensely grateful to them.

An experience like this tests the relationships around you, not just colleagues and friends but also your immediate family. Choosing to embark on this journey brought untold pressures upon those closest to me. I would like Nuncy, Edward and Isabel to know that it was the strong love between us which allowed me to hold things together.

Writing a book like this naturally brings many legal considerations and I have received advice from three different groups of lawyers as to what could be published. There were things I wanted to say but have not been able to. Nevertheless, I feel the heart of the story has been captured. Recording what took place was important to me because it provides an insight into the way people act in such circumstances, and hopefully encourages others faced with similar dilemmas to find the right way forward.

The book would never have happened without the support and encouragement of several people. Firstly, my literary agent, Patrick Walsh from Conville & Walsh. Patrick: you believed in me when I was at my lowest ebb and are one of the world's special people. I'm also appreciative to Carrie Plitt at Conville & Walsh for spending all those days with me developing the book's timeline and so diligently cross-referencing all the published material.

Acknowledgements

I would like to thank Matthew Gwyther, the editor of *Management Today*, for helping bring structure and some elements to the book I would never have thought about.

At Penguin, I'm eternally grateful to my editors, Joel Rickett in London and Brooke Carey in New York. Their editorial sensibilities were invaluable. Also at Penguin may I thank Ben Brusey, Ellie Smith and Richard Lennon for all their assistance and in ensuring this book was delivered on time. I'm in awe of the art of copy-editing and for this I would like to thank Trevor Horwood for checking continuity and a hundred other things.

It has taken me over 1,000 hours to write *Exposure* and all that goes with it. In this process one person I grew to be dependent on was Peter Maddern. Because I am the world's slowest typist, I turned to voice recognition software which is truly wonderful. But I had to be taught how to use it and how to recover the system when it crashed. Whatever time of day, Peter was always there, patient and ever helpful.

At times I felt very black about the world, but there were so many friends and members of my wider family, not mentioned in this book, who throughout those difficult months let me know they were always around and supporting me. I hope in the years ahead, I'll be able to repay just a little of your kindness.

Finally, my heartfelt gratitude to the people of Japan, who have shown me such empathy and encouragement.

Index

Index